WORKINGMEN OF WALTHAM

WORKINGMEN

HOWARD M. GITELMAN

OF WALTHAM

Mobility in American
Urban Industrial Development
1850–1890

The Johns Hopkins University Press · Baltimore and London

This book has been brought to publication with the
generous assistance of the Andrew W. Mellon Foundation.

The Johns Hopkins University Press, Baltimore, Maryland 21218
The Johns Hopkins University Press Ltd., London

Library of Congress Catalog Card Number 74-6822
ISBN 0-8018-1570-3

Library of Congress Cataloging in Publication data
will be found on the last printed page of this book.

Contents

List of Figures   vi

Introduction   ix

CHAPTER I: Early Waltham   1

CHAPTER II: Physical Mobility, 1850-90   23

CHAPTER III: Occupational Mobility, 1850-90   50

CHAPTER IV: Social Mobility, 1850-90   77

CHAPTER V: Government and Power   104

CHAPTER VI: Neighborhoods and Social Life   132

CHAPTER VII: Summary and Conclusions   164

APPENDIX I: Research Methods   182

APPENDIX II: Occupational Classifications   188

Index   190

List of Figures

Table

1.1	The Distribution of Assets among Males in 1822	10
1.2	The Distribution of Assets among Males in 1840	12
1.3	The Distribution of Assets among Males in 1850	16
1.4	The Distribution of Assets among Males, 1840 and 1850 (with deletions)	17
2.1	Male Population Growth and Mobility, 1850–90	28
2.2	Quinquennial and Decennial Migration Measures, 1860–1870	30
2.3	Male Population Growth and Mobility, 1850–90, by Religion	37
2.4	Male Population Turnover, by Age, 1850–90	39
2.5	Employment at Boston Manufacturing and Waltham Watch Companies, 1850–90	40
2.6	Rates of Population Increase, Waltham, Massachusetts, and Selected Towns	43
2.7	Persistence, 1830–90	45
2.8	Long-Term Persistence, 1850–90	47
3.1	The Structure of Occupations, 1850–90	56
3.2	The Major Occupational Groupings of Catholic Males, 1850–80	61
3.3	Money and Real Wages at Waltham Watch Co., 1860–90	65
3.4	Occupational Mobility among Persisters, 1850–80	66
3.5	Inter-Generational Occupational Mobility, 1850–90	67
3.6	Three Measures of Occupational Mobility among Male Workers at Waltham Watch Co., 1860–90	69
4.1	The Current Value of Taxable Assets, 1850–90	80
4.2	The Distribution of Assets among Males, 1822–90	83
4.3	Asset Holding among Persisting Heads of Households, 1850–90	86
4.4	Asset Mobility among Persisting Heads of Households, 1850–90	88
4.5	Upward Mobility among Long-Term Persisters, 1850–90	97
4.6	Upward Inter-Generational Mobility	100
5.1	Fiscal Trends, 1850–90	106
5.2	Municipal Budgets, 1850 and 1890	107
5.3	Municipal Offices, 1890	111
5.4	Assets and Occupations of Public Officials	113

5.5	Characteristics of Selectmen, 1850–84	114
5.6	Assets and Occupations of Selectmen and Aldermen	116
5.7	Election Returns, November 1880	120
5.8	Poll Tax Payers and Voters, 1860–90	121
6.1	Length of Service at Waltham Watch Co., 1860–90	155
6.2	Arrests, 1872–90	159

List of Maps, Diagrams, and Illustrations

1.1	Waltham	7
2.1	Waltham Population Growth, 1790–1970	24
2.2	Age Distribution of Males, 1850 and 1880, by Religion	36
6.1	Settlement Patterns, 1854, 1874, and 1890	135
6.2	Residences of the Irish, 1854, 1874, and 1890	139
Photographs of Waltham		142

To My Parents

Introduction

During the last half of the nineteenth century approximately seventeen million immigrants arrived in the United States. Many remained in the port cities of their arrival, while many more dispersed inland in search of a livelihood and a home. Wherever they settled and wherever they moved, these newcomers became members of still other population movements, for large numbers of the native born population were also on the move; heading westward toward land and agriculture or heading cityward to find a place in the growing industrial economy. The railroads, and the mining and manufacturing firms of the era were generally able to locate wherever they chose, secure in the knowledge that enough men to meet their needs could be induced to follow them by one means or another.

It is perhaps understandable that of all of these population movements, the movement westward should have attracted a disproportionate amount of attention. Frontiers have too much dramatic potential ever to suffer from neglect. And generations of Americans, through both the make-believe of Hollywood films and the more serious ministrations of scholars and teachers, have had this potential exploited for their amusement and for their edification. Indeed, from the zeal with which we have fixed upon our heritage of frontier settlement, it might be supposed that Thomas Jefferson's vision of a land of independent freehold farmers had truly come to pass and that it is this development which has to be explained and understood. In consequence, we know more about the development of select counties in Iowa than we know of the population processes which shaped Elizabeth, New Jersey or Cleveland, Ohio. We are more knowledgeable about life in the mining camps of California and the homesteads of Wisconsin than of the fortunes of Haverhill shoe workers, New York City store clerks, or Harrisburg shopkeepers. We are heirs to more concrete detail and more intellectual debate about our vestigial past than about those elements of the past which have demonstrably become the informing characteristics of our present and future. Finding ourselves in an urban industrial society, we have very little sense of how we got here.

In the absence of specific knowledge of the rates and roles of mobility in urban industrial development, casual observations have all too often gained the standing of demonstrated fact. In my own field of labor history, mobility has come to play the role of *deus ex machina*. It is put forth as a major factor in virtually all explanations of: the weakness of nineteenth-century labor organizations; the failure of radical ideologies to gain acceptance among workingmen; the absence of class consciousness; and the development of that distinctively American brand of unionism known alternatively as pure and simple or business unionism. Yet, until most recently, the literature of American labor history included no research bearing upon the rates, modes, or consequences of mobility among workingmen. It was simply assumed that the mobility experiences of American workers differed in some unspecified way or ways from those of workers in Western European countries. Because of the lack of specification, it was not even clear whether mobility meant physical mobility, occupational mobility, or social mobility.

Having come to this realization, it seemed intellectually dishonest to continue to rely upon vague and unsubstantiated assertions about the rates and consequences of mobility. Nor was it possible to find much reliable and useful mobility data elsewhere. Historical studies of physical, occupational, or social mobility among American workers were too few and often too limited in scope to be of much assistance.

How much mobility had in fact occurred during the latter half of the nineteenth century? What was the relative importance of each of the three forms of mobility? What were the consequences of mobility, and the precise means by which those consequences were produced? In developing a research design to get at these issues, a number of considerations led to the decisions to employ the case-study method and to include only males, but all of them regardless of their status in or outside of the labor force.[1] These decisions in turn added a new dimension to the project. The information required to accomplish the original objectives of the study provided the basis for a new approach to the analysis of urban industrial development. The data which had to be assembled for each male individually could be aggregated and would, when followed through time, expose the processes of development as reflected in the changing size, character, and composition of the male population. Hence, the lives of men would bear witness to urban and industrial change rather than the other way about.

It was clear from the outset that all three forms of mobility—physical, occupational, and social—would have to be examined if the necessary distinctions between them were to be drawn. Or could it be, for it seemed increasingly plausible, that the best reason for examining all of the mobilities was that they *combined* to produce the results so often attributed to

---

[1]One consideration was that the almost exclusive interest in blue-collar workers which has long dominated labor history was too narrowly restrictive. This tradition was stimulated by a labor force trend—the increasing proportion of blue-collar industrial employments at the beginning of industrial development—and might not inappropriately be ended by another labor force trend—the current relative decline of blue-collar and expansion of white-collar employments. From such a perspective, labor history appropriately encompasses the entire labor force.

each of them independently? The very obvious and real differences between the mobilities would appear to argue against such a view. Each form of mobility involves movement through one of three distinct kinds of space, each of which has its own unique dynamics. And physical mobility, in contrast to the other two, is more nearly an act which can be undertaken at will. Yet, on at least one level, mobility of any kind subjects movers to a common experience of considerable impact. Almost all movers are obliged to sever some ties with their past and to suffer some degree of disorientation for a time. They are also compelled to make some adjustment to either or both their new surroundings and their new position within their surroundings. It is this cutting-off from the old self and the development of the new self which, in varying degrees, characterizes the experience of mobile persons regardless of the form or direction of their movement. This common experience may provide a basis for generalizing about some of the consequences of mobility.

Because an industrial social system is always going somewhere—perhaps the least controversial statement of where it is going takes the form: "toward a sustained rise in real income per capita"—it is routinely change-laden. Mobility opportunities are generated by this unceasing change. As men must move through physical space in response to changes in, say, the location of economic activity, so they must move through occupational space (i.e., the volume and distribution of gainful employments) in response to technological changes, to increasing specialization, and to shifts in the demand for output. And they must also move through social space (i.e., the volume and distribution of status attributes) in response to such factors as rising incomes, altered occupational and institutional structures, and shifts in the loci of power. From such a perspective, urban industrial development may be seen as a process involving the sustained reallocation of men in physical, occupational, and social spaces.

While mobility may be caused by the locational, the demographic, the technological, and the institutional changes we associate with and often call development, it is also a cause unto itself. Who moves, how much movement takes place, and how men are equipped for or barred from movement are among the critical shaping factors of the social order which emerges. A physical movement composed of single men produces distinctly different consequences at its terminus from a movement of families. Large-scale movements create different absorption problems from small-scale movements. Any one basis for rationing employment opportunities or occupational entry may result in quite different stresses and strains from those created by any other rationing device.

Since the influences of lineage, long-established residence, and tradition have always been very weak in the United States, the accommodation of men in physical, occupational, and social space through mobility must have been that much more important a determinant of the American social order. Several recent studies of early colonial settlement suggest that the "heavy hand of the past" was indeed restrained by the mobility oppor-tunities afforded by land availability.[2] Urban industrial development sub-sequently compounded the number and variety of mobility opportunities. Hence, the analysis of this mobility experience should lay bare some of the main roots of American exceptionalism. The passion for results that ex-presses itself partly in the form of high productivity, the overweening materialism, and the aggressive individualism which set this country apart from others (by degrees) can be seen to bear direct relation to its experi-ence of mobility.

Of necessity, the analysis of all three forms of mobility requires an interdisciplinary approach. Had it been possible simply to borrow con-cepts and measurement techniques from one or more of the social sciences, the tasks of data organization and analysis would have been reduced greatly. This was not to be, however, Several preliminary investigations were made, partly to test the adequacy of the data available and partly to explore alternative approaches to the treatment of the data.[3] These, to-gether with a review of much of the empirical and theoretical literatures bearing upon each form of mobility indicated that wholesale borrowing would be impossible.

Few conceptual or measurement problems arose in connection with physical mobility. Those males not enumerated in successive decennial censuses, less those recorded as having died in Waltham during the decade following enumeration, were counted as out-migrants. Those males making their first appearance in a census, less those recorded as having been born in Waltham during the decade preceding enumeration, were counted as in-migrants. The number of in-migrants minus the number of out-migrants yielded the number of net in-migrants, a measure of the con-tribution of physical mobility to population growth. In an effort to gauge the extent to which decennial census tallies understated actual population flows, the Massachusetts census of 1865 was employed to provide two comparative five-year tallies for 1860–65 and 1865–70.

The measurement of occupational mobility was considerably more problematic. To compute rates of movement, it was first necessary to establish the occupational boundary lines which had to be crossed. My pilot study of occupational mobility suggested that there were at least four different bases upon which such lines could be drawn. Each of these yielded differing estimates of occupational mobility. Which of them is the best depends entirely upon the perspective brought to the subject. An

---

[2]Sumner C. Powell, *Puritan Village* (Middletown, Connecticut: Wesleyan University Press, 1963) and Kenneth A. Lockridge, "The Population of Dedham, Massachusetts, 1636–1736" *The Economic History Review*, 2nd Ser., Vol. XIX, No. 2 (August, 1966).

[3]"The Labor Force at Waltham Watch During the Civil War Era" *Journal of Economic History*, Vol. 25, No. 2 (June, 1965); "Occupational Mobility Within the Firm" *Industrial and Labor Relations Review*, Vol. 20, No. 1 (October, 1966); and "The Waltham System and the Coming of the Irish" *Labor History*, Vol. 8, No. 3 (Fall, 1967).

economist, for example, might prefer to define occupational mobility as a movement between skill levels. A sociologist might prefer a definition which reflected income, status, or associated life-style differences. A historian might wish to define occupational mobility as whatever change the population under investigation viewed as occupational mobility. In the absence of a well-defined and widely accepted theory of occupational mobility, there is no obvious basis for selecting *the* best definition or *the* best estimate. Each of the different measures developed has been presented in Chapter III so that comparisons can be drawn between the estimates they yield.

Measurement of social mobility was even more vexatious, for here there was little agreement upon what was to be measured, let alone how this was to be done. Even if it were agreed that wealth, income, occupation, power, and lineage, for example, were the constituent elements of social status, there was no agreement upon the relative weights to be assigned to each or upon the basis for establishing cutting points between social standings. While it is comparatively easy to provide evidence of social stratification by citing objective differences between men, we lack a clear definition of social class that is of any practical value as a guide to the measurement of social mobility. The quite arbitrary indices which sociologists have developed in their efforts to define social standings and to mark status differences are useless in historical research because they require interviews with living respondents.

In estimating social mobility in this volume, the records of changes in assets, occupational mobility, power wielding, and roles played in voluntary associations were examined independently. No attempt has been made to attach weights to each element or to combine them. The estimates provided are admittedly of the most controversial sort. They rest ultimately upon an interpretation of the subjective evaluations of status differences in the study population. For this reason the estimates are higher than they could be under any alternative hypothesis. Since my primary object was to derive estimates, the hypothesis employed in doing so is spelled out, but only in outline form.

The estimates and analyses of all three forms of mobility were derived from: the manuscript federal census returns for Waltham from 1850 through 1880 (almost all returns from the 1890 census were lost in a fire); the Massachusetts census returns of 1865; municipal birth, death, and marriage registers; municipal tax rolls and annual reports of the local government; city directories; company record files; diaries; church and club records; and newspapers. Every census-enumerated male has been followed through these records until he either out-migrated or died, or until the terminal date of the study, 1890. Each male figures in the measurement and analysis of physical mobility. The estimates of intra- and intergenerational occupational and social mobility necessarily encompass only those males who remained in Waltham for a time and whose record files satisfied certain specified criteria. The procedures employed in making estimates are indicated in the text and amplified in Appendix I.

A word now about the limitations of the study. The first of these has to do with the fact that Waltham was not a typical American place. Neither Waltham nor any other single place could possibly give adequate representation to the diverse elements which then marked the American environment. If Waltham shared anything in common with other places, it was only the bare outlines of the processes by which mobility contributed to the creation of an urban industrial society. The timing, the rates, the personae, and even many of the consequences of these processes were particular to it. It is, however, this bare outline of mobility processes and the singular history of Waltham and its populace which are the objects of the study. The presumption has been that this case study can effectively demonstrate the fruitfulness of mobility analysis as an approach to our understanding of American labor history and urban industrial development.

A second limitation stems from the exclusion of females from the study. Since females always outnumbered males, their inclusion would have more than doubled the task of data collection. There appeared to be no sampling technique which might have been used and which, by reducing the size of the male component, might have permitted the inclusion of females. More importantly, however, most females were neither lifetime labor force participants nor primary status carriers. For these reasons their occupational and social mobility experiences were likely to have been too few or too insignificant to merit attention. But in consequence of the neglect of females, very little can be said about the significance of social mobility accomplished via marriage, about the economic contributions of females to male asset holdings, or about the relationships between family size and mobility.

A third limitation arises from the very objective of the study. As mentioned above, it appeared to be impossible to devise a sampling technique which could provide a study population of the desired size. If many men died or out-migrated over each decade, there might have been too few persisters to permit statistically significant conclusions to be drawn at many points. The study population, therefore, had to be the entire enumerated male population. This requirement was not viewed with misgiving, since the study was aimed at the anonymous masses of men who had lived history but whose lives had never been treated as its concrete substance.

It was necessary to extract the records of these men from censuses, tax rolls, and the like, only to re-enter them upon those presumed most anti-humanistic of artifacts, computer punch cards. But this is not where the irony lay; computers by themselves are merely machines which can be rendered impotent by disconnecting a circuit. The irony resided in the fact that the attempt to get as close as possible to the experiences of masses of individual men resulted in the loss of all individuality because of the numbers involved. It became necessary to suppress the experience of any one man, once having taken it into account, in order to reveal the experience of the generality of men. Most of the results presented in the chapters on physical, occupational, and social mobility are presented as numbers or proportions rather than as events which marked the lives of personified individuals. But, at a minimum, every man is counted and counts in the history he made.

Presumably, what we wish to know about mobility, industrial development, and urbanization is not only what happened when, why, and how, but also the consequences of such changes for the quality of life. It might be hoped that the collection and analysis of perhaps more information about a population, individual by individual, than ever before attempted, would provide a basis for answering some of the following questions. In what ways did the lives of the men of 1890 differ from those of the men of 1850? Were they happier or less happy in the sense that their lives were less or more problematic, less or more full of experiences and opportunities for experiences in day-to-day living? Had the progressive specialization of work and non-work roles had adverse results? Had the increasing scale and complexity of the urban environment strained the credibility of belonging to and being responsible to society? Had specialization and increasing scale raised barriers to the creation and maintenance of close interpersonal relationships? Had secularization combined with specialization to cast men adrift in skepticism and uncertainty, and diluted the wholeness of life?

Perhaps it was naive ever to believe that such questions might be answered unequivocally, for in the final analysis they cannot be by any of the methods available in social science. Such judgments are for novelists to make who can create a credibility out of their own private visions of reality. The social scientist who makes such an effort must finally come to recognize that his "answers" are judgments; that as such they have no standing save as the ephemeral insights of one man in one time and place. No amount of replication of data can or will compel the same judgments. Are these judgments then not to be made? No, they will be made, simply because the questions they respond to are so important. Facts by themselves are intellectually indigestible without a recipe for their combination. But it remains that a novelist such as Charles Dickens has probably given us a better and more secure understanding of the quality of life during the English industrial revolution than any social scientist will ever be able to do. No future can ever make his portrayals incomplete or inadequate.

How, in the present context, can the men of 1850 and of 1890 be compared when they were different men living in different worlds? Were their problems and concerns more or less weighty for being different, their joys and satisfactions qualitatively discrete from having derived often from different sources? The dimensions of men's objective circumstances can be compared over time, but not their or our estimates of the quality of life. For, at bottom, problems and concerns and joys and satisfactions were not and are not separable from the views of life which provoke their recognition. Retrospectively, we may believe that we now know what was right or wrong, good or bad about other men's pasts. But the vanity we invest in such judgments should be chastened by a recognition of the considerable difficulty which men at all times face in the living of their presents. The study of mobility is more likely to impress upon us the relative nature of historical change than to sustain views of evolutionary stages and the qualitative and often gratuitous judgments which such views foster.

Before concluding this brief introduction, I wish gratefully to acknowledge the assistance of Jean Colely, Richard Williams, William Spector, and Leonard Oshinsky, who helped compile the data on which this volume rests. I stand equally in the debt of the Waltham Historical Society, the Waltham Public Library, Mayor Richard Dacey, the Baker Library of Harvard University, and the archivist of the Commonwealth of Massachusetts, for their kind and wholehearted cooperation. To Mrs. Kay Woolston, Mrs. Joan Catherwood, and Professor David Reimers I owe very special notes of thanks.

The National Science Foundation, under grant GS-1477, and the College of William and Mary provided financial support for a portion of my research. The computer center at the College, and particularly Mrs. Sandra Duncan, were helpful beyond all bounds.

Permission to draw upon previously published work was granted by the *Journal of Economic History*, from Vol. 25, No. 2, (June, 1965); by the *Industrial and Labor Relations Review*, from Vol. 20, No. 1, (October, 1966); and by *Labor History*, from Vol. 8, No. 3, (Fall, 1967).

The data compiled and many of the materials collected in conjunction with the preparation of this volume have been deposited at the Brandeis University Library in Waltham.

I · Early Waltham

Waltham, Massachusetts, was organized as a town in 1738 for what would strike us today as eminently American reasons: its citizens thought the walk to the meetinghouse too far and wished to be separated from Watertown so that they might organize their own parish; there was also an east (Watertown)-west (Waltham) dispute over the equity of town disbursements of tax receipts. At the time, a little more than 100 years after the arrival of its first Puritan settlers, Waltham had 112 adult male residents and an estimated population of 450.[1]

Viewed from the perspective of its future growth, the most important facts of Waltham's existence were its location ten miles due west of Boston, its access to the Charles River, and the relative paucity of its natural resources. Proximity to Boston conferred a number of advantages. It was from there that the capital came for Waltham's initial industrial development. Boston also provided a market for Waltham's manufacturing and agricultural output, and if over time the manufacturing output was not consumed in Boston itself, the city provided a transportation and communication link with other American cities and with Europe. The second factor in Waltham's life was the Charles River which provided, along with fish, ice, and amenity, the water power for early industrial growth. As we shall see, the river as a source of power conferred a benignly limited advantage.

Except for the fertile plain which extended for a distance of about one mile along the river bank, much of the town's area was hilly, covered by a hard, loamy soil studded with rocks, and only moderately fertile. In consequence, although Waltham was an agricultural settlement from its beginnings, its agricultural development was neither so easily undertaken nor so profitable as to produce intensive land use or high land prices. Nonethe-

---

[1]Apart from the primary source materials employed in this brief sketch of early Waltham history, the following accounts were also relied upon: Edmund L. Sanderson, *Waltham as a Precinct of Watertown and as a Town, 1630-1884* (Waltham: Waltham Historical Society, 1936); John W. Barber, *Historical Collections* (Worcester, Mass.: Dorr, Howland, 1839); Harriet Martineau, *Society in America* (New York: Sanders and Otley, 1837); and Rev. Samuel Ripley, "A Topographical and Historical Description of Waltham, in the County of Middlesex, January 1, 1815" in *Collections of the Massachusetts Historical Society*, 2nd ser., Vol. III (Boston, 1815).

less, until well into the twentieth century, much of the town's land area was taken up by small, widely dispersed farms. It comes as something of a surprise to find that, along with its growth as a city and a manufacturing place, Waltham continued for so long a time to incorporate freehold farming into its make-up.[2]

By the time of the first federal census of population in 1790, Waltham had 882 residents. In the first fifty years of its corporate existence, the town had not quite managed to double its population. But the constants in its destiny—proximity to Boston and the Charles River—had already begun to shape its development. Along the Great Country Road leading from Boston to the interior, a number of inns and taverns had been established to cater to the needs of travelers. Locally, this development served to fix Waltham's main street. The town had also gained something of a reputation as a summer retreat. Several Boston merchants built grand country seats, and these added a touch of aristocratic and architectural elegance to the tidy but otherwise commonplace homesteads of working farmers. Finally, a number of small manufacturing ventures had been launched, including, most notably, two paper mills. In association with these, the first dams across the Charles had been built.

Just as the inns and taverns along the high road became the nucleus of Waltham's commercial district, so the two paper-mill dams served the community's industrial development. In 1807 one of the mill properties was sold and converted into a fulling mill. Shortly thereafter, a trio of capitalists, two of them from Boston and the other from Watertown, rebuilt and enlarged this mill and entered into the production of cotton and woolen textiles. In 1814 the second paper mill was sold and a large cotton textile mill was built upon its site. The textile industry, the first "leading sector" of industrialism, had arrived. Waltham found itself an early American entrant into the industrial era.

The establishment of the Boston Manufacturing Company, the second of the two textile ventures, was undoubtedly the single most important event to befall Waltham in the first one hundred years of its existence. Not only did the Company have a profound impact upon the town, it also influenced much of the subsequent development of the American textile industry. For the latter reason, Boston Manufacturing has probably received more attention than any other firm in American history. But it is for the former reason that we must investigate it here.[3]

---

[2]In keeping with New England usage, the "town" of Waltham was truly a township. The first concentration of population within this township was referred to as "the village." With still further growth, the village became "the town." With the granting of a city charter in 1885, the city of Waltham became colloquially coterminous with the township, as it had always been in political terms. In this volume, "town" is always understood to include the entire township.

[3]For additional detail, the reader may consult the author's "The Waltham System and the Coming of the Irish," *Labor History*, Vol. VIII, No. 3 (Fall, 1967).

In providing a synthesis of some British and some American technological and organizational practices, a synthesis known as the Waltham System, the Boston Manufacturing Company was distinctly innovative. The Waltham System most properly includes all of the practices—technological, financial, and managerial—which characterized Boston Manufacturing's operations. It was this entire package that was later reproduced at Lowell and in other New England towns to the west and north of Boston. In a more restricted sense, however, the Waltham System was also taken to designate Company policies toward its workers. It was in this sense that, after the fact of financial success, the entrepreneurs of Boston Manufacturing came to be regarded as beneficent innovators. It was also in this sense that the Company had its greatest impact upon the town.

Instead of following the established practice of recruiting whole families, children and all, for work in its mill, the new company relied most heavily upon young women for the bulk of its work force. Its complements of mechanics, overseers, building tradesmen, and common laborers were made up of adult males. The employment of children was limited to a small number of bobbin boys and pickers.

The female employees, most of whom were between the ages of 18 and 25, were provided with room and board in Company houses. They were paid in currency, net of their lodging fees, and given an opportunity to save from their incomes, at interest, in company accounts. The Company took steps to protect the mill girls from any loss of virtue by formulating regulations, such as obligatory church attendance, and by providing "house mothers" in the boarding houses. Of paramount importance, however, was the fact that, since most of the girls entered the mill with short-run objectives (e.g., to accumulate dowries, to help pay off the mortgage on the family farm, etc.) they remained industrial workers for only short periods of time, probably on the order of four years or less. In consequence, the mill girls did not come to constitute a permanent factory proletariat. Boston Manufacturing had accomplished, or so it seemed, a grand American *coup*: it engaged in manufacturing without creating at the same time a dependent and debased laboring class.

In truth, however, it was not so much the mechanics of the living-working arrangements offered by the Company that made the Waltham System distinctive. The Company had to use relatively mature females in its work force. It had, in consequence, to provide the assurance—to the girls, to their parents, to the Company owners themselves, and to the community at large—that the social standards of the day regarding the oversight of virginal maidens would be maintained and enforced. What was unique was the girls themselves. No successful enterprise had ever relied so heavily for its work force upon literate, pious, and healthy country girls. And when, in the 1830's at Lowell, the mill-girls working under the Waltham System engaged in literary and other intellectual pursuits, they testified in the most impressive way possible just how unique a work force they were.

There were, in addition to those already mentioned, a number of other acts of the Company (or more precisely, acts of the Company and characteristics of its workers) which were compounded into the Waltham System. Most of these were directly related to the Company's impact upon Waltham.

Upon their arrival in Waltham, the entrepreneurs of Boston Manufacturing found a town of approximately 1,250 persons, many of them lifelong residents who, in every sense of the word, owned the town. The initial Company work force of 175 was not quite as large as that of the earlier Waltham Cotton and Woolen Factory Company. Moreover, few of the members of this work force could or did become members of the "society" of the town. The female employees were both socially insignificant—for being females—and physically transient residents. Among the mechanics, who might have been expected to be more important and less transient, it has been found that only five out of thirty-one remained over the period 1817-23.[4] Even the Company's first resident agent, Patrick Tracy Jackson, was too deeply committed to Boston to become a true citizen. Thus, while the Company's presence broadened the employment base of the community and brought population growth, and while the Company may be said to have dominated the town economically, Waltham did not become a company-town in the strictest sense of the word.

Waltham was not sufficiently developed to meet many of the needs of the Company or its employees. As was the case with the construction of its own boarding houses, the Company was obliged to compensate for the town's deficiencies. In doing so, it served its own needs, those of its employees, and those of the town. For example, when the Company absorbed the Waltham Cotton and Woolen Factory Company, it continued to maintain the grammar school which the latter had established. This freed the town of the need to make such provision itself. When the Company purchased a fire engine, it granted use of the equipment to the town. The members of the first volunteer fire company were mill employees. When the Company donated funds to the local minister for the purchase of books, and eventually underwrote the establishment of a reading-room, it extended the use of these facilities to all townspeople. The Company contributed to the subsequent development of the reading-room into a public lyceum, the Rumford Institute. The Company also supported the community church above and beyond its legal obligation to do so.

It is clear from the minutes of board of directors meetings that these company contributions to the Waltham community were prompted in the first instance by self-interest.[5] This is not surprising since, like most

---

[4]George S. Gibb, *The Saco-Lowell Shops* (Cambridge: Harvard University Press, 1950), p. 53.

[5]All information pertaining to internal operations of the Boston Manufacturing Company were drawn from the extensive collection of Company records held at the Baker Library, Harvard University, Cambridge, Massachusetts.

American towns and cities, the public entity called Waltham was to be more largely the product of unrelated, privately made decisions, heaped one atop another, than the result of consciously conceived and directed community action.

Boston Manufacturing, like most companies entering industrially undeveloped communities, faced its testiest problems on the input side of its operations rather than on the demand-for-output side. In particular, the difficulties involved in recruiting and retaining workers would have increased immeasurably had the Company not acted to offset the deficiencies of Waltham. It is in this light that the Company's contributions to education and to intellectual and religious pursuits are to be understood. What was required was that there be enough diversion in Waltham to make it attractive. The precise types of diversion provided—above and beyond relatively high monetized earnings—were those most likely to satisfy the work force: a school for workers who wanted their children to be literate; a lyceum for mill girls and mechanics; church support for a religious population; and, inevitably, the opportunities for socializing, created by bringing together a large number of previously isolated farm girls.

In essence, if the view taken here is correct, there was no such thing as the Waltham System, when defined as an innovative scheme of corporate labor policy. What there was was a set of consequences, derived from the employment of capable Yankee girls, and from the undeveloped nature of Waltham itself. As we shall see, when poor Irish immigrants entered the mills and reduced any need on the Company's part to make the community attractive, the consequences were radically different from what they had been earlier.

Because of its proximity to Boston and because of its water power, Waltham underwent its first industrial development relatively early. Because of the limits of its water power resources, it was spared wholesale conversion into a mill town. When, flushed with their financial success, the owners of Boston Manufacturing sought to expand their operations, they were compelled to search elsewhere for a source of power. The ultimately dubious distinction of boom-town mill-town growth fell to Lowell (1823). Waltham, in sharp contrast, was to have a period of about forty years in which to digest and integrate its first industrial growth. By the time of its second industrial surge, marked by the arrival of the Waltham Watch Company in 1854, the impact of Boston Manufacturing was so deeply imbedded in the fabric of the community as to be inseparable. Memories of the heroes of the first development—Francis Cabot Lowell, Patrick Tracy Jackson, Nathan Appleton, and Paul Moody—had already been enshrined as street names. The Company and its employees were no longer a source of wonderment.[6]

---

[6]A history of nineteenth-century Waltham could probably be written by tracing the origins of its street names. It was not until 1842 that the town began to name its paths and ways to pro-

The population impact of the Waltham Factory Company and of Boston Manufacturing is readily discernible in federal censuses.[7] In the decade prior to the establishment of these companies, 1800–1810, Waltham's population increased from 903 to 1,014, or by 8 percent. In the decade of establishment, 1810–20, the population grew by 65 percent, to 1,677 persons. In the following decade, the rate of increase declined to 11 percent. This one-time population surge undoubtedly increased physical mobility into and out of the town, since it increased the proportion of the population known to be transient. But whether the additions to population were transient or not, it was the absolute increase in size that influenced the course of town development. New stores were built, new churches organized, and the tempo of town life increased. This secondary impact of population growth upon the economic base of the community was confined to servicing the needs of mill employees and townsmen. It was commercial and social rather than industrial. No new firms arose to cater to the needs of Boston Manufacturing because, on the one hand, the Company was so completely integrated economically that it provided most of its own services (e.g., the Company built and serviced much of its machinery and provided its own local transportation facilities). On the other hand, for financial and marketing services, the Company turned to its Boston connections.

An 1830 map of Waltham reveals the first semblance of village development.[8] Because workers had to walk to their jobs and to shops, the location of the mills influenced residence patterns, which in turn influenced the location of retail shops. The first population cluster took the form of two rows of houses and shops, arranged like strands of beads along the Great Country Road for a distance of one mile. At one end of this settlement corridor, where the road passed closest to the river, stood the mills and houses of Boston Manufacturing; at the other end, but more distant from the road, stood the company's bleachery and surrounding houses. Away from this concentration were the randomly scattered settlements of freehold farmers. The federal census of 1830 and town tax records make it possible to examine some of the salient aspects of the population.

If many of the mill girls entertained high hopes of finding a marriage mate in Waltham (their reputed preference was for mill foremen), it seems

---

vide for uniformity in local usage. For some time to come, it was the residents of a street or locality who provided the government with place names. Streets were most often named for local men of prominence, for their first residents, or to signify the presence of an important institution (e.g., Church Street). Names could be changed to reflect any loss in esteem. Thus Crescent Street was once named Dennison Street until the watch company changed it to reflect Aaron Dennison's fall from grace within the company.

[7]The manuscript federal census returns for Waltham are held at the National Archives of the United States, Washington, D.C. The manuscript returns of the Massachusetts censuses for 1855 and 1865 are held at the State House, Boston, Massachusetts.

[8]All of the maps examined in the preparation of this study are held at City Hall, Waltham, Massachusetts.

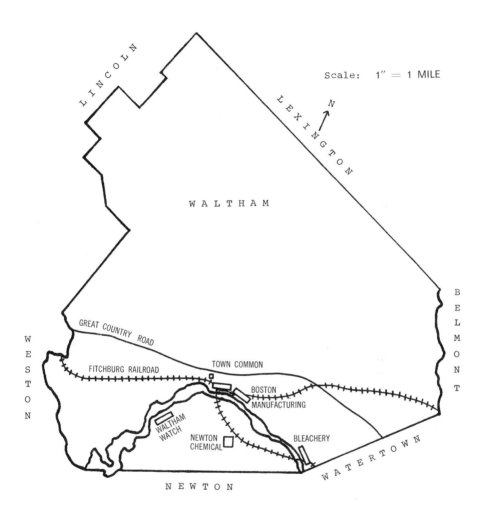

Figure 1.1 *Waltham*

that such hopes were doomed to frustration. Females outnumbered males three to two in the marrying ages 15 to 40. The entire sex distribution of the population was weighted in favor of females by the presence of the mill girls and by the greater survival rates of females: there were 137 females present for every 100 males. The mill girls also influenced the age distribution of females, but the average age of the female population, 24.8 years, was remarkably similar to that of males, which was 24.3 years. Almost three-quarters of the male population was within the economically active ages of 10 to 60.

The age distribution of the population in 1830 provides evidence to support the view that much of Waltham's population growth since 1810 had been the result of net in-migration. There were, to illustrate, 217 males and 332 females aged 20 to 30 present in 1830. In the same year, there were only 165 males and 289 females aged 10 to 20, and 176 males and 182 females aged from birth to 10 years present. Neither the numbers of those in their teens nor of those younger still would have been sufficient to eventually replace the number of persons 20 to 30 years of age present in 1830. Barring a rapid rise in the rate of natural increase in the decade 1800–10 or a rapid decline in the decades 1810–20 and 1820–30, neither of which is likely to have occurred, many of those present in 1830, in the 20-30 years grouping (the largest single age grouping) must have been in-migrants.

Another, more direct, estimate of the importance of net in-migration is afforded by an analysis of residential longevity among male heads of households. Such an analysis provides us with the information that, out of the 224 such persons:

67   (30.0%) had been born in Waltham;
3   (1.3%) had arrived prior to 1800;
14   (6.3%) had arrived at least as early as 1800–09;
16   (7.1%) had arrived at least as early as 1810–19;
74   (33.0%) had arrived at least as early as 1820–29;
50   (22.3%) had no record of arrival prior to 1839.[9]

These data, which reveal that upwards of two-thirds of the male heads of households present in 1830 had migrated into Waltham, are subject to two qualifications before anything can be said about the entire population. First, the household heads were not representative of the entire population, given the large number of unmarried mill girls present. If these girls could be taken into account, the proportion of native-born Walthamites in the entire population would have been even smaller than

---

[9]These estimates were derived from a search of the birth, death, and marriage rolls, preserved in *Vital Records of Waltham, Massachusetts to the Year 1850* (Boston: New England Historical Geneological Society, 1904). All post-1850 data of similar nature were collected from the manuscript records on file at Waltham City Hall.

30 percent. On the other hand, this unrepresentativeness was offset to some unknown degree by the fact that many heads of households were also the parents of Waltham-born children (as the mill girls were obviously not). Perhaps slightly less than one-half of the resident 1830 population had been born in Waltham.

In demographic terms, Waltham in 1830 had a clear concentration of young, working-age men and women, many of whom had migrated to the town in the past two decades in response to the employment opportunities created by the textile mills. Ninety-nine out of the 224 male heads of households appeared on the Boston Manufacturing payroll in 1830. The entire population, old and new alike, was composed overwhelmingly of native-born Yankees. There were only five adult Irish Catholics on the payroll of Boston Manufacturing, and probably no more than another handful in the rest of the town. In economic and political terms, however, the town was more the property of the older, native-son residents than of the newcomers.

Unfortunately, the tax rolls for 1830 have not been preserved among Waltham's records. The earliest nineteenth-century tax rolls available are for an earlier year, 1822. An analysis of this tax list is provided below as a base point against which future changes in the distribution of assets within the community may be gauged.[10]

Of the 475 male taxpayers in 1822, 231 or 48.6 percent had no taxable assets whatever, i.e., neither real or personal property, nor income high enough to be subject to taxation. They appeared on the tax rolls as poll-tax payers only. The average tax paid by those males who had assets represented an average asset holding of $1,849. However, the top two percent of the male taxpayers—nine in number—held 36.9 percent of all of the community's assets. A clear view of the distribution of assets is provided in Table 1.1.

Of the top twelve asset holders in 1822, seven were Waltham born, three (including a former governor of the state) had settled in the town in the eighteenth century, one had come to town with Boston Manufacturing in 1815, and one was mentioned in town records for the first time in the 1822 tax list. Out of the next twenty-five highest asset holders, all but four were born in Waltham. It seems clear from this that the distribution of assets within the community was strongly influenced by inheritance and by length of residence. Alternatively, a large portion of the inequality in asset holdings in 1822 was attributable to the influx of the new people who had come to work in the textile mills.

Asset holding and economic power can be, and in this instance were, two different things. For all their assets, Waltham-born residents were not the prime movers of the community in economic terms. This role fell to the resident agent of the Boston Manufacturing Company. For example, when (in the 1840's) the state legislature authorized the construction of

---

[10]All tax data presented were taken from the manuscript tax rolls on file at Waltham City Hall.

TABLE 1.1   *The Distribution of Assets among Males in 1822*

Asset Holdings	Male Taxpayers		% Of Total Assets Held
	Number	% Of Total	
None	231	48.6	0.0
Some, but less than $1,000	125	26.3	8.1
$1,000, but less than $5,000	107	22.5	50.5
$5,000, but less than $10,000	8	1.6	10.7
$10,000 or more	4	0.8	30.7

a Boston-to-Fitchburg railroad to pass through Waltham, the Company agent influenced the exact route of the road to insure that it serviced the company mills. More obviously, the Company was by far the largest employer and source of income in the town.

It appears, however, that the Company exerted its influence only when its own interests were directly involved. The day-to-day decisions of the community were left to other hands, most often to the older, Waltham-born population. In 1822, for example, all of the selectmen, two of the three tax assessors, and the tax collector were Waltham born. The third assessor had been resident since at least 1802.

Such functionaries, while undoubtedly respected members of the community, were not, however, the ultimate repositories of community trust and wisdom. Despite its industrial growth and population change, Waltham continued into the 1820's and even into the 1850's to preserve vestiges of its theocratic beginnings. The single most influential townsman in the 1820's was the Reverend Samuel Ripley. Over the length of his tenure as the Congregational minister, Reverend Ripley was the acknowledged spiritual and intellectual leader of the community. Until at least 1822, his salary continued to be paid from public tax monies. (The constitutional separation of church and state was not effected until 1833 in Massachusetts). It was to him that Boston Manufacturing turned for assistance when it established its library and lyceum. It was at his feet that the abler children of the town received their post-grammar school education.

A generation later, in the 1850's, another Congregational minister, the Reverend Thomas Hill, would lead the community. But by that time Reverend Hill had to lead by the sheer force of his character. The secular institutional vacuums that had been filled by his predecessor and the unchallenged authority of the Congregational Church no longer existed to confer automatically high status and community leadership.

Waltham continued to grow during the 1830's to the point where, in 1840, it achieved the status of an urban place. It had experienced a 35 percent increase in population over the decade and now had 2,504 residents. Of the additions to population, one-third had resulted from natural increase (the surplus of births over deaths) and two-thirds from net in-migration. The growth of population 1830–40 attributable to natural increase alone was greater than the growth 1820–30 from all sources. Although it is not known whether this was due to an increase in birth rates or to a decline in death rates, there is presumptive evidence that it was the latter of the two.

The earlier suggestion that the surplus of females over males in the ages 15 to 40 made for dim marriage prospects is not supported by the data on marriages over the decade 1830–40. During this period, 44.4 percent of the average number of females aged 15 to 40 took husbands. Since many females were either too young to marry or already married, it seems clear that a large number of the mill girls did find husbands during their stay in town. The same conclusion follows when we look at marriages from a different perspective: slightly better than one-third of the male heads of households who had first arrived in town during the decade and were enumerated in the 1840 census were newly wed in Waltham. This finding in turn suggests that many of the single male in-migrants were fairly young.

The high rate of marriage which prevailed may have resulted in a slightly higher birth rate since, although the proportion of children aged birth to 10 years was virtually the same in 1840 and 1830, the proportion of females present in the child-bearing ages 15 to 40 had declined slightly. However, the extremely low death rate which prevailed over the decade— 9.6 deaths per 1000 population—undoubtedly accounted for most of the natural increase in population. It is impossible to account for this abnormally low death rate except to note that, until the financial panic of 1836–37, the decade had been one of unprecedented prosperity. (There is no readily apparent reason why vital statistics records-keeping should have been significantly worse in this decade, but that may have been the case.)

The primary impetus to migration into Waltham came from the expansion of Boston Manufacturing Company. By 1840 the Company had three mills and a bleachery in operation, and employed approximately 550 workers. (In contrast, Lowell in 1844 had 11 mills employing 7,430 females alone. In 1840, Lowell's population was almost ten times the size of Waltham's.) In response to this expansion, and contributing to further population growth, the number of shops and stores had risen to forty-six and the number of churches to six: three Congregational, and one Methodist, one Universalist, and one Catholic. The town now boasted its first hotel and bank. In all, there were 275 dwellings, making for a ratio of nine persons per dwelling—which was more reflective of the presence of boarding houses than it was of large families.

As the existence of a Catholic church suggests, the number of Irish Catholics in the population had grown somewhat. There were now at least eight Catholic households, enough to prompt a part-time ministry by a priest who divided his energies between Waltham and Watertown. There were also, in the first census count available, ten Negroes resident in the town. But overwhelmingly the town continued to be composed of native-born Yankees.

A comparison of the male heads of households present in 1830 with those in 1840 provides a clearer picture of the processes of population growth and change. Of the 224 household heads present in 1830, 27 had died by 1840, 121 had remained in Waltham, and 76 had left. Those who died and those who persisted accounted for 66.1 percent of the 1830 household heads. Of the 335 male heads present in 1840, 121 were persisters, 35 were sons risen to household head status, 18 were first mentioned in the census but are believed to have been present in the town sometime prior to 1831, and 161 were in-migrants over the decade. The number of in-migrant household heads exceeded that of the resident household heads. The proportion of Waltham-born heads of households had declined from 30 percent to 23 percent.

The distribution of assets within the community in 1840 was, if anything, more inequitable than that which had obtained in 1822. The 1840 figures are presented in Table 1.2.

Although the proportion of those with no assets had increased by 10 percent between 1822 and 1840, the proportion of young men aged 20 to 29—those who might have been expected to have the fewest assets—declined slightly. Therefore, the youthfulness of the male population cannot explain the increased inequality in asset holding. But mobility into the community can. Of the 389 men without assets in 1840, only 18 had been present in 1830. All of the rest had in-migrated during the decade. Most in-migrants, 71.8 percent of them to be exact, were without assets at the end of the decade of their arrival. In contrast, 87.8 percent of those who in 1840 had been present a decade or more had some assets. Thus, both the 1822 and 1840 data suggest the same conclusion: residential longevity and the possession of assets went hand in hand. Those without assets were most likely to be the most recent in-migrants. This was so even though the absolute number of in-migrants with assets exceeded the number of persisters with assets.

Since between 1822 and 1840 the aggregate value of all assets had just about doubled, and since among males a smaller proportion had assets in the latter year, those with assets in 1840 were on the average much richer than their 1822 counterparts. The average value of assets among males with assets rose from $1,849 in 1822 to $3,344 in 1840. This meant, of

TABLE 1.2   *The Distribution of Assets among Males in 1840*

Asset Holdings	Male Taxpayers		% Of Total Assets Held
	Number	% Of Total	
None	389	58.5	0.0
Some, but less than $1,000	91	13.7	4.7
$1,000, but less than $5,000	133	20.0	37.6
$5,000, but less than $10,000	42	6.3	30.0
$10,000 or more	10	1.5	27.7

course, that the gap between those with and those without assets had widened considerably. However, it must be recognized that whatever anguish and frustration might have flowed from this growing inequality was largely mitigated by the fact that most of the assetless men were new to Waltham. They had not been present to witness the success of others where they had failed. Nor were they doomed to spend the rest of their lives having their noses rubbed in their "failure." There was no failure, only newness. Following the pattern of those without assets in 1822, these most recent in-migrants were only beginning to strive to succeed. Should they succeed, many of them would settle down in Waltham. Should they fail, they would move on to try their luck elsewhere. The potential torment associated with economic inequality was diminished by the absence of a permanently poor group of permanent residents.

During the 1840's, Waltham's development was quickened by a series of events of lasting consequence. The first railroad linking Waltham to Boston and to western Massachusetts went into operation in 1842. The town added to its land area by annexing from Newton a 600-acre tract south of the Charles River. The population increased at the unprecedented rate of 76 percent, from 2,504 to 4,464, and encompassed, in a growing number of Irish Catholics, more diversity than heretofore.

Singly, these changes marked no discrete break with the past. In combination, however, they pushed Waltham along the path of urban industrialism at such an accelerated speed that the decade 1840–50 can be taken as a benchmark. What had previously been a community of small-scale farmers and a summer retreat, with a single large-scale manufacturing firm grafted on, now became a town linked by the railroad, by population scale and heterogeneity, and by a growing volume of manufacturing activity to the whole complex of changes transforming New England and the northeastern United States generally.

In testament to these broader changes, it may be noted that several of the events of the forties stemmed from actions over which Waltham had little or no control. The Fitchburg Railroad was built through Waltham under the authorization of the state legislature. The road passed through the town simply because it lay abreast of the most direct route from Boston to the west. It may have been a feather in Waltham's cap to have the railroad, but the town itself had had little to say in the matter. The same was true of the population influx. One stream of in-migrants was composed of Irish Catholics fleeing the ravages of famine and fever in their homeland. The other stream was made up of native-born Yankees abandoning an increasingly unprofitable New England agriculture. Both groups were more strongly pushed than pulled, and their decision to come to Waltham owed very little to the design or the desires of the town.

Only in the matter of the land annexation did the town have a choice and, therefore, the power of decision. The development of the area involved had been undertaken by Waltham men and by Boston Manufacturing. Apart from farmsteads, this development had taken the form of the Newton Chemical Company, which supplied dyes to the textile firm. When a dispute arose over the maintenance of a bridge connecting the area with Waltham, Newton ceded its jurisdiction (in 1849) for the token sum of $1,000. Within a decade Waltham Watch was located upon this tract and "south of the river" became the scene of rapid and extensive growth.[11]

Of the net additions to the population during the forties, just better than 9 percent was accounted for by natural increase. Slightly less than another 9 percent was accounted for by the land acquisition. More than 80 percent of the new people in the town in 1850 were in-migrants.

Some new people were introduced into the town by the railroad. Depot and baggage masters, gate attendants, and maintenance and operating crew members appeared for the first time. In addition, there was some expansion of employment at Boston Manufacturing and at Newton Chemical. New industrial activities included an iron foundry, several small-scale shoe factories, and a garment-making establishment. A number of new retail shops also arose to serve the needs of the growing population. The mere listing of new enterprises, however, does little justice to the drama of the changes which occurred. Two of the major consequences of expansion, increased assets and a housing boom, come closer to indicating how very considerable the changes were.

The total value of all assets held within the town increased at the phenomenal rate of 130 percent over the decade. This is the rate of increase with no allowance having been made for the fact that, nationally, the consumer price index was 20 percent lower in 1850 than it had been in 1840. If tax assessments were made in terms of current prices, and if an adjustment is made for the price decline, then true asset values increased by better than 190 percent.[12] One reflection of this increasing wealth took the form of a housing boom. Over the decade, the stock of houses in the town nearly doubled. Nearly as many new houses were built 1840 to 1850 as were standing in 1840 after two hundred years of settlement. A boom of such proportions would in and of itself have attracted numbers of workers into the town.

The reliability of the asset and housing figures employed can be gauged in a number of ways. The true value of assets, as reported by the tax assessors, was divided into two categories for tax purposes, real property and personal property. Bearing in mind that prices were lower in 1850 than in 1840, the increase in asset values cannot have been merely the product of an altered assessment of real property values (land, houses,

---

[11]With the sole exception of the grant of a small, unoccupied parcel of land to Belmont in 1859, Waltham's boundaries remained unchanged through 1890.

[12]Throughout this volume, I have employed the price index prepared by Ethel Hoover, which appears in "Employment, Growth, and Price Levels," *Hearings Before the Joint Economic Committee*, U.S. Congress (Washington, G.P.O. 1959), pt. II, p. 397.

and buildings) for the value of personal property (including farm stock, business inventories, carriages, furniture, stocks and bonds, savings at interest, and income taxable beyond the first $2,000) rose even more rapidly than did the value of real property. There were, moreover, by actual count, almost twice as many houses and buildings standing in the town. These structures, in turn, did not represent an inflated count based upon the development of a shanty town among the Irish in-migrants. Waltham had no shanty town. The assessments upon Irish-owned houses and upon rental houses occupied by Irish families were too high for this to have been the case. Against a Yankee average value of $1,800 for a house and lot, Irish-owned homes had an average value of $1,200, while in the five known instances of house rentals to Irish (listed in the tax rolls as "5 Irish Houses") the houses were valued at $500 each. These rental properties were undoubtedly quite modest, but they were by no means rude shanties.[13]

The Irish population of Waltham skyrocketed during the decade. Where there had been only eight or so Irish households in 1840, there were 163 in 1850. From an insignificant minority, the number of the Irish increased to the point of comprising one-quarter of the town population.

Many of these newcomers were refugees in flight from Ireland's devastating famines. Others were pre-famine immigrants, some of whom may have been prompted to migrate to Waltham by the backing-up of immigrants in Boston. Although it was impossible to distinguish between the famine and pre-famine Irish in many instances, the distinction is an important one. For example, there were, in 1850, twenty-five Irish home-owners in Waltham. This surprising finding—given our image of the destitution of the famine Irish—is largely explained by differences in the timing of Irish arrivals in the United States. Of fifteen Irish families known to have been resident in the U.S. for a decade or more prior to 1850 (including four families present in Waltham in 1840), eight had assets and six of these owned houses. In contrast, of the five families definitely known to have immigrated within the past three years, not a one had assets.[14] What was true among Yankees held with equal force among the Irish: asset holding was associated with persistence in the town, and with the further factor of longevity in the United States.

Although townsmen as a group were more than twice as wealthy in 1850 as they had been in 1840, the distribution of assets did not materially change over the decade. Since there is one sense in which this assertion is true and another in which it is false, let us examine and qualify Table 1.3.

[13]The average value of Yankee houses and lots was derived from a sample of 50 owner-occupied houses. Some portion of the higher value of Yankee real property stemmed from higher land values rather than from the greater value of dwellings. This was so because, on the average, Yankee-owned homes and lots were in the older, more improved, areas of settlement.

[14]The birth places of children under three as given in the federal census or in the town death rolls were used to establish longevity or recentness of arrival in the country.

TABLE 1.3   *The Distribution of Assets among Males in 1850*

Asset Holdings	Male Taxpayers		% Of Total Assets Held
	Number	% Of Total	
None	698	61.7	0.0
Some, but less than $1,000	137	12.1	3.1
$1,000, but less than $5,000	203	17.9	24.6
$5,000, but less than $10,000	56	5.0	20.1
$10,000 or more	37	3.3	52.2

A comparison of the distributions for 1840 (Table 1.2) and 1850 reveals an increased polarization of asset holding. The proportion of those with no assets rose slightly; the proportions in the next three categories declined; and the proportion of those with $10,000 or more in assets and the proportion of the assets held by this category rose considerably. While absolutely more people had absolutely more assets, the number of those with the largest assets rose fastest along with the amount of assets they held. The gulf between rich and poor had widened.

It happens, however, that very special circumstances explain the very large proportion of the assets held by the richest taxpayers. The seven largest asset holders, who among them accounted for thirty percent of all the assets, were men with business interests in Boston who used Waltham, in modern parlance, as a suburban bedroom. Five of the seven were merchants, while two were listed in the census as gentlemen, meaning, presumably, that they did not work but lived off of investment returns. The availability of trains into Boston (perhaps a forty minute trip, station to station) made it practicable for this group to travel between their counting-houses and their Waltham estates.

Apart from the service of several of these men as vestrymen in a Waltham church, there is no evidence that they took any interest or active part in the conduct and life of the town. It is, of course, entirely possible that they made their influence felt in informal ways, by a few well-chosen words to key townsmen while attending a musicale or a lecture. Even in the absence of overt influence, their mere presence, as exemplars of wealth and well-being, may have had a subtle impact upon townsmen. But none among this group sought public office, or served on the directorates of voluntary associations, or participated in town meetings.

If, for all practical purposes, these seven richest men were *in* but not *of* the town, if their eyes were upon their Boston enterprises, their Boston clubs, newspapers, and entertainments, may it not be presumed that in the view of townsmen they constituted part of the Boston rather than the Waltham aristocracy? Unquestionably this was the case for three of the seven, the Lymans, the Cabot Lowells, and the Copely Greenes, who already possessed what has come to be styled Brahmin status. To get some sense of how townsmen compared themselves with one another, such non-comparable aristocrats may meaningfully be excluded from the analysis. When this is done, the distribution of assets in 1850 is much more like that of 1840.

It is possible further to refine our view of the distribution of assets by allowing for the fact that all of the remaining rate payers were not meaningfully equal. In the asset distributions presented thus far, this point has been neglected, but the taxable male population was differentiated by age, marital status, kinship, and newness of arrival. By taking such factors into account, it is possible to move closer to the actual and more relevant distribution of wealth in the community.

Some 46 percent of all the male heads of households had assets. Most asset holders were married men, while most of those without assets were single and without familial obligations. These facts serve to reduce the social significance of the inequality manifest in Table 1.4. This inequality is further reduced by the knowledge that most of the heads of households without assets were young men relatively new in that status. Irish inmigrants, many of whom were famine immigrants, accounted for a disproportionate share of the assetless household heads. Though they composed only a fifth of all of the household heads, the Irish made up almost a third of the family heads without assets. Their newness in the country and the circumstances of their flight from Ireland are alone enough to account for their lack of assets.

Finally, a small number of heads of households were without assets for having passed them on to sons in advance of their deaths, while another group of single sons without assets had asset-holding fathers present. All in all then, the asset distributions presented in the foregoing tables tend to overstate the inequality of asset holding. Inequality there certainly was, but the raw distribution of assets when corrected for differences in age,

TABLE 1.4   *The Distribution of Assets among Males, 1840 and 1850*
(with deletions)

Assets	Male Taxpayers		% Of Total Assets Held
	Number	% Of Total	
1840			
None	389	58.5	0.0
Some, but less than $1,000	91	13.7	4.7
$1,000, but less than $5,000	133	20.0	37.6
$5,000, but less than $10,000	42	6.3	30.0
$10,000 or more	10	1.5	27.7
1850			
None	698	62.1	0.0
Some, but less than $1,000	137	12.2	4.5
$1,000, but less than $5,000	203	18.1	35.5
$5,000, but less than $10,000	56	5.0	28.9
$10,000 or more	30	2.7	31.1

marital status, kinship, and newness of arrival in the United States, is decidedly less inequitable.

Of the 335 male heads of households enumerated in the 1840 census, 187 (55.8 percent) persisted to 1850, 56 had died prior to 1850, and 92 (27.5 percent) had outmigrated.[15] In 1850, as in 1840, more in-migrants held assets than did persisters. In part, this can be explained by the fact that in 1850 the in-migrant household heads were more than twice as numerous as were persisting heads and rising sons. In part, also, it can be explained by the rise in wealth that marked the in-migrants' decade of arrival. But what is troublesome is that, in the face of so many asset holders among the in-migrants, so many persisting heads of households fared so poorly. Of the 195 persisting heads;

92 experienced an increase in assets,
25 came to possess assets for the first time,
10 with assets experienced no change,
38 without assets experienced no change,
29 with assets suffered a decline,
 1 unknown

Over-all, most persisting household heads improved their asset positions, but almost 40 percent either realized no gain or lost assets. Apart from the size of this latter group, what is truly striking is that it included a number of men who, it might have been thought, would have been most likely to accumulate assets. In particular, there were in this group several foremen from Boston Manufacturing. That such men—the recipients of relatively high wages and stable employment—were unable to claim any assets whatever, in a decade when all assets more than doubled, is remarkable. It engenders a note of incredulity about the likelihood that many in-migrants accumulated their assets *after* their arrival in Waltham.

The possibility that many in-migrants brought assets with them and made Waltham the richer thereby—even though such a possibility runs counter to the expectation that most physically mobile persons move without assets—may be inferred from both the extraordinary changes sweeping the larger New England community and from other characteristics of Waltham's in-migrants.

The 1840's witnessed the first truly massive population movement away from the New England countryside. Of two streams of migrants, one moved westward toward the frontier, while the other remained within the region and resettled in cities and towns.[16] Industrially developing urban

---

[15]Of the 92 out-migrants, eight were carried on the 1850 tax rolls. These eight have been included in following remarks and figures.

[16]That this movement affected all of New England except Connecticut is indicated by Jeffrey G. Williamson in "Antebellum Urbanization in the American Northeast" *Journal of Economic History*, Vol. XXV, No. 4 (December, 1965).

places attracted most of the migrants, just as they simultaneously attracted a disproportionate share of incoming Irish famine immigrants. The net result of these movements was an unprecedented acceleration of urban population growth. While Waltham increased its population by 76 percent over the decade, Lowell grew by 221 percent, Newburyport by 80 percent, West Cambridge by 62 percent, and Watertown and Newton by 57 percent each.

The age distribution of the 1850 Protestant male population in Waltham, when compared with that for 1840, provides additional substance for this argument. Over the decade, the proportions of male children (infants to 15 years of age) and of young men (ages 15 to 30 years) declined relative to the proportion of men 30 years and older. This suggests that the in-migrant Yankees, although married, as many of them were, brought relatively few children with them. It also suggests that, when confronted with a choice between western homesteading and urban relocation, the older and the more well-to-do among rural New Englanders chose the latter course. It appears to have been as true among Protestant in-migrants as it was among the 1850 Irish population in Waltham that assets held, age, and the number of dependents were closely related. Those who possessed assets were most likely to be over 30 years of age and to have only one or two children.[17] The comparative wealthiness of the Yankee in-migrants of the forties perhaps explains the very rapid response of the housing market to population growth.

In sum, Waltham's growth during the forties was part of a general movement into urban places. The pull of Waltham's employment opportunities was fed by pushes out of New England agriculture and out of famine-stricken Ireland. Many of the married Yankee in-migrants appear to have brought assets with them, whereas their Irish counterparts brought none.

Admixed in these population movements, even in so small a place as Waltham, was the outward pull of the California gold strike. Just one month after a local paper carried the news from California (in mid-December of 1848), a company of 28 young men, including at least eight from Waltham, organized for sea travel to the gold fields. When still another townsman sent back a bag of gold dust, it had the effect of mobilizing another party of men. Independent of these events, a group of men—including three of the 1840 non-persisting household heads—departed in 1849 for Mexico, to staff a newly organized cotton mill. Such wide-ranging movements suggest that physical mobility at the time was not severely limited by the difficulties and perils of long-distance travel.[18]

[17]Estimated from a sample of men with and without assets. It is possible that, in view of the higher average age of asset holders, some of their children had already left the parental roof and hence that asset holders only appeared to have fewer dependents.

[18]Critics of mobility studies have rather consistently called for information on the destinations of out-migrants without, it would seem, much sense of how difficult it is to find such data.

The decade of the 1840's was not entirely as roseate as the other indices of growth suggest. The average annual death rate rose to 15.2 per thousand, up from the abnormally low rate of 9.6 per thousand during the thirties. Among the factors contributing to this trend were the high death rate among recent Irish immigrants and an outbreak of cholera in 1848.[19]

As a result of the patterns of mobility and the small scale of natural increase, Waltham's 1850 population was more "normal." There were more older men present, and the ratio of females to males continued its decline. From 127 females per 100 males in 1840, the ratio declined to 118 per 100 in 1850. But the very same forces served to make Waltham more "abnormal" in the sense that its native population and its old-timers were now overwhelmingly outnumbered by new people. Who was in Waltham, how people acted, and what kinds of lives they led, were increasingly subject to fewer and fewer internalized social controls. Population newness, heterogeneity and scale, and industrial development presaged a new order of things. The task of the next several generations of men would be to attempt to accommodate themselves to this new order; to make this abnormality somehow a normal and liveable state of affairs.

But in the 1840's, the life of the community remained as yet wonderfully uncomplicated. Early in the spring of each year, the townsmen gathered at the town meeting to deal with the agenda prepared by the board of selectmen. There were few controversial issues. The election of town officials generated little excitement, since the same men appear to have served in office for extended periods. In any event, there were no more than a dozen public offices of consequence (3 selectmen, 3 assessors, 5 school board members, and the town clerk), and all of these functioned on a part-time basis. Public servants were very literally servants who contributed their energies to the community for only token rewards.

Something of the magnitude and scope of public affairs can be provided by the town's financial statement for the fiscal year ending March 1, 1842:

Paid in support of	
schools	$2,367.00
fire department	2,796.00
road repairs	1,779.00
incidentals	1,890.00
Balance on hand	$2,047.00

Newspaper reports of departures, such as those mentioned above, were few and far between, and even then dealt only with select portions of the population. A check of the 1850 tax rolls for the whereabouts of non-resident property owners, yielded information on only four 1840 out-migrants (two were in Boston, one in Concord, and one in Keene, N.H.) These four, plus the three venturers to Mexico, account for the whereabouts of less than 10 percent of all 1840 non-persisters. It appears that there is no simple way to deal with out-migrant destinations in a systematic fashion.

[19]Although town statistics indicate that deaths exceeded births three times during the decade,

At the time, the community supported nine common schools with 500 students and no more than 12 teachers. The fire department was composed of volunteer companies. The road repair crews were hired on an ad hoc basis. Even the care and maintenance of school buildings and grounds were left to voluntary neighborhood committees. In short, with the exception of the school teachers and the collector of taxes, no one looked to the town government for his primary income. There were as yet no professional politicians, firemen, or city workers.

The town still had no lock-up and no police force, for crime was a rarity. Indigency was also so rare that instead of providing its own poor farm, the town boarded what few aged paupers it had in private homes at public expense. What limited public assistance there was was most likely to take the form of payments in kind—e.g., a pair of shoes, a cord of wood—rather than cash. Limited public activity and frugality were the hallmarks of town government: even the grass upon the town common was harvested and sold as fodder to add to the public purse.[20]

The social life of the community revolved around the churches and Rumford Institute. Well into the 1870's, religious enthusiasm gripped the Protestant townsmen, and in the absence of revival meetings, the churches organized fairs and socials around the year. Rumford Institute—the town's lyceum, meeting-hall, and library—at one time or another brought before the public such notables as Ralph Waldo Emerson, Horace Mann, Louis Aggasiz, George Bancroft, and Edward Everett. In addition, there were numerous diversions afforded by the river, the taverns along Main Street, and by the snow and ice of long and often bitter winters. Still, the pace of town life was not sufficient to keep alive a local newspaper in competition with the Boston press. Despite numerous efforts, Waltham was not to have its own successful paper, a weekly, until 1856.

In consequence of the lack of an extensive printed record, the events which took place in the 1840's confront us as disjointed bits and pieces of history. Nonetheless, these events represented so large an amount of change that they may be taken to form a major turning point in the town's development. It would be a serious mistake to suppose that at this turning point the men of Waltham consciously set out to build a new society or that they were aware of having any options whatever in this regard. Least of all is it likely that they imagined the possibility of creating (for it had not previously existed) that sense of community the loss of which is today so incontinently mourned. We may suppose, instead, that they looked forward to a changed future because its prospects were more attractive than

---

this result was probably due to a recording mix-up of some sort. Reported births, for example, gyrated wildly from 38 to 105 to 33 to 151 to 60 to 133, over the period 1844–49.

[20]Information pertaining to the activities of town government was taken from annual reports on file at Waltham Public Library. The library also possesses complete runs of town newspapers, the minutes of some voluntary associations, published and unpublished reminiscences, and other miscellaneous records. These sources, along with smaller holdings of the Waltham Historical Society, provided the basis for the descriptions of town life and events presented.

any past they had known. In the face of increasing population size and anonymity, in the face of a mutual animus between Yankee and Irishman, and in the face of increasingly new possibilities for living and working, their primary goals very likely became—if they had not always been—simply to cope with existence, and to cope in materially successful and emotionally satisfying ways.

II · Physical Mobility
1850-90

The analysis of physical mobility requires something of the same peripatetic vision which railroad conductors must develop in the course of their work. On the trip through time with which we deal in this chapter, starting at 1850 and ending at 1890, the census returns for Waltham provide the ticket stubs. Each time we look into a fresh set of returns we can expect, like a conductor making his rounds, to find new ticket holders amidst a dwindling number of familiar ones. At any one moment in time, the passengers on board will have been present for varying lengths of time, and the most recent arrivers may easily outnumber those who have travelled most of the distance. In all, there will have been many more passengers than the sum of those at the start and at the end of the trip indicates. The ticket stubs alone accurately reflect the whole number of travelers.

Unlike the railroad conductor who makes his rounds after every stop, the analyst of physical mobility has to contend with the fact that the federal census of population provides him with information for only sixty days out of every 3,652. There is, in consequence, a difference of unknown proportions between *actual* population movements and movements among the *enumerated* population. Physical mobility in the enumerated population must always be less than that which actually occurred.

In addition, the student of mobility has many more questions to ask than just "Tickets, please." It matters to him who it is that comes to a place and who it is that departs. He wants to know, if possible, why this movement takes place and what influences its rate. Beyond this, he also wants to know what the consequences of physical mobility are for the individuals and for the community involved. How does the process of physical mobility work to transform the shape and character of a community?

During the forty-year period from 1850 to 1890, Waltham experienced uninterrupted population growth. When viewed within the perspective of the population record stretching from 1790 to 1960 (Figure 2.1), this period clearly marks the emergence of Waltham as an industrial city. From 1850 onward the population rose decennially from 4,464 to 6,397, to 9,065, to 11,712, and to 18,707 in 1890.

23

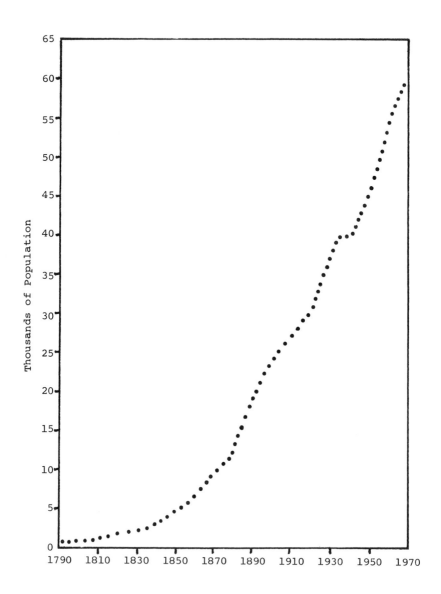

FIGURE 2.1   *Waltham Population Growth, 1790–1970*

Demographically, the two sources of Waltham's population growth were the surplus of births over deaths (the natural increase) and the surplus of in-migrants over out-migrants (net in-migration). An initial impression of the relative importance of these may be gained from the following figures: Between 1850 and 1880, the male population increased from 2,048 to 5,435, that is by 3,387 males. Over the same period, 3,376 males were born, while 1,991 males died, resulting in a natural increase of 1,385. This natural increase accounts for 40.9 percent of the growth of the male population. Residually, net in-migration amounted to 2,002 males, and accounted for 59.1 percent of the male population growth. These are the proportions of natural increase and net in-migration that would, as a matter of convention, result from the use of the kinds of data generally available to demographers. They are, however, quite deceptive. The birth and death figures employed were collected on a daily basis, and therefore apply to the actual population. The population figures themselves refer to the decennially enumerated population. A better estimate of the contributions of natural increase and net in-migration to population growth can be gained by adjusting birth and death statistics so that they apply only to the enumerated population.

In the decade 1850-60, only 29 percent of the males who died in Waltham had been enumerated in its 1850 census count. The comparable figures for 1860-70 and 1870-80 were 32 percent in each case. Even on a five year basis, less than 50 percent of those who died had been enumerated in the most recent census. (The exact figures are: 47 percent over 1860-65 and 42 percent over 1865-70). One reason why such small proportions of the deceased were to be found among the enumerated was that many of them were recent in-migrants. A second reason was that many of those who died were children who were born and who perished between two censuses.

Slightly better than one-quarter (26.5 percent) of all male deaths between 1850 and 1880 were accounted for by the mortality of infants under one year of age. Almost half (46.3 percent) of all male deaths in the same period involved children five years old and younger. Such grim statistics distort not only the value of mortality figures, but also the value of birth figures as they apply to the contribution of natural increase to the enumerated population. If most of those who died had never been enumerated, and if many of those newly born perished soon afterwards, then they could not have played a part in the growth of the enumerated population. The appropriate birth and death figures are those which include only those males born who survived to be enumerated and those males who died after having been enumerated. We have already seen that deaths in the enumerated population involved only about a third of all recorded male deaths in each decade. Correcting the number of recorded births for infant and child mortality and for out-migration, it appears that slightly less than a third (30.3 percent) of all male births resulted in additions to the enu-

merated population. Hence, while the actual birth and death figures indicated that natural increase made up 40.5 percent of the population growth
between 1850 and 1880, the corrected vital statistics suggest that natural
increase contributed only 11.9 percent to the growth of the enumerated
population. This points to the conclusion that net in-migration played
by far the largest part in Waltham's growth.[1]

Net in-migration is of primary importance in the analysis of population growth. By comparison, the measurement of *gross* in- and out-migration has an independent and an equal if not greater significance. For
while it is important from one point of view to know whether population
grew or not, and why and at what rates, from another point it is just as
important to know whether the over-all movements of population were
large or small. If a community's population increased by 10 percent as
the result of small amounts of in- and out-migration, the consequences
would differ significantly from a situation in which the same size of increase resulted from wholesale population turnover. What is potentially at
stake here are such matters as the security and effectiveness of institutions and organizations, the distribution and character of power relationships, and the provision and maintenance of many public and private
investments.

In the absence of comparative data, there is no firm basis upon which
to judge whether the rates of in- and out-migration of the Waltham population were high or low. But when one considers what the observed rates
must have meant for individuals, for inter-personal relationships, and for
the life and character of the city itself, there is no question that these rates
were exceedingly high. The figures presented immediately below were
derived from individual-by-individual comparisons of successive censuses. They overstate out-migration to the unknown degree by which
census enumerations were incomplete.

By 1860, 57.4 percent of all the males present in 1850 had out-migrated;
by 1870, 53.5 percent of all the males present in 1860 had out-migrated;
by 1880, 50.0 percent of all the males present in 1870 had out-migrated;
by 1890, 38.6 percent of all the males 20 years of age and older in 1880 had
out-migrated.

[1]To measure natural increase in the enumerated population:

$$EP_2 - EP_1 = EB_2 - ED_1$$

where EP_2 = enumerated male population at end of decade

EP_1 = enumerated male population at start of decade

EB_2 = born in Waltham during the decade and enumerated at its end.

ED_1 = deceased in Waltham during the decade and enumerated at its start.

In practice, EB_2 was found by subtracting from the total number of recorded births, (a) the
number of the Waltham-born deceased in the appropriate age brackets, and (b) an estimated
number of Waltham-born out-migrants. This latter estimate was arrived at by applying the
proportion of out-migrants in the starting male population to the surviving population of
new-born males. ED_1 was computed by matching the male death rolls with the appropriate
census listing.

On the average, almost half (49.1 percent) of the males present at any one moment in time were not likely to be present a decade later. This level of population turnover was solely the product of out-migration. Those who died within a decade of their last enumeration have not been included. If they are included, then on the average 57 percent of the males present at any one time were not to be found in residence ten years later.

Since Waltham continually grew in population during the period, and since the contribution of natural increase to this growth was quite small, the town experienced more in-migration than out. Once more, shortcomings of census enumeration would lead to overstatement.

68.6 percent of the 1860 male population had in-migrated since 1850;
67.8 percent of the 1870 male population had in-migrated since 1860;
54.5 percent of the 1880 male population had in-migrated since 1870;
58.8 percent of the 1890 male population 20 years of age and older had in-migrated since 1880.

On the average, 61.2 percent of all the males present at any one time had in-migrated within the decade. This proportion would be higher still had it been possible to include the sons born in Waltham to in-migrant parents during their decade of arrival. Table 2.1, below, provides the details which underlie the foregoing calculations. Since in the absence of manuscript census returns for 1890 the city tax rolls for that year were employed, the 1880–90 figures apply, where noted, only to the male population twenty years old and above.

Neglecting the upward bias introduced by the incompleteness of census counts, over half the males present at any one time disappeared within a decade, most of them as out-migrants. Approximately two-thirds of the males present at any one time had only arrived in Waltham within a decade. These proportions, it must be remembered, are *underestimates* of actual population flows. They exclude all moves out of and back into Waltham that occurred in between census years, and all moves into and back out of Waltham in between census years. In a moment we shall attempt to gauge the difference between actual population flows and enumerated population flows. Before doing so, let us turn our attention to the trends in migration.

As indicated previously, the rate of out-migration declined steadily over time. The rate of in-migration also declined steadily until 1880, and then it rose over the next decade. At least three alternative hypotheses can be put forward in explanation of these trends. Which of these provides the most accurate explanation cannot be said at this time.

One hypothesis runs to the effect that the rates of physical mobility in Waltham were the product of regional rather than purely local factors. Since rates of physical movement were slowing down in New England as a whole, their decline in Waltham was simply part of a larger trend. Alternatively, it could be argued that perhaps it was the changing composi-

TABLE 2.1   Male Population Growth and Mobility, 1850–90

	1850–60		1860–70		1870–80		1880–90	
	No.	%	No.	%	No.	%	No.	%
Start of decade population								
Total	4,464		6,397		9,065		11,712	
Males	2,048		2,961		4,227		5,435	
Male:								
Population Increase	913	44.6	1,266	42.8	1,208	28.6	2,000[a]	60.3
Enumerated Births	180		221		623		(516)[b]	
Enumerated Deaths	123		236		261		(362)[c]	
Natural Increase	+57	+6.2	−15	−1.2	+362	+30.0	not applicable	
Out-Migration	1,177		1,586		2,115		1,280[a]	
In-Migration	2,033		2,867		2,961		3,126[a]	
Net In-Migration	856	93.8	1,281	101.2	846	70.0	1,846[a]	92.3

[a] Figures are for men 20 years of age or older in 1880 and 1890
[b] Number of persisters among 1880 males 10 to 19 years of age
[c] Number of deceased males 20 years or older in 1880

tion of the Waltham population which accounts for these trends. If later in-migrants were, for some reason, more likely to settle-in than their predecessors, this would result in reduced rates of mobility. Or, lastly, it could be contended that Waltham had grown to where it had achieved a critical mass sufficient to reduce outward movements. The size and number of its opportunities may have become large enough to weaken the incentive to go elsewhere in the pursuit of opportunities.

It should be pointed out that, whatever the trends in rates of migration, the absolute numbers of migrants steadily rose. (The possible but unlikely exception to this occurs with regard to 1880–90 out-migrants, when the figures exclude all males under twenty in 1880). Whether it was the proportion of new men to old or the absolute number of new men to old, Waltham was in both regards continually recomposed with new people. If we take females into account, recalling that they out-numbered males and were likely to be even more transient, total population flows probably exceeded those we have computed.

Up to this point we have examined Waltham's population growth by combining observed mobility in the enumerated population with the natural increase in population corrected so as to apply to the enumerated population. Now we shall reverse procedures and combine the natural increase of the actual population with estimates of mobility in the actual population. As a first step in this direction the Massachusetts census for Waltham in 1865 was employed to derive two quinquennial measures of mobility. By comparing mobility for 1860–65 and 1865–70 with the mobility computed for 1860–70, we can discern how greatly the use of decennial data results in an understatement of mobility in the actual population. By extrapolating from these five-year counts, we can then attempt to estimate the mobility of actual population over the entire period.

As indicated in Table 2.1, the use of decennial census data for the decade 1860–70 reveals a male population increase of 1,266. This increase was the result of an enumerated natural decrease of 15 males and the net in-migration of 1,281 males. Out-migration totaled 1,586 males and in-migration 2,867 males. The results obtained for the same decade using quinquennial measures are as follows:

Table 2.2 indicates that the role of natural increase in population growth was greater than the decennial measure would lead us to believe; the role of net in-migration was correspondingly smaller. Out-migration as measured over the decade understated the two five-year counts by 958 males or by 60.4 percent. In-migration was understated by 886 males or 30.9 percent. If the results for this one decade are at all representative of the entire era, we could conclude that each of the out-migration figures in Table 2.1 understates actual out-migration by at least 60 percent, while each of the in-migration figures understates actual in-migration by at least 31 percent.

TABLE 2.2   *Quinquennial and Decennial Migration Measures, 1860–70*

	1860–65	*1865–70*	*Differences between two five-year measures and one ten-year measure*
Population Increase	168	1,098	0
Enumerated Births	141	238	+158
Enumerated Deaths	158	164	+86
Enumerated Natural Increase	−17	+74	+72
Out-Migration	1,291	1,253	+958
In-Migration	1,476	2,277	+886
Net In-Migration	185	1,024	−72

Now let us attempt to estimate the mobility of the population as if we possessed a daily census register comparable to the birth and death rolls. Actual male births during the decade 1860–70 (1,039) and actual male deaths (738) resulted in a natural increase of 301 males. Since the male population increased by 1,266, net in-migration must have totaled 965 males. Assuming that the ratio of the understatement of actual out-migration to actual in-migration was the same as that of the quinquennial measures (i.e., a 60 percent underestimate of out-migration and a 31 percent underestimate of in-migration), what levels of in- and out-migration will yield a net in-migration of 965 males? The answers are 3,460 out-migrants and 4,429 in-migrants. Under the assumptions employed, actual mobility into Waltham was 55 percent greater than that recorded in Table 2.1. Out-migration in the actual population was 119 percent greater than that recorded.

These estimates do not in any way alter the percentage figures for in- and out-migration presented earlier. The increase in out-migration reflects the movements between censuses of in-migrants only, not the stationary population. Thus while there were an estimated 3,460 out-migrants instead of 1,594 as recorded, it remains the case that 53.8 percent of the 1860 population out-migrated by 1870. What does change is the volume of in- and out-migration. Extending the estimates for 1860–70 to the period 1850–80 yields 10,682 out-migrants as opposed to the 4,878 recorded, and 12,185 in-migrants as opposed to the 7,861 recorded. These figures, however, have little meaning except as very crude estimates of actual mobility. Given the assumptions underlying their derivation, it would be too much to expect that they, in conjunction with the actual natural increase would yield the actual change in population, and they do not.

An alternative impression of the proportions of short-term (between census) physical mobility is potentially available in the measurement of what, for want of a better term, may be called slippage. Slippage is the number of men 20 years and older who in a census year appeared in the census but not on the tax rolls plus the number of men who, in the same year, appeared on the tax rolls but not in the census. The proportions of slippage were as follows: in 1850, the number of men involved equaled 20 percent of the enumerated male population; in 1860, 20 percent; in 1870, 28 percent; and in 1880, 13 percent.

Slippage may have resulted from the incompleteness of the censuses, of the tax rolls, from physical mobility, or from all of these. Since the tax rolls were prepared early in the spring of each year while the census was conducted during the summer, it is possible that much of the observed slippage was a product of short-term physical mobility. The men who appeared on the tax rolls but not in the census may have out-migrated in the months between the two listings. Those who appeared in the census but not on the tax rolls may have in-migrated during the same period. A check of men taxed in 1850 but not enumerated revealed that only a few of them appeared in the 1860 census. This suggests the possibility that they had out-migrated before the 1850 enumeration. On the other hand, since the number of men who failed to be taxed consistently exceeded the number who failed to be enumerated, some slippage may have been the product of inadequacies in tax assessment procedures. Which of these, mobility or incompleteness, was the larger cause of slippage cannot be determined.

In summarizing we can note that Waltham's population growth was the product of interactions between a high but declining rate of out-migration, a high and mixed rate of in-migration, and an increasing rate of natural increase. Over each decade from 1850 to 1880, at least half of the population resident at the start of the decade left Waltham. At the end of each decade, between one-half and two-thirds of the resident population had in-migrated within the decade. The numbers of males who moved into the city and then moved out without ever appearing in a census was roughly equal to the number of observed out-migrants and roughly half the number of observed in-migrants. In absolute numbers, the growth of the male population by 3,387 males, between 1850 and 1880, involved 4,878 recorded and 10,682 estimated out-migrants, and 7,861 recorded and 12,185 estimated in-migrants.

We can only imagine, at this point, some of the consequences of mobility experienced in such volume. Individuals must routinely have had to accommodate themselves to frequent disruptions of interpersonal relationships. The boy who grew to manhood in Waltham was likely to have seen many of his chums depart. Adults—at work, in church, in clubs, and in their neighborhoods—had to interact with constantly changing groups of peers. And with what success could the work of town government and of voluntary associations be carried on, in the face of this shifting population?

In pondering upon such matters, we run the risk of imputing too much force to mobility, of romanticizing its impact. All mobility does not occur simultaneously. When an individual loses one friend or acquaintance through out-migration, he may well have established a new relationship before the next of his friends departs. The same sort of continuity prevails within organizations; there may always be enough interested men present and arriving in town to maintain an organization in spite of the fact that it loses some of its members through physical mobility.

Several imputations do, however, seem warranted. One is that the high rate of physical mobility contributed, along with the increasing scale and heterogeneity of town society, to the growth of impersonal human relationships. In a growing number of daily activities, people were obliged to interact with comparative strangers. Trust and confidence in these strangers, the felt assurance that they would act within the framework of one's own understanding of right and wrong, was a concomitant necessity. Anyone who was strange, who seemed unaware or unobservant of one's unwritten rules of behavior, was held suspect. Here was the rooting ground for stereotypes and for discriminations based upon invidious comparisons. For example, "All Irishmen are drunkards and hooligans" could be believed by even the most respectable native son because the Irish were different in a number of respects. As always, it took a certain amount of understanding to appreciate which of these differences were permanent and which were transitory, and a goodly amount of personal flexibility and tolerance to accept such differences as facts of life. As we shall see at a later point, some native sons rose to the challenge represented by the Irish, just as some rose to meet the other problems raised by industrial and urban growth, while some native sons did not.

A second imputation relates to the force with which institutions pursued their objectives in view of the wholesale turnover of their leaders and their members or constituencies. How strongly could a church, for example, have influenced the lives of its members when as an institution its congregation was neither stable nor in any sense a community of the spirit? Many parishioners could not know one another or even, in the face of the turnover of clergymen, their spiritual leader. For what constituency should the town leaders have planned and guided the activities of town government? If half of those they served were soon to depart only to be replaced by an even larger number of newcomers, whose or what interests were they obliged to serve? To foreshadow a later argument, it would be wholly unrealistic on our part to have expected them to have formulated and pursued goals based upon an idealized image of Waltham as a place. Waltham was an ever-changing population, and it was in light of this fact that its public leaders groped along the path of least public resistance.

In the course of its development, the composition of Waltham's population was substantially altered. Approximately 75 percent of all of the males enumerated between 1850 and 1880 were native-born Americans. By far, most of these native sons were born in Massachusetts. Twenty percent were born in other New England states, and three percent were born elsewhere in the United States. The proportion of the native population born outside of New England and New York was negligible. Given the high proportion of in-migrants in each enumeration, the origins of the native-born population as a whole reflect the origins of in-migrants as well. Most native-born movers into Waltham came from Massachusetts and from its neighboring states. Most of the foreign-born population came from southern Ireland. The Irish composed a high of 83 percent of the foreign-born in 1860 and a low of 62 percent in 1880. Most of the remaining foreign-born hailed from England, Scotland, and Canada. Steadily over time, Canadians displaced the English and Scots as the second largest foreign-born group. Very small numbers of Germans and Swedes were also present in the population.

Homogeneously white and predominantly native-born, the population was most seriously split along religious lines. Nativity tends to be deceptive on this score. For example, numbers of the native-born were the offspring of Irish parents, while numbers of the English and Canadian-born were also of Irish descent. For such persons and for the Waltham community, their Catholicism was likely to have been a more significant personal attribute than was their nativity.

It has been assumed here that the differences in church affiliations among Protestants were relatively unimportant. The basic religious cleavage in Waltham was that between Protestants and Catholics. In deciding religious affiliation, it was assumed that all persons of Irish birth or parentage were Catholics and that all other persons were Protestants. Small numbers of Jews, and of Germans who might have been either Catholic or Protestant, have been omitted from consideration. The error involved in these procedures, which is the sum of those Irish who were not Catholic (a portion of whom were positively identified as Protestants) and those non-Irish who were, is likely to have been very small.

In 1850 Catholics constituted 24 percent of the male population. This proportion rose to 38 percent by 1860 and to 44 percent by 1870. Then there appears to have been a leveling off, for Catholics still formed 44 percent of the male population in 1880. After 1880, French Canadians began arriving in numbers, to be joined by Italian immigrants in the early decades of the twentieth century. Waltham was eventually to have a majority Catholic population. But by 1890 this had not yet come to pass. We shall examine the social and political consequences of the Catholic-Protestant division in subsequent chapters. At this point, let us consider some of the demographic differences between these two segments of the population.

Much of the increase in the proportion of Catholics in the population was a result of their higher and sustained birth rates. In contrast, birth rates among Protestants declined over time. No effort has been made to compute these rates from the birth rolls. It is known that there was a general decline in Protestant birth rates during the era. It is also known that in one year, 1863, when Catholics constituted approximately 40 percent of the population, they were responsible for 70 percent of all Waltham births. Trends in birth rates can, however, be inferred from changes in the composition of households.

Where the Protestant population, in spite of its absolute growth, had a declining proportion of dependent male children, the growing Catholic population had a higher and stable proportion of dependent male children. That these differentials derived from differential fertility rather than from physical mobility is supported by the long-term increase and convergence of Catholic and Protestant rates of persistence (examined below). In 1850, 36 percent of the male Protestant population as compared to 30 percent of the male Catholic population was composed of dependent children. From 1860 onwards, when Catholic dependents rose to 37 percent of the Catholic population and remained at that level, the proportion of Protestant dependents steadily declined, first to 31 then to 27 and then to 25 percent.

In absolute terms, these trends produced the following results: where in 1850 the numbers of dependents in both groups just fell short of equaling the number of heads of households in each group, by 1880 Protestant dependents numbered slightly better than one-half tne number of Protestant household heads, but Catholic dependents exceeded the number of Catholic household heads. Since these results were not produced by migration patterns, and since death rates over the long run moved closer to convergence, Catholics must have maintained higher birth rates than Protestants.

These inferred differences in fertility appear to have been a function of economic and possibly of theological differences. The hypothesis that Protestants restricted their births so that their progeny would not have to compete with Catholics or with immigrants generally, appears to be unsupportable. As we shall see, there was too little economic or social competition to warrant such an action. Waltham Protestants as a group were simply wealthier than Waltham Catholics. In consequence of better diets, better living conditions, and more medical attention, they enjoyed a lower infant mortality rate. Hence their need to have many children in order to have surviving children fell more rapidly than was the case among Catholics. It is also likely that Protestants chose to restrict their births because of the greater degree of economic security they enjoyed. They needed fewer income-earning hands now and in their old age.

To foreshadow later considerations, we can now point to some of the issues raised by the fertility differentials associated with religion. For one, in view of the fact that the growth of the Catholic population was in some measure attributable to large families, the voting strength of that population was disproportionately smaller than its aggregate size would lead us to believe. Many Catholics were too young to vote and, given the greater likelihood that Catholics were foreign born, many Catholic adults were less likely to register to vote. Secondly, there was the issue of public expenditures for education. If, in comparison with Protestants, Catholics contributed smaller amounts to the public purse via taxation (as they did) and at the same time created the largest demands for public education by virtue of their numbers, how would the Protestant majority respond? Would it liberally spend public monies for schooling when, from 1870 onwards, a majority of the children in the city were Catholics, or would it not? We shall examine this and related issues of public activity in Chapter V.

If a large portion of the growth of the Catholic population came about as the result of natural increase, much of the growth of the Protestant population came from the net in-migration of males of labor-force age (taken as 12 and older). The results of these changes are readily discernible from the age distribution diagrams presented below. The Protestant population was, on the average, older to begin with in 1850 and older still in 1880. The Catholic population became younger, on the average, with the passage of time. The noticeable bunching of ages at rounded five-year intervals—e.g., 30, 35, 40—suggests something of the extent to which census age reports were not reliable. Indeed, there were some men who refused, for census purposes, to age at all, while a few grew younger with every passing decade.

Table 2.3 provides a clear picture of the population processes at work within the two main religious groupings. The males present at the start of any decade could have met with one of three fates. They might have remained in Waltham, or perished, or out-migrated. Those who persisted would find their ranks replenished by in-migrants and by new-born males. Differences in the rates of change between processes produced changes in the religious composition of the population.

In-migration and out-migration streams were more largely composed of Protestants than of Catholics throughout the period. This, however, was due to the predominance of Protestants in the population. The *rates* of in- and out-migration were higher among Catholics. Thus, for example, 832 Protestant males as compared to 345 Catholic males out-migrated between the 1850 census enumeration and that of 1860. The former figure constituted 53.4 percent of the 1850 Protestants while the latter figure constituted 70.4 percent of the 1850 Catholics.

The most remarkable piece of evidence supplied by Table 2.3, however, bears upon similarities rather than differences. Rates of persistence and out-migration among Protestants and Catholics had converged by 1890. Convergence was also likely to have been approached in rates of in-migration. What is remarkable about this is not that it took only thirty to forty years for two very diverse populations to be mobile and persistent at the same rates, but that there was convergence at all, to any marked degree. For to be making the same decisions at the same rates implies that Protestants and Catholics were on an equal socio-economic footing in 1890. That just wasn't the case, as we shall see. Some other factor or factors must account for the trends evidenced in Table 2.3.

Between 1850 and 1880 about one-fifth of both the in- and out-migrants were dependent children. Single men accounted for two-fifths

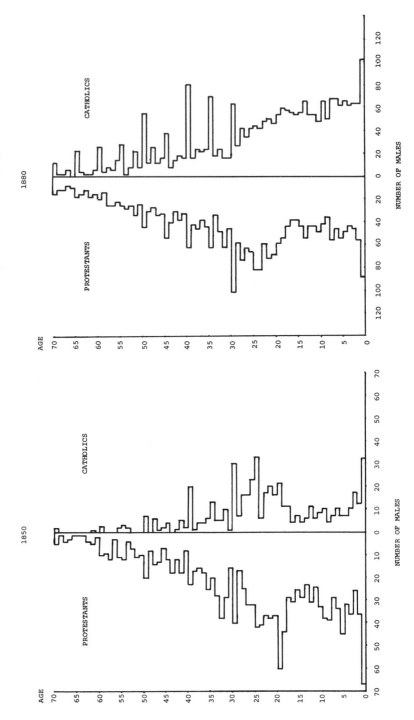

FIGURE 2.2   *Age Distribution of Males, 1850 and 1880, by Religion*

TABLE 2.3　　Male Population Growth and Mobility, 1850–90, by Religion

	1850–60		1860–70		1870–80		1880–90[a]	
	No.	%	No.	%	No.	%	No.	%
Persisters:								
Protestant	629	40.4[b]	776	42.4[b]	1,110	47.4[b]	1,325	50.0[b]
Catholic	119	24.5[b]	360	32.1[b]	735	39.4[b]	857	48.6[b]
Deceased:								
Protestant	97	6.2[b]	161	8.8[b]	165	7.0[b]	240	11.3[b]
Catholic	26	5.1[b]	74	6.5[b]	96	5.2[b]	228	12.9[b]
Out-Migrants:								
Protestant	832	53.4[b]	892	48.8[b]	1,069	45.6[b]	988	38.7[b]
Catholic	345	70.4[b]	691	61.4[b]	1,031	55.4[b]	697	38.5[b]
In-Migrants & Births:								
Protestant	1,200	65.6[c]	1,568	66.9[c]	1,920	63.4[c]	—	—
Catholic	1,006	89.4[c]	1,466	78.7[c]	1,649	71.1[c]	—	—
Population Growth:[d]								
Protestant	271	30.0	515	42.4	686	56.8	—	—
Catholic	635	70.3	701	57.6	522	43.2	—	—

[a]Male population 10 years and older in 1880 and 20 years and older in 1890
[b]Proportion computed on start of decade population
[c]Proportion computed on end of decade population
[d]Figures may not agree with those in Table 2.1 because of omissions or other religious categories

of the out-migrants and for a slightly higher proportion of the in-migrants. Married heads of households accounted for the remainder. In terms of household statuses then, the same kinds of males both came to and departed from Waltham. This conclusion holds with equal force when the asset positions of migrants are considered. Most adult in-migrants were without assets at the time of their first enumeration and most adult out-migrants were without assets at the time of their last enumeration. Table 2.4 provides evidence to the point that in- and out-migrants were also pretty much alike in their ages. Most in- and out-migrants were at all times 30 years of age or younger. (The inclusion of births and deaths unfortunately complicates the picture. Deaths have their most marked effect among the 1-to-10 and over-60 age groups. The effects of births are entirely concentrated in the 1-to-10 age group.)

The similarities between in- and out-migrants suggest two different points. The first of these is that since both population flows were pretty much alike, most trends in the Waltham population were either caused by or experienced by the persisting population. In spite of the very large volume of physical mobility, it was that smaller number of men who stayed in Waltham for a decade or more who influenced and/or felt the changes in the age, household status, and asset distributions of the aggregate population.

The second point takes us back to the argument that mobility studies are incomplete when they fail to deal with the destinations and experiences of out-migrants. This cannot be done, and the evidence now in hand suggests that there may no longer be any reason to make the attempt. The men who came to Waltham were very much like those who left. They took the same jobs, lived in the same houses, and were demographically and in asset terms fair equivalents of one another. For these reasons the experiences of in-migrants to Waltham may well have been very similar to the experiences of Waltham out-migrants elsewhere. Waltham, from such a perspective, was simply one of a large number of possible stopping points along a stream of migration. Some men found their niche here and settled in, while others moved on in pursuit of their ambitions. For some men time undoubtedly ran out or hope was lost. But many realized their goals and became, like the persisters of Waltham, the successful and respectable permanent citizens of other towns and cities.

The number and variety of motives which prompted movement into and out of Waltham by so many families and individuals from 1850 to 1890 can neither be known nor even exhaustively presumed. Few migrants leave records upon such matters. To resort to conjecture, when conjectural variations are without limits, would be foolhardy. Still, of necessity, we may presume that some men came to the community to wed, to join family or friends, or to be independent of family; and that others departed for some of the same and for still other reasons. As we have seen, a goodly portion of the mobility was accounted for by the fact that numbers of male

TABLE 2.4 Male Population Turnover, by Age, 1850–80

| | 1850 to 1860 | | | | 1860 to 1870 | | | | 1870 to 1880 | | | |
| | Out-Migrated and Died | | In-Migrated and Born | | Out-Migrated and Died | | In-Migrated and Born | | Out-Migrated and Died | | In-Migrated and Born | |
Ages	No.	%	No.	%	No.	%	No.	%	No.	%	No.	%
1–10	263	20.2	716	32.3	377	20.5	944	30.3	443	18.5	1,208	33.6
11–20	310	23.8	389	17.6	458	25.0	538	17.3	525	21.9	524	14.6
21–30	392	30.0	547	24.7	472	25.7	782	25.1	672	28.1	814	22.7
31–40	159	12.2	304	13.7	252	13.7	427	13.7	319	13.3	531	14.8
41–50	83	6.4	155	7.0	138	7.5	251	8.1	198	8.3	282	7.9
51–60	57	4.4	74	3.3	82	4.5	90	2.9	123	5.1	139	3.9
61–70	20	1.5	16	0.7	31	1.7	55	1.8	69	2.9	70	1.9
71+	21	1.5	14	0.6	25	1.4	24	0.8	43	1.8	22	0.6

children moved into and out of town in response to decisions made for them by their parents. Having said this much, it is necessary to add that probably the largest part of the mobility among adult men was rooted in economic motives. Waltham attracted men primarily through the force of its employment opportunities. It lost men to the even more attractive pull of opportunities elsewhere.

After 1850, the main engines of Waltham's economic and population growth were the Boston Manufacturing Company and the Waltham Watch Company. (Although the watch company had several different names during the period, it will be referred to throughout this volume by its most popular name.) Over each of the following four decades, employment rose at both companies. This maintained them in their standing as the major economic forces within the community. It would not be wide of the mark to suggest that probably a majority of the adult males ever present in the town worked—at one time or another, for greater or lesser periods—at one of the two enterprises. Moreover, because of their importance, the decisions of the companies on such matters as whom to hire and what terms of employment to offer strongly influenced the composition and the standards of living as well as the size of the population.

In a number of respects the two companies set in motion forces which pulled in opposite directions. Boston Manufacturing, for its part, employed relatively few skilled males and, for that reason, paid a low average wage. It also experienced relatively high rates of worker turnover. Its labor requirements resulted in a relatively poor, unskilled population marked by large numbers of transients. In contrast, Waltham Watch employed a much higher proportion of skilled and semi-skilled men, and paid a higher average wage. Its turnover rates were significantly lower. Hence its impact upon incomes, occupational standings, and the physical mobility of the population differed at each point from that of Boston Manufacturing.

Both companies, however, followed parallel courses in a number of other regards. Both employed Irish Catholics long before many com-

TABLE 2.5 *Employment at Boston Manufacturing and at Waltham Watch Companies, 1850–90*

Year	Boston Manufacturing Co.	Waltham Watch Co.
1850	620	——
1860	944	161
1870	1,129	524
1880	1,207	1,355
1890	Not Available	2,824

SOURCES: Boston Manufacturing Co. data from manufacturing schedules of the census. Waltham Watch Co. data compiled from payroll records.

panies in the Boston area were prepared to do so. Over the period, though, the watch company increasingly discriminated against Irish Catholics (but not Irish Protestants) in its employment policies. Both companies imported English workmen into the town. Both made efforts, through the provision of low-rent company housing, to provide their employees with wholesome living arrangements.

On balance, the differences between the companies were of more consequence than their similarities. Some of these differences stemmed from differences in company managements, but the greater portion of them derived from such factors as competitive position and the technologies employed. These were matters which were beyond the scope of direct company control and yet they shaped company behavior and, through that medium, the mobility, the composition, and the welfare of a large portion of the Waltham population.

A graphic illustration of the force of external circumstances upon the two companies and Waltham is provided by their experiences during the Civil War. During several of the war years, Boston Manufacturing was compelled to shut down because it could no longer get cotton. By itself, this closing would have increased out-migration and reduced in-migration into the town. Out-migration was also raised by military enlistments and the draft. But the war prompted a boom of unprecedented proportions at Waltham Watch. The company's cheaper line of watches found a new and mass market in the demands of soldiers for time pieces. The consequent expansion of employment served to reduce out-migration and to increase in-migration. In combination, these opposing pushes and pulls just offset one another. Between 1860 and 1865, the male population grew by only 168. In contrast, in the post-war quinquennium, the male population grew by 1,098. Most of the post-war increase was occasioned by significantly higher rates of in-migration and a slight decline in out-migration.

In addition to the opportunities created by expanding employment at Boston Manufacturing and Waltham Watch, three further sources of economic opportunity may be identified. One of these took the form of new firms organized as suppliers or competitors to Waltham Watch. As early as 1857 the first such spin-off had taken place. This, like a number of subsequent branchings, involved a movement out of Waltham rather than the development of new firms within it. (Waltham Watch, for having been the first to develop the techniques for the mass production of watches, was also subjected to repeated raids upon its work force by its competitors. There developed, in consequence of such raids, a mobility ambiance between Waltham and other watchmaking centers, such as Elgin, Illinois.) But over the years, numbers of employees undertook to organize their own firms in Waltham. In response to inventions they had made, to personality clashes within the firm, and to specific firm problems, a number of small specialty shops—producing such items as watchmakers' lathes and emery wheels—a school for watch makers, and a full-scale rival to Waltham Watch, were established. These developments progressively enhanced the town's reputation as a mechanical trades center especially qualified for work involving close tolerances and mass production.

Population growth itself stimulated a considerable amount of economic opportunity. The town government expanded and entered into the provision of many new services, creating new employment openings. New stores and shops, new services and trades emerged to meet the demands of the growing number of people. To all appearances, the readiness with which individuals ventured their capital in small retail and service enterprises suggests that, in an urban setting, the single proprietorship took the place of freehold farming in a rural setting. But as rates of attrition were high in farming, they were high also in shopkeeping. For example, six out of every ten small businesses present in 1880 had disappeared by the end of the decade. Not all of these disappearances represented business failures, but probably most of them did. There were, nonetheless, ever larger numbers of men ready to risk their savings in business in hopes of achieving, simultaneously, higher incomes and the personal independence associated with being one's own boss.

A final source of employment opportunities derived from the decisions of several manufacturers to locate their plants in Waltham. In at least one instance, a resident's discovery of a process (for purifying chalk) led to the establishment of a chalk and crayon factory. Other enterprises of some size included an iron foundry and a screw and bolt factory.

Those who left Waltham permanently spread out widely through the country. During one period in the late 1860's, a town paper carried items from former townsmen now settled in California, Minnesota, Iowa, Missouri, and Colorado. Letters were also received from India, Ireland, and Liberia. Some Waltham men participated in the westward march of the American population, while others moved to Boston, New York, and other nearby cities and towns. Numbers of men also left town temporarily. Among the well-to-do, a sojourn in Europe was not unheard of; nor was a southern journey to escape the New England winter. In the summer, many who could afford it—and this included workers—spent a week or two at the seashore or in the mountains of New Hampshire. Mount Desert in Maine was a favorite spa among Waltham Watch workers long before it became a rich man's retreat. No matter whether the move was permanent or temporary, one cannot help but be impressed with the frequency of travel in view of the known hardships it often involved.

Even within the bounds of Waltham, travel from home to work increased. Over the period 1850 to 1890, most of the people who lived in Waltham worked there, and most of the people who worked in Waltham lived there. Progressively, however, a growing number—but always a small minority—of the men resident in the town worked outside of it, while numbers of men who worked in town were non-resident. The direct association between workplace and residence was repeatedly weakened by improvements in the network of transportation.

As we saw earlier, the very first rail link with Boston had permitted a handful of men to commute to work from Waltham. The development of a street railway in 1865 increased the ease of two-way commuter traffic into and out of town. The opening of a second rail link in 1882 and the spread of a trolley system over much of the Boston metropolitan area served to further increase commuter traffic. Step by step, the historic one-to-one relationship between economic opportunity within the town and its population growth was weakened. Waltham became ever more tightly bound to an economic region broader than its own political boundaries. In time such boundaries would lose most of their relevance, but up to 1890 this trend had not gone so far as to reduce the usefulness of Waltham as the unit of study and concern.

Within Waltham, the advent of the street railway, an additional span across the Charles River, improved hack services, and improved road maintenance, all contributed to expand the area of residential settlement. Density remained high in the area of the town common, but increasingly over the period new houses encroached upon areas formerly under the plow. The area south of the river, in the neighborhood of the watch factory, progressively filled up. Settlement pushed out to the west and to the east. The "walk to work" came to be less and less of a commonplace.

To demonstrate most graphically how its industrial growth propelled Waltham along an entirely new course, we have only to compare its rate of population increase with those of neighboring towns untouched by industrial development. Weston, Lincoln, and Lexington, along Waltham's western and northern borders, remained agricultural centers, and as such could not match the expansion of their neighbor. As indicated in Table 2.6, Waltham's rate of growth also consistently exceeded that of the state as a whole.

In a growing community and in a community marked by considerable in- and out-migration, those who remain in residence, the persisters, are most likely to be those with the largest stake in the town. Such men, very often the owners of property, are likely to have been born in the town or to have reached middle-age there, all the while prospering from its growth

TABLE 2.6   *Rates of Population Increase, Waltham, Massachusetts, and Selected Towns*

Decade	Waltham %	Massachusetts %	Weston %	Lincoln %	Lexington %
1840–50	70	35	11	5	16
1850–60	43	24	38	-1	23
1860–70	36	18	1	10	-2
1870–80	29	22	15	12	8
1880–90	60	26	15	12	30

and development. In differing combinations, birth-place, material success, and ageing, with its attendant responsibility of family headship, are likely to influence who it is that stays put in the midst of whirlygig migration.

Persisters, as the maintainers of historical continuity, are also likely to be called upon in public service and in voluntary associations to lend their memories of custom and usage to the tasks of leadership. Length of residence, however, cannot by itself have been a major factor in such selections. In the conduct of most affairs, after all, it probably took relatively little time to pass on to newcomers the necessary information about how to proceed. The persisters at any one moment in time held few monopolies of any kind. In addition, many of the activities within the community—both of the public and the private sort—were themselves so new that persistence conveyed little or no advantage. The "build a better mouse-trap" mentality set more store in workability than in the authority of tradition.

What made many men persisters in the first place—their relative material success—also made them attractive as community leaders. Those who stayed on for other reasons, such as a lack of venturesomeness, advanced age, or dependent status, were much less likely (or wholly unlikely) to be called to leadership by the community. We shall see that the same criterion applied in regard to newcomers to the town. When the volume of community activity rose to a point where it was no longer possible to attract enough willing and able men from among the ranks of the persisters, relatively recent in-migrants were permitted to occupy positions of authority or prestige. More often than not, such "new" men had already achieved a measure of material success in their private lives. It was this success, along with an interestedness and a willingness to serve, that brought these new men to the attention of the community.

> In 1860, 36.5 percent of the males present in 1850 remained and formed 25.2 percent of the 1860 male population.
> In 1870, 38.5 percent of the males present in 1860 remained and formed 26.8 percent of the 1870 male population.
> In 1880, 43.8 percent of the males present in 1870 remained and formed 33.9 percent of the 1880 male population.
> In 1890, 50.5 percent of the males (ten years and older) present in 1880 remained and formed 41.4 percent of the 1890 male population twenty years and older.

As the foregoing figures indicate, there was from 1850 onwards an increase in the rates at which men persisted within Waltham. Where just better than one-third of the male population remained in Waltham over the decade 1850–60, one-half did so from 1880 to 1890. The numerical importance of persisters in the male population increased from one-quarter of the 1860 population to two-fifths of the 1890 population.

Most of the adult males who settled in were married men who were heads of households. Of the adult persisters over 1850-60, 74.6 percent were household heads. For the decades 1860-70, 1870-80, and 1880-90, the respective proportions were 71.7 percent, 70.7 percent, and 63.3 percent. Anywhere from one-quarter to one-third of the male persisters were single men, numbers of whom married during the decade over which they remained. There was, however, a very marked increase in the rates at which single men stayed on. In 1860, for example, persisting heads of households represented 43 percent of the 1850 heads of households, and persisting single men represented 19 percent of the 1850 single men. By 1890 these figures had increased to 57 percent and 41 percent respectively. The much faster increase in the proportion of single men remaining over a decade merits an explanation. Perhaps the answer is to be found in the dramatic increase in the rate of marriage. During the decade 1850-60 marriages annually averaged 6.15 per 1,000 population. In the terminal decade the annual rate was 11.72 per 1,000 population. Many of the single men who remained over each decade participated in this marrying trend, and in their new status as heads of households, freshly encumbered with brides and often with young children, reduced their penchant for physical mobility.

Taking household heads alone, census data permit a view of persistence rates stretching from 1830 to 1890. As indicated in Table 2.7, the rates among such men exceeded 50 percent in the 1830's and 1840's, then declined only to rise to new heights by the 1880's. The rates of the entire male population followed an identical course from 1850 onwards, but at consistently lower levels. In consequence of the rates of male population increase, remaining heads of households always constituted a small fraction of the population. This group, presumably the one from which community leaders were most likely to be chosen, composed as little as 9 percent of the male population in 1850 and a high of only 15 percent of the male population in 1880. When single males who both remained and became household heads over the decade of their persistence are added in, the pool of potential leaders is about 4 percent higher for each decade.

TABLE 2.7   *Persistence, 1830-90*

	Number		Persisters		Rate of Persistence	
	Household Heads	*All Males*	*Household Heads*	*All Males*	*Household Heads*	*All Males*
1830-40	224	––	121	––	54.0	––
1840-50	335	––	186	––	55.5	––
1850-60	759	2,048	330	748	43.5	36.5
1860-70	1,124	2,961	500	1,139	44.5	38.5
1870-80	1,661	4,227	806	1,851	48.5	43.8
1880-90[a]	2,075	4,336	1,195	2,189	57.6	50.5

[a] The all-males figures apply only to the 1880 population 10 years old and above.

Many of the heads of households who remained were, as suggested above, the owners of assets. The data reveal several significant trends: a tendency for growing numbers of household heads to settle in, even though they possessed no assets, and a progressive narrowing in the difference between those who owned homes and those who did not. Thus, for example, while 62 percent of the household heads who remained between 1850 and 1860 had assets, only 46 percent of those who stayed on from 1880 to 1890 had assets at the start. And where 58 percent of the 1850 homeowning heads of households remained until 1860, as compared with 44 percent of all household heads, the comparable figures for 1880–1890 were 64 percent and 58 percent. It seems clear that the relative importance of homeownership and of asset holding generally, declined as factors associated with persistence. If asset holding, along with persistence and household head status, were prerequisites for community leadership positions, then only 5 to 10 percent of the population were in a position to fill such roles.

In part, the trends in the composition of persisters as well as the secular increase in persistence appear to have been a product of the settling-in process of Irish immigrants and their progeny. A population new to the country was finding its place in physical space. This is what explains their initially much higher rates of internal migration and lower rates of persistence. Within a generation or so after their arrival, the Irish were just as persistent and just as mobile as the Protestant population. Over 1850–60, 40.4 percent of the male Protestant population stayed on as compared with only 24.5 percent of the male Catholic population. Fully 60 percent of the 1850 Protestant homeowners remained as compared with 35 percent of the Catholic homeowners. Thirty years later, Protestants ten years and older in 1880 persisted at the rate of 51.8 percent, while Catholics did so at the rate of 48.5 percent. Among 1880 Protestant homeowners the rate of persistence had risen slightly, to 63.8 percent, while among Catholic homeowners there had been a dramatic rise to 64.3 percent. But because, on the average, the Catholic population was poorer and had larger families, their impact upon the characteristics of persisters produced divergent results. It was largely on these accounts that more young males persisted over time and that more men without assets persisted.

Since there was a discernible increase in Protestant persistence rates as well, some portion of what was going on had little to do with changes in the composition of the population. The hypothesis that Waltham had developed a large enough attractive force to reduce out-migration—that by virtue of its size and diversity it seemed to afford so many opportunities that there was no need to look for them elsewhere—appears to provide a reasonable explanation for the slowdown of physical mobility rates and the increase in persistence rates.

One consequence of the increase in these rates after 1850 was that more and more residents were Waltham-born. Approximately one-third of the 1850-60 persisters was born in the town. Although computations have not been made for subsequent decades, there is every reason to believe that this proportion increased over time. Among other things, the high birth rates of Catholics combined with their increasing rates of persistence would alone have produced this result.

Thus far we have examined persistence over each decade as if it involved different men each time. Some of the males who remained over one decade, however, stayed on for two, three, and possibly four decades. In fact, slightly better than one-third of those who remained over any one decade were present over two or more decades. These men came, within the bounds of human mortality, as close as possible to representing the permanent Waltham population. They also constituted that portion of the population most appropriate for the study of occupational and social mobility.

To gain a perspective upon population persistence, we can start with the whole number of males recorded in the 1860, 1870, and 1880 censuses, and in the 1890 tax rolls, which was 17,938 males. Of this number, 12,014 males were enumerated in only one census, and so either out-migrated or died. There were, in addition, 5,924 instances of persistence, all of which were accounted for by 3,674 different individuals. If our previous estimate of actual (as opposed to enumerated) population flows is employed, the number of individual persisters remains at 3,674, but as many as 25,000 males may have temporarily settled in the city between 1850 and 1890.

Table 2.8 presents persistence data in detail. From it we learn, for example, that of the 2,048 males enumerated in 1850, 750 were again enumerated in 1860. Of these 750, 428 were enumerated in 1870, 272 in 1880, and 167 in 1890. These 750 different individuals accounted for 1,617 instances of persistence. Only 167 men spent as many as forty years in Waltham, while only 533 (272 + 261) had spent between thirty and forty years in residence by 1890. The number of males staying on for between twenty and thirty years up to 1890 was 1,550. How many fathers

TABLE 2.8   *Long-Term Persistence, 1850–90*

	1850	1860	1870	1880	1890[a]
All Males	2,048	2,961	4,227	5,435	5,315
New Males		2,211	3,088	3,588	3,127
Persisters		750	1,139	1,847	2,188
From 1850		750	428	272	167
From 1860			711	414	261
From 1870				1,161	708
From 1880					1,052

[a]Males 20 years or older in 1890

and sons remained long enough to allow inter-generational comparisons to be made remains to be seen. It is perfectly obvious, though, that very few men in Waltham were ever in a position to witness the whole lives of many other men. All that could be seen were bits and pieces of other lives. Most men knew only their own personal histories and those of members of their family.

One of the questions which can now be answered relates to the persistence of old Waltham families. Although a number of families could trace their residence back to the earliest days of colonial settlement, we shall class as "old" those families whose lines in the city ran to at least 1800. There were numbers of other families whose lines also ran back this far or further, but because the "seats" of these families lay outside of Waltham, they must, of necessity, be excluded from our consideration. Hence, for whatever the value placed upon old stock lineage in Waltham, our examination of old families understates the numbers of such persons actually present.

There were, in 1830, 29 families resident in Waltham whose presence in town dated at least as early as 1800. (This number neglects the possibility that within any one family there may have been more than one branch and one household.) Just sixteen of these families were direct descendants of the first or the very early Waltham settlers. These included, by family name: Bemis, Brown, Childs, Fiske, Garfield, Hager, Harrington, Lawrence, Livermore, Peirce, Sanderson, Smith, Stearns, Viles, Warren, and Wellington. By 1890, eleven of these families were still in residence. The Browns, Garfields, Livermores, Peirces, and Warrens had either died out in the male line or out-migrated. Of the thirteen non-colonial old families (which may have had colonial roots outside Waltham) only six had descendants present in 1890: Baldwin, Barnes, Bright, Clark, Dix, and Lyman. These six plus the eleven persisting colonial families are the only ones that, as far as we can know for a certainty, had claims to whatever prestige derived from early arrival. There were others, like the Mayos from Concord, the Robertses and Sawins from Watertown and the Hobbes and Greens from Weston, who could lay claim to colonial forebearers, but in the nature of the case, there is hardly any means by which all such old-stock residents can be identified. Since most of Waltham's residents were native-born Americans, drawn mainly from the New England states, it is likely that a high proportion of the population had colonial antecedents.

At this juncture we must turn away from most of the males we have been considering. Those men who came to Waltham only to depart, those boys who came of age in the city only to leave it, and those Waltham-born children who moved away with their migrating parents cannot enter into our considerations of occupational and social mobility. The persisters alone form the study population of the next two chapters.

*   *   *

SUMMARY   Sparked by the growth of Boston Manufacturing, Waltham Watch, and a number of smaller enterprises, Waltham quadrupled in population over the forty years from 1850 to 1890. Between 1850 and 1880, natural increase in the enumerated population accounted for only about twelve percent of the growth experienced. Net in-migration accounted for all of the rest.

The flow of in- and out-migrants produced a population in which a majority was at all times new to the city. On the average, sixty-one percent of the males present at any one time had in-migrated within a decade. And almost half (forty-nine percent) of all the males present at any one time out-migrated within a decade. In the process of adding 3,387 males to the population between 1850 and 1880, 12,739 enumerated males in- and/or out-migrated. In actuality, as many as 25,000 males may have passed in and out of Waltham residence during the thirty year period.

Most migrants were under thirty and unmarried. Among the in-migrants of native birth, those born in Massachusetts predominated. Among the foreign born, those born in Ireland predominated. Over time, Catholics of Irish descent came to constitute slightly better than two-fifths of the population.

The male Catholic population was generally younger and more physically mobile than its Protestant counterpart. More Protestants literally moved in and out, but the proportions of those moving was greatest among Catholics. There was, however, a remarkable degree of convergence in the rates at which both groups persisted and out-migrated. This development has yet to be explained. It does appear likely, however, that over-all rates of persistence and out-migration changed, as they did because of the increasing size of the city and the increasing number of economic opportunities which growth provided.

Older, married men were more likely to remain in Waltham for longer periods of time. Many of these men possessed assets and owned their own homes. This group, with its visible stake in the community, with its demonstrated economic achievement, and with its residential longevity, was the one from which leadership in both public and private voluntary affairs would most likely be drawn.

To convey with some finality how very mobile (and mortal) the population was, one last statistic may suffice. Out of the almost 20,000 males recorded in the 1850, 1860, 1870, and 1880 censuses and in the 1890 tax rolls, the number who persisted so as to appear in every listing was 167.

III · Occupational Mobility
1850-90

As the division of labor widens in the course of industrial development, it creates opportunities for occupational mobility for the very simple reason that occupations which had not previously existed are brought into being. If men already in the labor force enter such an occupation, they are, by definition, occupationally mobile (without regard to whether they move up, down, or horizontally on an occupational scale). If a new occupation is taken up by young men just entering the labor force, these men must be occupationally mobile vis-à-vis their fathers, since their fathers could not have had the same occupation. Either intra- or inter-generational occupational mobility, or both, must result when the division of labor increases.

The division of labor involves a distinction drawn in terms of *who* performs an economic function. It increases when men purchase or otherwise obtain goods or services which heretofore they had produced for themselves. Proliferation is the term adopted here for distinctions drawn in terms of *what* economic functions are performed. Proliferation may be said to occur when a wholly new occupation emerges as a result of a technological innovation. Railroad engineers, electricians, and photographers come to mind as examples of proliferation in the nineteenth century. The duties associated with these occupations were not previously undertaken as parts of other occupations: they were wholly new. Entrants into such occupations were necessarily mobile in occupational terms. To the extent that the innovations which created new occupations caused older occupations to disappear, they also compelled occupational mobility on the part of those displaced.

In Waltham between 1850 and 1890, the division of labor and proliferation resulted in the doubling of the number of occupations represented in the labor force. Where, in 1850, there had been approximately 100 occupations, there were approximately 200 in 1890. The opportunities for occupational mobility created by this doubling, however, must have been quite small. For such opportunities need have been generated for only a short time after new occupations came into existence. Subsequent entrants into these occupations may not have been occupationally mobile. The sons of electricians, for example, may themselves have become electricians and experienced no mobility. In addition, the large volume of physical mobility into Waltham increased the likelihood that new occupations were staffed by men who had already entered those occupations elsewhere. To the extent that this was the case, the increased division of labor and proliferation in Waltham was associated with less occupational mobility among its populace.

Many more men were involved in and directly influenced by the increases in specialization which occurred at Boston Manufacturing and Waltham Watch. Before examining these developments it will be necessary to clarify the meaning of specialization.

When the division of labor increases and a new occupation emerges, the members of that occupation are said to be specialists. When, for example, men go to barbers to have their hair cut instead of having this done at home by a family member or friend, barbering emerges as a specialization. In our own times few objections have been raised to specialization of this sort. We have the expectation that those who specialize develop an expertise that is both economically and socially beneficial. However, we also apply the term specialization to that process by which a single occupation is broken down into component parts. Men come to devote their energies on a full-time basis to fractional components of what may once have been a single occupational designation. Specialization of this sort is often decried, for it frequently reduces work to mindless, repetitive tasks or so narrows viewpoints as to be intellectually and emotionally stifling. We expect that this fission of tasks may be economically advantageous but tend to view its social and psychic consequences negatively.

The fission of tasks was carried to extremes at both of Waltham's largest employing units. At Boston Manufacturing, job assignments were divided from an early date along major process lines, such as spinning, carding, and weaving. Even the kinds of materials handled gave rise to divisions, so that some workers wove only sheeting while others wove only fancy goods or hosiery. At Waltham Watch, the fission of tasks was carried further still. By 1890, an estimated 3,700 discrete operations were required in the production of a single watch.

These developments served to compound the status differences within occupations, while the division of labor and proliferation brought about the same result between occupations. Not only were watch workers deemed "better" than textile workers, but weavers were "better" than spinners and watch finishers were "better" than pinion makers. Weavers of fancy goods were deemed "better" than weavers of sheeting, and enamelers who worked on high-priced watches were deemed "better" than those who worked on cheaper watches. And so it went over the whole gamut of tasks. Such intra-occupational distinctions virtually defy incorporation in the study of occupational mobility. Moreover, many of these distinctions were so subtle that, in the nature of things, they could not be known to those outside a particular plant or industry. They had limited rather than social relevance, and will be ignored in the present context.

The fission of tasks creates opportunities for occupational mobility in much the same way as proliferation and increases in the division of labor. The number of opportunities created by fission is also relatively small and limited in time. Thus it may be said that in Waltham, the fission of tasks, the increasing division of labor, and proliferation directly accounted for only a small proportion of the occupational mobility opportunities. Indirectly, however, they accounted for very many more, for these changes in the structure of occupations were occasioned by and necessary aspects of the growth of employment. This growth, in turn, created the bulk of the opportunities for occupational mobility. The inter-relationships between employment, the structure of occupations, and mobility opportunities are most clearly evident from the following sketch of the development of the Waltham Watch Company.[1]

In 1854, when the predecessor to Waltham Watch relocated in the town, it brought with it a complement of fifty men skilled in various aspects of watch and watch-tool making. The inspiration for the mass production of watches had sprung from Aaron Dennison's exposure to the idea of interchangeable parts. Dennison had worked for a time as a machinist at the Springfield Armory, the birth place of the idea and the center for its application.[2]

Reorganized under the ownership and management of Royal E. Robbins in 1857, the company weathered a business depression and found itself, on the eve of the Civil War, with 150 employees, the only large-scale producer of watches in the country. With the outbreak of the war, Dennison, now superintendent of the plant, sought to encourage the production of a low-priced watch that could be purchased by soldiers. A squabble ensued, and Dennison was ousted, leaving Robbins in complete control. But the idea which precipitated the dispute was soon adopted. A cheap watch was produced, and overnight the company was swamped with orders. Production rose from 12,300 watch movements and 6,100 watch cases in 1860 to 44,600 movements and 14,500 cases in 1865. Employment climbed from 161 to 476 over the same period. Nor did this boom cease with the end of the war. Output and employment rose steadily until the depression which followed the panic of 1873. In that year 79,000 movements and 44,000 cases were produced by a work force numbering 698.

As early as 1863, owner-manager Robbins had discovered the existence of economies of scale: the more inputs he employed, the larger still.

---

[1]The primary sources of information on the company include: the extensive collection of its records held at the Baker Library, Harvard University; records in the possession of The Newall Company, Waltham, Mass.; and those owned and graciously loaned by Mr. D. Dumaine of Weston, Mass.

[2]See: Henry G. Abbot, *History of the American Waltham Watch Company* (Chicago: American Jeweler Print, 1905); and Charles Moore, *Timing a Century* (Cambridge: Harvard University Press, 1945), Ch. I.

the increment to output. In his annual report to stockholders he put the matter as follows:

> It being considered essential to make cheaper watches to meet the demand for goods of that class, it was essential to make them in larger numbers, thus reducing the cost of each on the obvious principles which regulate all manufacturing. That this course has proved in our case to be true economy I will state that whereas in 1859 we employed two hundred hands in producing about fifty movements per day we now find that three hundred hands will produce one hundred movements per day, in other words an increase of fifty percent in the force will double the production.[3]

This result was produced by the fact that increases in employment in response to increases in demand permitted an ever greater fissioning of tasks. The more narrowly men, machines, and supervision were concentrated upon individual tasks, the greater the productivity of labor in those tasks.

When the demand for watches declined with the depression of the 1870's and no longer spurred employment and the fission of tasks, competition arose to provide an equivalent stimulus. Up to this time, the company had not worried much about its competitors. However, while it had basked in success (in 1864 alone, profits equaled 164 percent of the capital investment), that same success had encouraged entry into the industry. Faced with a slackened demand and with competition, Robbins now turned his attention to the preservation of his enterprise.

On the one hand, he compensated for the decline in domestic demand by developing positions in English, Canadian, and Australian markets. On the other hand, he attempted to join with competing firms to fix prices and to divide the domestic market. These collusive (but not yet illegal) arrangements repeatedly failed after a time, as they did in most other industries. Some parties to the agreements saw an opportunity for aggrandizement if they violated the pact, and they did so. Robbins was not wholly unhappy to report that, on at least one occasion (1879), a price-fixing agreement had collapsed because at equal prices "our goods are preferred by the public."[4]

Competitive pressures, however, goaded him to seek more and more economies. Several times he reduced wages, salaries, and dividends, and periodically he resorted to layoffs. But he did not view these measures as more than short-run expedients. Instead, he believed that economic security and profitability were to be had only in growth. He expanded the physical plant, added new machines, and hired more workers. He rationalized supervision and created several new departments. "This year's

---

[3]Treasurer's Reports 1859-87, Volume AD-1, Waltham Watch Collection, Baker Library.
[4]Ibid.

selling price is the cost of last year" he reported to the stockholders in 1876, "and so it has been these three years [past]. And these reductions have been largely due to improvements in mechanical means and methods, the end of which we have not even approached."[5] In spite of the depression and occasional layoffs, employment continued to grow throughout the seventies. By 1880, 1,355 men and women were employed. By 1888, output totalled 341,000 watch movements and 110,000 watch cases. In 1890, employment stood at 2,824.

We can see at work, in this one firm, Adam Smith's doctrine that the division of labor is limited by the extent of the market. Initially, the market for watches was expanded by producing a cheap watch which met a demand never before tapped. Subsequently, competitive pressures stimulated a race for economies of scale and new markets. In both instances, the resulting growth of employment went hand in hand with the progressive fissioning of tasks, and because there were more jobs in the watch factory (and in the textile mill, and the iron foundry, etc.), many more men could enter occupations which neither they nor their fathers before them had practiced.

A host of problems stand in the way of a full understanding of the amount of occupational mobility in the Waltham population. Many of the native born in-migrants to the city and most of the Irish immigrants came from rural places. Given the relative decline of Waltham agriculture, most of these men could not find employment in agriculture. Presumably, many of them had no desire to do so. Hence, many of these newcomers were occupationally mobile vis-à-vis their fathers, and many were mobile in terms of their own previous work experience. But since the censuses provided no information about past occupational experiences or about the occupations of fathers not present in Waltham, there is no way of estimating what was probably the single greatest volume of occupational mobility. We are left totally in the dark about the extent to which occupational and physical mobility went hand in hand.

In addition, much of the occupational information which was provided in the Waltham census returns is of limited use. As often as not, respondents gave place of work as their occupation. There is no way of knowing from the census whether a man listed as "cotton factory" was skilled or unskilled, worker or supervisor, blue- or white-collared. Payroll records have been used where possible to correct for this. Even where clear occupational designations were used, there was often no effort made to distinguish men by their employment status. It is not clear, for example, whether a "hatter" produced hats, retailed hats, was an employee, or an employer. To some extent this problem has been reduced by checking the manufacturing schedules of the censuses to identify proprietors.

[5]Ibid.

There are a number of other data problems stemming from the then current double usage of some occupational titles. An "agent," for example, might have been the manager of a factory or a salesman, and a "clerk" might have been an important official in a manufacturing firm or a salesman in a store. In the case of the largest single occupational category in the census, "laborer," there is reason to believe that some of the men so listed were not laborers at all. A few to our knowledge were farmers, and others were undoubtedly occupied across the entire spectrum of blue collar occupational possibilities. Without stretching the imagination too far one can conceive of a Irish housewife being confronted by a strange Yankee at her door and responding to his query that her husband was "a workingman." Down on the records he went as "laborer." Not that most Irish men were not laborers during the period, but some so classed probably belonged in other recognized occupational groupings. The record is so ambiguous in so many ways that we cannot tell whether the only joke in the entire census run—which went something like this:

James Donlan, age 46, occupation: doing nothing
John Donlan, age 19, occupation: helping his father—

was a joke or an expression of bitterness, came out that way from Mrs. Donlan, or was a commentary provided by the census taker.

Many of these data problems are lessened somewhat when changes in the aggregate structure of occupational groupings are examined. For many of the same inadequacies of the census data tended to affect each decennial occupational profile in the same way, although, on balance, the census does seem to have improved with time. In reading Table 3.1 it should be borne in mind that the numbers of self-employed and of industrial employers are likely to be underestimated. The 1890 "unknown" category is too large for comfort, but the city directory listings employed were much more incomplete on this score than were the censuses. Over-all, the data presented in the table should be viewed as crude estimates rather than precise quantities.

A detailed list of the occupations encompassed within each of the categories used in Table 3.1 is provided in Appendix II. For those who do not care to search this through, we can suggest some of the larger anomalies concealed by the table. For example, all building-trades men were classed as blue-collar skilled, even though this group included some unskilled hod carriers. The number of skilled and unskilled among textile workers and watch workers was pro-rated on the basis of the ratios known to have prevailed at Boston Manufacturing and Waltham Watch. The decline in the number of self-employed farmers between 1850 and 1860 was occasioned by the inclusion of working sons in 1850 and their subsequent exclusion. From 1860 onwards, sons of farmers were usually classed as farm laborers (blue-collar unskilled) until they became farm operators,

TABLE 3.1   The Structure of Occupations, 1850–90

Occupational Group	1850 No.	1850 %	1860 No.	1860 %	1870 No.	1870 %	1880 No.	1880 %	1890[a] No.	1890[a] %
Blue-Collar Unskilled	463	33.9	965	48.0	1,406	49.4	1,701	45.9	1,755	33.0
Blue-Collar Skilled	363	26.6	546	27.2	763	26.8	1,008	27.2	1,484	27.9
White-Collar Unskilled	18	1.3	77	3.8	80	2.8	170	4.6	236	4.4
White-Collar Skilled	6	0.4	7	0.3	37	1.3	71	1.9	145	2.7
Self-Employed	124	9.1	135	6.7	232	8.1	284	7.7	341	6.4
Self-Employed Farmers	178	13.0	115	5.7	146	5.1	159	4.3	184	3.5
Managers-Officials	29	2.1	35	1.7	43	1.5	70	1.9	170	3.2
Technical-Professionals	34	2.5	48	2.4	59	2.1	64	1.7	108	2.0
Industrial Employers	12	0.9	8	0.4	15	0.5	10	0.3	12	0.2
Unknown[b]	138	10.1	71	3.5	63	2.2	172	4.6	880	16.6
Labor Force Participants[c]	1,365	100.0	2,009	100.0	2,848	100.0	3,709	100.0	5,315	100.0
Male Population Ten Years and Older	1,597	—	2,392	—	3,496	—	4,336	—	—	—

[a] All figures are for men 20 years and over.

[b] Those 20 years and over with no occupational listing were classed as unknown. Those under 20 with no listing were not counted in the labor force.

[c] Percentage columns may not total 100 percent because of rounding.

if they did. Some clerks categorized as white-collar unskilled should more properly have been designated as managers-officials, while numbers of blue-collar skilled and unskilled were actually self-employed.

For all these shortcomings, the data in Table 3.1 suggest that a very considerable amount of opportunity for occupational mobility was available during the period. To illustrate the theoretical maximum of such opportunity, consider the possibilities opened to a blue-collar unskilled worker in 1850. If this man remained until 1860 and acquired over the decade either the requisite skills or capital, there were at least 183 new skilled positions open to him in 1860 plus as many more positions as were vacated by the out-migration and deaths of 1850 skilled men. There were 59 new white-collar unskilled vacancies plus those created by the out-migration and deaths of 1850 white-collar unskilled. In all, there were approximately 207 possibilities for upward occupational mobility created by the growth of the labor force and an equally large if not larger number created by the disappearance of 1850 men.

Almost half of the labor force appears to have been composed of blue-collar unskilled workers throughout the period. (Note that this proportion is lowest when the proportion in the "unknown" category is greatest. This is probably another manifestation of the tendency for under-reporting to most strongly affect those at the bottom of the social hierarchy.) The blue-collar skilled comprised another quarter of the labor force, while all the remaining groups put together composed another twenty-five percent.

If the data accurately reflect the relative stability of most of the occupational groupings, they support the view that most of the opportunities for occupational mobility were generated by the growth of employment rather than by shifts in the character of employment.

The barriers to mobility raised by skill or capital requirements should not be overestimated for this time and place, even though they must be taken into consideration. There were no personnel departments collecting applications and verifying them. Formal skill qualifications were subordinated to the need for men who could pass muster on the job. Similarly, the barriers to going into business for oneself on a small scale were negligible. It took the proverbial shoestring, courage or folly, and little else.

Perhaps a more substantial barrier to mobility was ethnicity or, more accurately, religion. If our hypothetical man of the fifties was an Irish Catholic, the number of real possibilities open to him—partly because of his own traits and partly in consequence of discrimination—was likely to have been fewer than if he had been a Protestant. As we shall see, one consequence of this was that the routes of occupational progress among Catholics remained quite narrow. Catholics did not attempt to compete with Protestants across the entire occupational spectrum. Instead they made inroads into selected occupations and then used those occupations as their main channels for advancement.

Our hypothetical man of the fifties might have found himself slightly advantaged in his quest for occupational mobility by virtue of his persistence and by the out-migration of so many of his potential competitors. Recall that 63.5 percent of the males present in 1850 had either died or out-migrated during the next ten years. Some persisters might have been more knowledgeable about new employment opportunities and job vacancies than were recent in-migrants. To the extent that this was so, they could be near the head of the line when it came to new job opportunities.

None of the foregoing remarks are meant to imply that occupational opportunities or persistence by themselves were responsible for occupational mobility. Ultimately mobility depended upon the character of the individuals involved. A lazy, dull-witted man might not have become occupationally mobile even when opportunities went begging. But the only basis upon which to gauge whether an observed amount of mobility was high or low depends upon knowing how much mobility was possible in the first place.

At the start of the period, a preponderance of the adult males in town were educational peers. They had attended grammar school and were literate. The only illiterates (so designated in the census) were to be found among the recent Irish immigrants. A few townsmen had attended private academies in the absence of a local high school, and a smaller number still had gone to college. Access to jobs, therefore, did not rest upon educational differences so much as upon access to privately sponsored training. Even in the professions, and most particularly in law, proficiency was gained by an apprenticeship of one sort or another rather than through formal schooling.

The most common sort of training, aside from learning one's father's trade (most fathers had no trade to teach) was simply to take a job and learn about it by watching more accomplished workers. Waltham Watch developed a formal apprentice program, as did Boston Manufacturing in its machine shop. Individual craftsmen also took on apprentices. It appears, however, that picking up a trade or a set of skills by observation and experimentation was much more common than formal apprentice training. Hence a young man's occupational future was likely to be most strongly influenced by the level of skills to which he was exposed while "breaking-in" to the labor force.

The formation of a local public high school in the late 1840's did not immediately, or even for some time to come, signal an increase in the importance of formal education in the labor market. In the twelve-year period 1866 to 1878 only fifty males received high school diplomas.[6] Had employers made sizeable demands for high-school graduates, they probably could not have found enough of them to satisfy their needs. Literacy alone

[6]Compiled from annual newspaper reports of commencement proceedings.

appears to have been the formal educational requirement of most jobs until 1890. Still, over the period, there was a steady increase in educational-training levels. Men in the professions had progressively more formal education. A school for watch-making was privately established and provided entry to the better-paying jobs at Waltham Watch. Publicly sponsored night classes and vocational training programs were instituted. These developments suggest not only that there was a growing demand for education and training, but also that employers in their hiring and clients in their purchases of professional services were increasingly influenced by educational and training attainments.

The argument has frequently been made that Catholics were occupationally disadvantaged in the latter part of the nineteenth century because of the relatively low value they placed upon secular education. Any such attitude, however, was irrelevant to considerations of the occupational experiences of Waltham Catholics and, at least until 1890, it was probably irrelevant elsewhere as well. For not only did the formal educational requirements for most jobs remain quite low, but, given the small number of high school graduates, Protestants were almost as unlikely as Catholics to acquire high school diplomas. To the extent that the ability to read and write were the sole educational prerequisites for most jobs, Catholics cannot have been disadvantaged in this quarter, for most 1890 Catholics like most 1890 Protestants had completed grammar school and were literate. Only in the sense that Catholics, as a minority victimized by discrimination, did not seek to combat discrimination by over-compensating in the realm of formal schooling, could a case be made that their attitudes were harmful at this time.

Catholic children did tend to enter the labor force at an earlier age than Protestant children. We know this from payroll records and from reports of attempts to enforce mandatory school attendance laws; Catholic parents were much more likely to fudge the ages of their children so that they could get work permits or leave school entirely.[7] This suggests that, while Catholic children were literate, they had less formal schooling than Protestant children, on the average.

It was the practice of early labor-force entry which, in conjunction with discrimination, shaped the occupational destinies of the Catholic population. Catholic parents did not, as many Protestant parents did, seek out positions for their children in which a skill or trade might be learned. Many positions of this sort were closed to the Irish, and some of their children were, by the standards of the day, too young at the outset for this sort of placement. Instead, Catholic children tended to enter the labor force in the dead-end jobs, like those in the textile mill, which were simple enough for them to perform and on which there was little to be learned.

[7]*Waltham Free Press* 10/5/77.

Such patterns of entry into the labor force were almost a guarantee of little occupational mobility and of low occupational standing in their adult lives.

Economic want played a part in shaping this result, too. Many of the famine Irish were in such desperate straits that they were compelled to send their children to work at an early age. A job, any job, was acceptable, so long as it provided a supplement to family income. It is debatable, however, if children were in all cases put to work for the income involved. In 1860, for example, a number of children ranging in age from 8 to 12, worked a ten-hour day, 22–23 days a month and earned as little as $1.29 to $3.54 a month for their efforts. At the time, an adult day laborer earned $1.25 per day while working. A family would have to have been hard-pressed in the extreme to have benefited from a $1.29 increase in income gained at the expense of a child's education and 220 hours of textile mill work.

It must be recognized that child labor was a norm of the times. Children were meant to work, lest in their idleness they create havoc in the home and get into trouble in the streets. Sending them to school was neither an obviously desirable nor a free alternative. Books and clothing had to be provided and income foregone. There was also the problem that many boys didn't like school and wanted to leave it as quickly as possible. Moreover, in the eyes of some parents, schooling itself was probably viewed as a form of idleness. The time might better be used in earning income and learning the ways of the world. Esoteric school learning was also potentially dangerous, for it might produce skepticism toward received answers about the nature of things. Too much book-learning was also tainted as unmanly.[8]

As a result of wants and attitudes and of early labor-force entry and discrimination, Catholic males from the beginning to the end of the period constituted the bulk of the blue-collar unskilled work force. In Table 3.2 the most important occupational groupings in which Catholics were represented are indicated along with the number of different groupings in which at least ten Catholics were present. The very low numbers reported in textiles for 1850 and 1860 stem from failure to report child labor in those censuses and from the classification of most adult textile workers as laborers. This accounts in large measure for the very sharp decline in the proportion of laborers.

The building and metal trades, textiles, and self-employment represented the growing sectors of employment for Catholics: The metal trades flourished with the growth of the Davis and Farnum foundry which, by a stroke of luck, expanded on the eve of Newton Chemical's disappearance.

---

[8]Prejudices of this sort were undoubtedly fanned by the facts that most school teachers were females and that schooling was an indoor, non-physical activity. Among the graduates of the high school from 1866 to 1877, females outnumbered males four to one.

TABLE 3.2   The Major Occupational Groupings of Catholic Males, 1850–80

	1850		1860		1870		1880	
	No.	%	No.	%	No.	%	No.	%
All Occupations	343	100.0	714	100.0	1,149	100.0	1,484	100.0
Laborers	247	72.0	338	47.3	389	33.9	445	30.0
Textiles	18	5.2	1	0.1	298	25.9	337	22.7
Watches	0	0.0	195	27.3	51	4.4	106	7.1
Metal Trades	14	4.1	46	6.4	91	7.9	91	6.1
Building Trades	4	1.2	17	2.4	91	7.9	111	7.5
Boots & Shoes	13	3.8	58	8.1	21	1.8	10	0.7
Self-Employed	7	2.0	19	2.7	48	4.2	115	7.7
Railroad	0	0.0	0	0.0	34	3.0	31	2.1
Unknown	26	7.6	12	1.7	23	2.0	50	3.4
All Other	14	4.1	28	3.9	103	8.9	188	12.7

Presumably numbers of those displaced by the latter's closing found employment in the former firm. Boston Manufacturing readily employed Catholics but afforded them—children and adults alike—few opportunities in skilled and none in supervisory positions Some boys were put to work in the machine shop where they may have picked up some skills, but if they did so, they did not remain with the company to practice them. Most men and boys were assigned to low-paying and often the dirtiest jobs.

Several of the more significant sources of employment open to Catholics disappeared or declined over time. The Newton Chemical Company, for one, ceased to operate after 1872. The boot and shoe industry, which at one time gave considerable promise, was ruined by the Civil War. Most of the Waltham output had been sold to Southern slave owners. At Waltham Watch, few Catholics were at any time employed in the production of watch movements. Most were employed at the low-skill task of watchcase making. This operation was at times sub-contracted within the factory, so that few Catholics ever appeared on the company's payrolls.[9] When case-making was subcontracted outside of the factory, Catholic employment declined sharply.

Throughout the period Catholics were less widely diversified occupationally than were Protestants. The latter were represented by at least ten men in three times as many occupational groupings in 1850 and in twice as many groupings in 1880. Although occupations in which Catholics were concentrated also had concentrations of Protestants, members of the two groups rarely competed directly against one another. This may not have been the case in day laboring, but from what is known about the structure of work assignments at Boston Manufacturing and Waltham Watch, it is clear that, with some exceptions, there were Irish assignments and Yankee assignments. If a bleacher or a case maker were wanted, he was likely to be Catholic; and if it was a machinist or a pinion maker, he was likely to be a Protestant.[10]

It appears that it was not so much discrimination in hiring itself which worked to the disadvantage of Catholics—except perhaps in the important instance of Waltham Watch—as it was discrimination in the job assignments of Catholics. Though willingly hired, they were rarely given an opportunity either informally or through apprenticeship to acquire skills. In consequence, their status as low-income earners tended to be perpetuated over time. Even here, though, a subtle process of improvement was at work as we shall see in connection with the occupation of "laborer."

From 1850 to 1880 the number of laborers among the Catholic population rose while among the Protestant population it fell. Ostensibly then,

[9]For a description of this practice see John Buttrick, "The Inside Contract System," *Journal of Economic History*, Vol. XII, No. 3 (Sept. 1952).

[10]Evidence from Boston Manufacturing Company records indicates that males suffered more than females from intrafirm ethnic discrimination in job assignments. See the author's "The Waltham System and The Coming of the Irish," *Labor History*, Vol. 8, No. 3 (Fall, 1967).

the predominance of Catholics in such work pushed Protestants out and up the occupational ladder. There were, however, still 103 Protestant laborers in 1880. If there was pushing, all Protestants did not automatically benefit from it. Moreover, many of the laboring jobs existed in the first instance *because* of the presence of Catholics in large numbers. Had Waltham's population growth not benefited from the influx of Catholics, many of the laboring jobs would not have been called into being by the growth in the demand for goods and services.

Within the class of Catholic laborers, a change of major importance took place which the numbers in Table 3.2 cannot reveal. In 1880, 355 of the 448 Catholic laborers had been born in Ireland. This means that most of the 1880 Catholic laborers were either older men or relatively recent immigrants. The younger, American-born Catholics, were therefore avoiding the most arduous and unstable day laboring jobs and were finding other work. Even if they turned to unskilled factory labor, this was, in the comparative stability of employment and income it afforded, a step up for many from the positions of their fathers. Slight as it may seem, this shift testifies once more to the importance of length of American residence in influencing the fortunes of immigrant groups.

As indicated in both Tables 3.1 and 3.2, growing numbers of men were able to launch their own business ventures over the period. This trend prevailed even though the capital required for many ventures rose over time. A comparison of the 1850 and 1880 manufacturing schedules of the census reveals that among self-employed carpenters, for example, an average of $2,400 was invested in equipment in 1880 as compared with $720 in 1850. Among blacksmiths the average investment rose from $625 to $1,025. Even after allowing for higher prices in 1880, there was still a sizeable increase in the capital employed in many businesses. Although entry was still to be gained in many fields with investments of only a few hundred dollars, successful competition or survival often required more.

The largest opportunities for self-employment appeared in retail trade and services. Protestants, quite naturally, were represented here across the board. Catholics also opened shops, some of which, like neighborhood groceries, catered to the needs of their co-religionists, but some of which, particularly those along Main Street, served the general public. By 1880, stable keeping, furniture moving, and contracting had become predominantly Irish fields of endeavor. The latter two fields suggest one of the few comparative advantages of the Irish: they became entrepreneurs in those trades where it was necessary to muster work crews on a job-to-job or day-to-day basis. Since the proportion of casual laborers among the Catholic population was high, men with access to this pool of labor were in the best position to draw upon it as the need arose.

Catholics had also begun by 1880 to provide a limited number of professional men from their own ranks. These included five attorneys, a single physician, and two clergymen. One of the attorneys, Thomas B. Eaton, was among the first Catholic graduates of the local high school. The son of a laborer, he had nonetheless been able (or was he compelled?) to return to Ireland to take an academic law degree, and returned to Waltham to practice. He and his fellow professionals, however, were quite uncommon men in the 1880 Catholic population.

Farming as a form of self-employment continued to attract men despite or perhaps because of the increasingly urban character of Waltham. The agricultural schedules of the census listed 110 farm proprietors in 1850 and 109 in 1880. Some of the men listed were not primarily engaged in farming but rented their land and equipment to tenants. This accounts, along with the inclusion of some farm laborers, for much of the discrepancy in numbers between farmers in the population schedules and those in the agricultural schedules.

Among the farmers were descendants of some of Waltham's earliest settlers. These men worked homesteads that had supported their families for the past 150–200 years in some instances. Most of them were among the 63 farmers present in 1850 who were also listed in the 1880 agricultural census.

Most Waltham farms were relatively small and had low capitalizations. Only one-fifth of the farms in 1880 exceeded 100 acres, and barely two-fifths were valued—land, buildings, equipment, and livestock, combined—at $10,000 or more. Only 9 Catholics were listed as farmers in the 1880 schedules. In spite of small scale and low capitalization, farming was not an important source of opportunities for self-employment.

Most men came by the means to go into business by saving, while some undoubtedly borrowed from friends and relatives. One of the two banks then in existence made its savings account ledgers available for this study, but these proved to be much too chaotic and contained too much useless information to warrant extensive use. Perhaps the single most conclusive piece of evidence to the effect that saving was widely undertaken derives from the high frequency with which families were able to purchase their own homes. We shall examine this point in the next chapter.

Workers saved not only in local banks, but in company accounts at Boston Manufacturing and in a stock purchase plan at Waltham Watch. A group of 74 textile workers held accounts with an average of $325 per account in 1864. At Waltham Watch, 203 out of 504 employees in 1869 held an average of seven shares of stock each.[11] The value of these shares at the time is not known, but two years previously the stock had traded in Boston at $190 to $197 per share. One employee noted that although it was fast becoming impossible to learn a range of skills in the company,

---

[11]The company's employee stock ownership scheme was the very first in the country. Nicholas P. Gilman's *Profit Sharing* (Boston: Houghton, Mifflin, 1890) and his *A Dividend to Labor* (Boston: Houghton, Mifflin, 1899) recorded none earlier.

this was of little consequence. The premium pay offered for even narrowly defined skills, he contended, was such that a man could save up and go into business for himself.[12]

Unemployment, however, brought on the "rainy days" for which most savings had been put aside. Most of the savings bank accounts were quite small and were probably liquidated when current incomes fell. Waltham Watch's stock ownership scheme was abandoned by most rank-and-file workers when layoffs were made during the depression of the 1870's. For the period as a whole, though, most economic indicators suggest that the population had progressively larger real incomes from which to save. After 1873, wages fell and then rose slightly, while prices fell more rapidly and continued to decline. The decline in real wages occasioned by the inflation of the Civil War was more than offset by these later developments.

TABLE 3.3   *Money and Real Wages at Waltham Watch Co. 1860–90*

	Average Daily Money Wage	Index of Consumer Prices[a] (1860=100)	Index of Real Wages (1860=100)
1860	$1.88[b]	100	100
1865	2.73	169	95
1870	3.08	142	127
1875	2.54	124	120
1880	1.80	110	95
1884	1.90	104	107
1890	2.24	103	127

[a]Source: Ethel D. Hoover, "Employment, Growth and Price Levels," *Hearings Before the Joint Economic Committee, U.S. Congress,* Part II (Washington: G.P.O., 1959) p. 397.

[b]The 1860 money wage was payment for an eleven-hour day. All subsequent money wage rates were tied to a ten-hour day. This difference has been taken into account in the computation of the index of real wages.

Thus far the discussion of occupational mobility has dealt with the opportunities for mobility created by the growth of employment, by the changing structure of occupations, and by out-migration and deaths. Some of the problems confronting the potentially mobile—problems of skill, capital acquisition, and discrimination—have been touched upon. The occupational mobility of Catholics as a group has been examined. In each of these connections mobility has been discussed without reference to the experiences of individual men, so that in the discussion of mobility among Catholics, for example, we were talking about different men at different points in time. An alternative and much less ambiguous perspective upon occupational mobility is to be gained from an examination of the mobility of persisters, the same men over time.

[12]*The Waltham Sentinel* 10/26/66.

In the decade 1850-60, 133 out of the 442 adult persisters (men 20 years of age and older) changed occupations. Since some adult persisters could not have registered any change, either for want of occupational data or for movements into and out of the labor force, the 133 mobile men may represent as much as 40 percent of all possible occupation changers. Employing the occupational categories presented in Table 3.1, Table 3.4 registers horizontal shifts (e.g., from textile employment in 1850 to watch factory employment in 1860, but with no change in skill level) and vertical mobility upwards and downwards among adult persisters.

TABLE 3.4   *Occupational Mobility among Persisters, 1850-80*

	1850-60		1860-70		1870-80		Totals	
	No.	%	No.	%	No.	%	No.	%
Adult Persisters[a]	442	100.0	699	100.0	1,139	100.0	2,280	100.0
Mobile:								
Horizontal	57	12.9	86	12.3	102	9.0	245	10.7
Upward	45	10.2	105	15.0	142	12.5	292	12.8
Downward	31	7.0	38	5.4	53	4.7	122	5.4
Immobile	309	69.9	470	67.2	842	73.9	1,621	71.1

[a] Includes all males 20 years and older and those 16-19 with an occupation.

Most adult persisters who were occupationally mobile during the period moved either horizontally or upward. But the most important conclusion provided by Table 3.4 is that 71 percent of the adult persisters were immobile. Even after allowing for shifts into and out of the labor force, it remains that most adult persisters were immobile. Quite possibly it was their occupational immobility that explains why many of these men were persisters in the first place. They had found occupations and employments in occupations which satisfied them and made them content to remain in Waltham. This was obviously the case among men of old families engaged in farming (though there was more to their persistence than just occupational content) and it was undoubtedly true for some locally successful businessmen, professionals, foremen, and blue-collar workers as well.

On closer examination, it turns out that most of the occupational mobility among persisters was experienced by the younger men in that group, by men in their 20's and 30's, who were comparatively unsettled in trades or occupations. This was true particularly of the horizontal and upward movers. Older men were more numerously represented among the downward mobile.

Many of the upward and downward moves in the decade 1850-60 were occasioned by mobility into and out of self-employment. The comparative ease with which men could establish retail shops and the preferred status of independence associated with shop owning made self-employment the main exception to the generalization that most occupational moves occurred between neighboring occupational categories.

In the light of the flow into and out of small businesses, it is all the more surprising to discover that many of the men who were downwardly mobile in occupational terms experienced increases in assets at the very same time. This was true of 19 of the 31 downwardly mobile over 1850-60 and of 18 out of the 38 downwardly mobile over 1860-70. Perhaps the presence of older men in these groups explains these apparently contradictory movements in occupations and assets. Perhaps instead of failing in their business ventures, some of the older men simply sold out and then took blue-collar jobs just to keep busy. One such semi-retirement job may have been that of janitor. On more than several occasions, men listed with this occupation had considerable assets and previous occupational listings above the blue-collar level. It also appears that the job title "janitor" may have encompassed more responsibility and much more prestige than at present.

Inter-generational comparisons of occupational standing have been made for 273 sons and their fathers. These indicate that most sons held occupations similar to those of their fathers at the same age. This result, however, was partly a reflection of the ages at which comparisons were made and partly a reflection of the composition of the study group. The younger the age of the son at the time of comparison, the more likely he was to have been either upward or downward mobile relative to his father. The older the age at comparison, the more father and son were occupationally alike. A number of the sons and fathers whose records permitted comparisons at advanced ages were old family members engaged in farming. This minority in the population strongly influenced all inter-generational tallies because of its disproportionate inter-generational persistence. (The procedures employed in making inter-generational comparisons will be elaborated upon in the next chapter.)

TABLE 3.5   *Inter-Generational Occupational Mobility, 1850-90*

Age at Time of Comparison	Upward Mobile	Equal To Fathers	Downward Mobile	Totals
Men in their 30's	53	65	20	138
Men in their 40's	21	50	13	84
Men in their 50's	8	21	6	35
Men in their 60's	3	12	1	16
Totals	85 (31.1%)	148 (54.2%)	40 (14.7%)	273

To the extent that fathers who persisted were likely to be relatively high up in the occupational hierarchy (i.e., employers, professionals, or self-employed), sons who achieved similar occupational levels cannot be regarded as mobility failures. The higher up the occupational ladder the father was, the fewer the rungs left for his sons to climb. Indeed, it might be argued that the ability of sons to maintain the high standings of their fathers was itself a species of success.

The limited amounts of occupational mobility that took place both intra- and inter-generationally are not, in themselves, conclusive evidence that the volume of such mobility was negligible when compared, say, to the volume of physical mobility. The measurements made thus far have involved the use of broad occupational categories to compensate for the limitations of census occupational data. The lack of data on the occupations of some men and on the movements into and out of the labor force by other men, have served to increase the proportion of the occupationally immobile and to decrease the proportion of the mobile. Moreover, the largest pool of potentially mobile men, the physically mobile in-migrants, has been excluded from consideration altogether, since there was no way of comparing pre-Waltham and Waltham occupations. Even in the face of these very considerable limitations, we find that an average of 29 percent of the adult male persisters were occupationally mobile over each decade between 1850 and 1880 (an average of 12.8 percent were upwardly mobile) and that 46 percent of the persisting sons were occupationally mobile vis-à-vis their fathers (31 percent were upwardly mobile).

Going beyond the census into company payroll records affords an alternative approach to the measurement and analysis of occupational mobility. The basic limitation of such an approach is that it focuses most intensively upon the mobility of blue-collar workers, to the exclusion of other occupational groupings. But most labor force participants were, after all, blue-collar workers. Payroll data, moreover, permit an examination of occupational mobility at a level of detail never before attempted, and one which is quite impossible using census records alone. Fairly complete sets of payrolls for both Waltham Watch and Boston Manufacturing have been preserved. The records of the former have been examined and provide the basis for the following discussion.[13]

The narrower the field of study, it seems, the greater the degree of refinement pursued. When census data were employed, it was thought appropriate to define occupational mobility as a move within or between broad occupational classes. When payroll records were examined, the question of definition arose anew. Is occupational mobility a move from an unskilled position to a skilled one (or vice versa for downward mobility)? Is it a movement within a job classification system? Or is it any positive or negative change in the terms of employment under which an individual works? Occupational mobility appears to be all of these; it depends upon what one wants to know that determines which definition is the best. If, from a sociological point of view, the differences between unskilled and skilled workers are thought to be associated with significant

---

[13]The following discussion has been adapted from the author's "Occupational Mobility Within the Firm," *Industrial and Labor Relations Review*, Vol. 20, No. 1, (Oct. 1966).

differences in behavior and attitudes, then mobility across skill lines is important. If, from an economic point of view, a job classification system is best thought to reflect differences in skill and productivity, then mobility within such a system is important. And, finally, if it is thought that the subjective evaluations of workers themselves must be incorporated into any understanding of a historic reality, then such evaluations form the proper basis for mobility definition and measurement.

All three of these alternative definitions have been employed to provide measures of the amount of occupational mobility within Waltham Watch. The results are presented in Table 3.6 for successive five year

TABLE 3.6   *Three Measures of Occupational Mobility among Male Workers at Waltham Watch Co. 1860-90*

	Quinquennium	Upward Mobile		
		As Percent of All Unskilled Starters	*As Percent of All Unskilled Persisters*	*As Percent of All Skilled Vacancies*
Measure I Mobility From Unskilled to Skilled	1860-65	15	42	16
	1865-70	14	45	38
	1870-75	7	23	12
	1875-80	15	24	20
	1880-84	15	24	24
	1884-90	12	25	29
	Weighted Average	13	26	24
		Percent Upward Mobile	*Percent Downward Mobile*	*Percent with No Change*
Measure II: Mobility in Terms of Job Class (Persisters Only)	1860-65	35	19	46
	1865-70	72	0	28
	1870-75	15	26	58
	1875-80	25	17	58
	1880-84	38	1	61
	1884-90	36	7	57
	Weighted Average	36	8	57
		Upward Mobile as Percent of All Daily Rated Males		
		Starters	*Persisters*	
Measure III: Mobility in Terms of Worker Evaluations	1860-65	45	98	
	1865-70	47	99	
	1870-75	21	46	
	1875-80	24	35	
	1880-84	50	72	
	1884-90	32	61	
	Weighted Average	36	63	

periods, from 1860 to 1890. Data for 1884 have been used throughout because certain computations could not be made from the 1885 data.

Measure I registers mobility among those men who moved from unskilled jobs to skilled ones as determined by pay rates at the beginning and end of each quinquennium. (Skilled pay rates were computed to equal 112 percent of the average pay rate. This is the rate received by carpenters, and the lowest rate among the skilled building tradesmen employed.) According to this measure, slightly better than one out of every four workers who started as unskilled and persisted for at least five years had become a skilled worker in five years time. On the average, the company filled a quarter of its vacancies in skilled positions by internal promotion.

Measure II registers mobility in terms of job class and hence includes the movements of skilled workers as well as those of the unskilled. Not only are more workers included, but the measure also increases the likelihood of mobility relative to Measure I by incorporating more categories across which mobility was possible. In Measure I, a worker could cross only a single unskilled-skilled line to be counted as mobile. In Measure II, a worker could cross any job-class line, of which there were as many as thirteen in any one year. The more categories or classes there are, the greater the volume of mobility is likely to be. According to Measure II, slightly better than one out of every three men who persisted for at least five years was upwardly mobile within that time.

Measure III maximizes the likelihood of mobility by registering any and all changes in the terms and conditions of employment which workers are likely to have viewed as improvements. Such changes include: money wage raises, shifts from daily rated to incentive wage payment, shifts from wages to straight salary, and promotions. By including money wage increases, the measure produces the anomalous results of higher mobility over 1860–65, when money wages rose but real wages declined, and lower mobility over 1880–84 when both money and real wages increased. How strong the money illusion truly was among workers cannot be said. On the average, the subjective evaluations of workers would have produced mobility for two out of every three workers over each five-year period. Since many of the men who persisted over a single quinquennium were likely to have remained for even longer periods, some of them must have improved their position more than once in terms of such evaluations.

Long-term persistence provides only a small number of individual records for examination. There were 103 men who, over the period, spent twenty years or more at Waltham Watch. Twenty-two of these experienced multiple shifts in the form of their wage payment, so that nothing can be said about their occupational mobility. Of the remaining 81 men, 41 were upward mobile over the length of their careers, 5 were downward mobile, and 35 ended in the same position as that in which they had begun. Mobility Measure I was employed in making these calculations, but it was modified to include mobility into foremanships and into salaried white-collar posts. Twenty-four out of the 35 men who were immobile had begun their careers as skilled workers or as foremen. Hence, in terms of Measure I, there was very little room for occupational mobility on their part. In all, only thirty-seven foreman vacancies arose between 1860 and 1890, and the number of salaried openings was not in excess of ten. Most men who could have been occupationally mobile, were. Most of those who were immobile probably remained with Waltham Watch because they were satisfied with their relatively high blue-collar standing.

Numbers of Waltham Watch workers were mobile outside of the firm both in Waltham and elsewhere. Because the company was for many years the main domestic source of the supply of skilled watchmakers, it was repeatedly raided by newly organizing firms. At one time or another between 1859 and 1870, former employees occupied managerial and top supervisory posts in most of the firms in the industry. Some employees left to go into business for themselves as watchmakers, jewelers, or machinists. Writing in 1889, the company historian noted with pride:

> It would be difficult to find another manufacturing concern, the ranks of whose workman (sic) have produced so many persons who have entered professional life, or adopted other forms of business as employers. Among the graduates from this factory there are several editors, lawyers, physicians, dentists and artists. Others have become merchants and manufacturers.[14]

Each of the four measures presented above reveals a higher incidence of occupational mobility than a reliance upon census data for the same men could possibly indicate. It happens, however, that Waltham Watch was so structured as to represent a polar case in the number of opportunities for mobility which it afforded. At the other end of the spectrum stood the Boston Manufacturing Company. This firm not only had far fewer persisters who might have been mobile—persistence is a prerequisite for intra-firm mobility—but it was also structured in such a way that the opportunities for mobility within it were very much fewer.

In contrast to quinquennial rates of persistence on the order of 42 to 49 percent at Waltham Watch, only 10 to 12 percent of the males present at one time at Boston Manufacturing were also present five years later, in the three quinquennia 1850-65.[15] The proportions of persisters who were mobile hinged largely upon the nature of job assignments within the two companies. In spite of the fissioning of tasks at Waltham Watch, the number of its tasks requiring high skills was large, and for these same tasks there existed a low-skilled equivalent. Hence a dial painter who started with the company by working only on cheap watches at a low wage rate

---

[14]E. A. Marsh, "History of Early Watchmaking in America," manuscript. dated 1889. Waltham Watch Collection, Baker Library.

[15]"The Waltham System and the Coming of the Irish," *op. cit.*

could pick up the experience that qualified him for work on expensive watches at a skilled wage rate. At Boston Manufacturing few such high-skill–low-skill equivalents existed among the jobs normally assigned to men. A man could not gain the experience which, if he persisted, was of any use for occupational mobility. For this reason, mobility at Boston Manufacturing was quite rare.

The large differences in the opportunities for occupational mobility in these two companies suggest that the fissioning of tasks and the growth of employment were not the determining factors. Both companies expanded in employment and both progressively divided tasks. What created mobility opportunities at Waltham Watch was the fact that variations in the quality composition of output depended upon variations in the quality of the labor input, as well as upon those in the materials used. What limited the mobility opportunities at Boston Manufacturing was the assignment of males to many non-production tasks where little could be learned. Females were employed in the jobs for which high and low skill equivalents existed. Females, in consequence, probably had more mobility opportunities than males. But because they were females, and because their participation in the labor force was of limited duration, occupational mobility cannot have been as consequential for them as it was in the careers of men.

Specialization then, in the form of minutely divided job assignments, did not by itself have adverse consequences for the volume of mobility opportunities. On the contrary, where the fission of tasks produced identical job assignments at low-skill and high-skill levels, it increased mobility opportunities. Only when such fissioning created assignments wherein the experience gained could not be transferred within a firm did it restrict opportunities.

Among the entire male population it seems clear that occupational mobility was a phenomenon of the young. Many of the in-migrants, about whose occupational mobility we can only speculate, were young men. Among persisters, young men were the most likely to be mobile. Among Waltham Watch workers, youthfulness and high rates of mobility within the firm went hand in hand. In contrast, the records of the older men who persisted strongly suggest that their comparative occupational immobility was linked with their persistence. Their occupational attainments were such as to make them content to remain in Waltham as permanent residents. Probably the single largest exception to the youthfulness of the mobile arose in conjunction with the efforts by workers to enter into business for themselves. Movements into and out of proprietorships involved older men to the extent that entry required the prior accumulation of assets and exit was associated with retirement.

Did the growth in size of Waltham's two major firms have any adverse consequences for workers? Did the fissioning of tasks divide workers one from another in ways that left them isolated and unable to combine to act in unison? Did work itself become less important in individual lives for having been fissioned into bits and pieces?

There is no readily available answer to the last of these questions. Workers rarely volunteer their views on this subject (do they have views, or is it only intellectuals who project them?) and not one did in the records available to us. A modern reader is nonetheless likely to be predisposed to answer this question in the affirmative, for he is likely to believe that the completion of whole tasks is more self-satisfying than is the performance of small segments of a larger task. Such a view, however, may overly romanticize the importance of work in the lives of most men. It assumes, among other things, that it is the nature of the work performed that provides an important source of gratification. Instead, it might be held that most men view work as an unavoidable necessity and that their satisfactions depend more strongly upon the terms and conditions of their employment than upon the nature of their work. Almost every modern study of worker behavior under conditions of narrow task assignments indicates that sincere displays of concern for workers as human beings generate enhanced performances. It is being respected and dignified as an individual that appears to provide the greatest emotional satisfaction of work, and not the breadth or narrowness of the work itself.

The Waltham record does provide evidence on the questions of whether intensive specialization acted to divide workers from one another or left them prey to anomie. In the case of Boston Manufacturing, such questions are hardly worth raising, for whatever went on within the company was experienced by only a few workers for any length of time. Specialization may have had adverse consequences—one might read this into the development of an intra-firm status pecking order—but if it did, few workers were exposed to these in a permanent and irretrievable way. At Waltham Watch, where rates of persistence were considerably higher, all of the evidence points away from division and isolation.

The watch workers were, if anything, a singularly gregarious social group. Within the company, they organized leisure-time entertainments and a variety of self-help and self-improvement activities, such as a mutual aid society and a brass band. In the city at large, they participated widely in church and fraternal activities. They came eventually to be a dominant influence in the city's public life and in its government, as we shall see. The depth and breadth of their involvement in group activities suggest that the watch workers were possessed of a strong and positive view of themselves. They displayed an élan and an activism that made them attractive to one another and to outsiders as well.

Most watchworkers were young—the turnover among females and the constant addition of male employees produced this result—and most of them were native-born Protestants. Because they were able to wear good clothes at work without fear of soiling them, they were a handsome group. Their workplace was also attractive. Very well lit, clean, and surrounded by company-maintained parks and the Charles River, the school-like factory was, as Robbins described it, "a true Palace of Industry." Wages were high on the average, and working hours as short as in the best companies of the day. On these accounts, townsmen of more than moderate means displayed no reluctance to permit their sons and daughters to take employment in the factory, and they themselves interacted with watch workers in churches and voluntary associations. Visitors from outside the city most often resorted to superlatives in describing what they had seen. The most credible of such reports was that of John Swinton, a famous New York labor reformer and editor of the day. Swinton was fully acquainted with prevailing industrial standards and conditions when he came to Waltham in 1888. After a week-long investigation, he described what he had seen in a pamphlet entitled *A Model Factory in a Model City.*[16] As this title suggests, he had nothing but praise for Waltham Watch and its employees.

In the initial stages of their respective developments, both Waltham Watch and Boston Manufacturing had made efforts to build integrated living-working arrangements for their workforces. So long as the firms were small and everyone lived close at hand, it was possible for workers, foremen, and even managers to know one another both on and off the job. The increasing scale of both firms weakened but did not altogether destroy these conditions. Both companies were throughout the era compelled to provide company housing, and they did so within walking distance of their factories. In consequence, clusters of workers and foremen continued to live together in fairly distinct neighborhoods. On the job, the fact that personnel functions still resided in the hands of foremen preserved opportunities for worker-management face-to-face dealings in spite of firm growth. Disparate as the firms were in so many ways, neither of them had a work stoppage during the era, and in neither company were trade unions organized. Some watch workers joined the Knights of Labor during the 1880's, but this appears to have been a fraternal rather than a collective bargaining affiliation for them.

Waltham's experience of occupational mobility, of economic growth, and labor specialization may have been untypical to the extent that these were shaped by so exemplary a firm as Waltham Watch (exemplary, that is, in every way, save for the blot of discrimination in hiring). Had Boston Manufacturing alone continued to dominate the local scene, things might have turned out much differently. But that did not happen, and hence it forms no part of Waltham's history.

*　*　*

SUMMARY   The expansion of employment in Waltham generated most of the opportunities for occupational mobility during the period 1850–90. The increasing division of labor, specialization, and the fission of tasks

---

[16]John Swinton, *A Model Factory in a Model City*, (New York, 1888). Waltham Public Library.

were necessary components of the growth process, but lesser direct causes of mobility opportunities.

Occupational advancement was largely dependent upon the nature of job assignments and experience rather than upon educational attainment or formal training. The earlier labor-force entry of Catholic boys and the discriminatory job assignment practices of major employers blocked access to some routes of mobility for Catholics. Generally, with the possible significant exception of day laboring, Catholics and Protestants were not in competition for many of the same jobs or clientele.

The capital required for successfully going into business increased during the period. Formal educational attainment became of increasing importance but, by 1890, this was visible only at the top of the occupational hierarchy. Over the period, there was also an increased emphasis upon formal skill training via vocational schools and apprenticeship programs.

How frequently those who were physically mobile into Waltham were also occupationally mobile cannot be known in the absence of information about pre-Waltham employment. Among adult persisters, about one-third were mobile upward, downward, or horizontally. The two distinct groups among the mobile were the young men who changed jobs or occupations and older men leaving self-employment. The high degree of occupational immobility among the persisters suggests a direct linkage between occupational-income satisfaction and persistence.

Inter-generational occupational comparisons indicated that the greater the age of father and son when the comparison was made, the more likely the son was to be immobile relative to his father. This result can be understood only if proper recognition is given to the fact that the greater the age at the time of comparison, the more likely was the father to be relatively high in the occupational hierarchy. The younger the fathers and sons at the time of comparison, the more likely was the son to have been mobile relative to his father.

The inadequacies of Waltham census returns and the availability of payroll records prompted more detailed intra-company estimates of occupational mobility among blue-collar workers. These estimates indicate how greatly results depend upon the definition employed. Measure I yielded an estimated average of one in every four men upwardly mobile from unskilled to skilled every five years at Waltham Watch. Measure II showed one in every three men upwardly mobile between job classes in the same periods. And Measure III indicated that two out of every three males were upwardly mobile because they experienced some improvement in the terms and conditions of employment. While Waltham Watch afforded its male employees many opportunities for promotion or advancement, Boston Manufacturing afforded very few. The nature of job assignments and the character of output were critical determinants of possibilities for intra-company mobility.

Although the fission of tasks was carried to great lengths at both Waltham Watch and Boston Manufacturing, it had no obviously deleterious effect upon the workers involved. At Boston Manufacturing this was true by default. Because rates of turnover were so high, few workers were ever with the company long enough to be adversely affected. At Waltham Watch, where turnover rates were very low, workers acted often and in unison both on and off the job to an extent that is the polar opposite of what might be expected had they been anomic or alienated.

IV · Social Mobility
1850-90

Industrial development alters the dimensions of social space by increasing both the size of the population it encompasses and the stock of worldly attributes available for division within it. Of equal importance, industrial development alters the distribution of hierarchical rankings in social space in the degree to which it modifies the routes of access to the growing stock of worldly attributes. How these trends work out, what kind of social system they help to produce, and what kinds of lives they make possible are among the ultimate questions of social science. "Among" is used advisedly, for the focus upon population and worldly attributes mischievously avoids concern for the essential but non-material aspects of life.

To be socially mobile, a man must experience a change in his social status as he sees it and as those with whom he interacts see it. This social status is compounded of the attributes by which men are commonly identified within a social system. These usually include: lineage, occupation, income, wealth, power, and roles in institutions apart from occupation. Some of these attributes may be changed, but some of them are immutable. A man may, for example, be able to change his occupation or his income, or he may be able to gain a new standing by the display of an exceptional talent. He cannot change his parentage; and, by degree, he is less able to alter or dissemble his racial, ethnic, and religious identifications.

The weight a society places upon each status attribute reflects its needs and values. Many pre-industrial societies rationed the opportunities (and the ambitions) for social mobility by placing considerable weight upon lineage, that attribute least subject to change. It might be contended that they did so because, apart from the mobility consequences of cataclysmic events such as wars and plagues, they normally generated few mobility opportunities. In contrast, most industrial societies give less weight to lineage and more to the variable attributes because more mobility opportunities are routinely created by the on-going changes within them.

In the final analysis, the attributes usually employed in defining social status appear to be less valued for themselves than for the degrees of freedom of choice which their possession connotes. Freedom of choice is employed here not in any political sense, nor in the sense that choosers and their choices are totally free. It is to be understood in the sense that men who are in a position to exercise personal discretion about what or when or where or how they will act (or have others act for them) are more highly esteemed than men who are able to make fewer choices. In such terms, social mobility takes place whenever the number of options available to an individual increases or decreases. The magnitude of these changes and the areas of life in which they are relevant can be used to identify and measure the dimensions of and hence the volumes of social mobility in different social systems.

In attempting to measure social mobility in Waltham, it was not necessary to attempt to reconstruct the entire social status hierarchy. It was only the *changes* in individual standings that were of interest, not the position of each man in relation to all other men. Nevertheless, the problems of determining what size of change and what kinds of changes were to be taken as social mobility required a sense of what divisions marked the status hierarchy as a whole.

The data themselves provided few clues as to the existence of classes, save for the small group of aristocrats distinguished in the earlier discussion of the 1840 asset distribution. That there were differences in wealth, occupation, power, familial origin, religion, and social leadership roles cannot be denied. For many men, however, there were marked discrepancies among their individual attributes, and the differences between men appear to have been arranged along a continuum and not in discrete clusters. Under these circumstances, any divisions employed as the lines across which mobility could occur had to be fairly arbitrary.

Unfortunately, contemporary sociology provides few tools which can be employed in the analysis of social stratification and social mobility in the past. Moreover, in the case of the United States at least, it has always seemed inappropriate to ask people to start thinking in class terms for sociological studies, in the face of the evidence that they do not habitually think in such terms. Distinct social classes either exist, or they do not. If they do, men will very often construe social statuses in class terms. If they do not, then the differences which actually combine to produce the ever-present social-status hierarchy must be comprehended in other terms. The men of Waltham certainly perceived that there was stratification, but they never publicly spoke or wrote of classes as if they were definitive social categories into which and out of which men moved. Nor is there any evidence that they viewed classes as the structural components of their society.

But to measure social mobility, there *must* be some standard of measurement. There must unavoidably be some decision as to what constitutes movement. My decision happens to be one which maximizes the likelihood of mobility. It presumes that most Americans in the latter half of the nineteenth century viewed any and all positive changes in their material circumstance as upward social mobility. This presumption follows from an elaborate line of argument which is presented in the concluding chapter. At this juncture, I would like merely to indicate the measurement procedure which this point of view has produced.

In this chapter, each of the most important attributes of social standing is examined independently, so that what is shown is how many men were mobile in terms of assets, how many in terms of occupations, social leadership roles, and power-wielding, by nativity, and by religion. No attempt has been made to combine attributes into social statuses. Asset mobility is taken as any asset change over a specified base period. Occupational mobility is registered as any movement between the divisions employed in Chapter III (presented there in Table 3.1). Mobility in terms of power and social leadership roles is taken as movement into and out of power positions and into and out of leadership roles in voluntary associations, in government, and in corporations which were not a man's primary employer.

Each attribute of social status is examined in turn. Changes in the volume of each attribute and in the distribution of each attribute are investigated in the effort to discern the dimensions of social space and the possibilities for mobility within it. Then the mobility of persisters, the intra-generational mobility of individual men and the inter-generational mobility of sons vis-à-vis their fathers is measured. It must be recognized at the outset that social mobility measurements can only be made for men who persisted in Waltham. This is a very select group of men. As we shall see, the selection process that influenced their persistence was distinctly associated with mobility in one or more of the attributes of social status. Hence it is to be expected that considerable amounts of mobility will be found to have taken place.

Asset holding or wealth is the least ambiguous aspect of social standing and the easiest to quantify and measure. For these reasons, the volume of assets, their distribution, and changes in their distribution form a central part of the analysis which follows. All asset figures are derived from manuscript tax rolls. Local taxes were levied upon heads (the male poll tax), upon real estate, and upon personal property. The poll tax was fixed by statute and was the same for all men. It has not been included in the asset figures employed. The value of real estate was assessed by public officials. Barring irregularities or discrimination of any sort on their part, it may be assumed that real property taxes were not subject to evasion and that they therefore accurately reflect real property values. Most of the men who held assets at any time during the period 1850–90, held assets only in this form; they owned a house and lot and nothing more. Personal property taxes were levied upon assets as reported by taxpayers. The following forms of assets were subject to such taxes: cash on hand, money at interest, out-of-state private securities, in-state bank securities, public securities, stock in trade, vessels, household furnishings in excess of

$1,000 in value, and income exceeding $1,000. The dollar figures employed here were subject to change over time. Those given were in force in 1870, the mid-point of the period. To the extent that personal property taxes were comparatively easy to evade, tax assessments understate actual wealth. Nonetheless, tax payments are the single best index of wealth available.

The assessed valuation of the assets held by adult males grew fourfold between 1850 and 1890. Since the number of taxable males grew at an even faster rate (364 percent versus 299 percent), per capita assets declined. Hence, while industrial growth generated a much larger stock of material assets, it stimulated an even faster rate of population increase, such that the share of the stock which any one man might have possessed in an equal division declined. This decline did not signal an equivalent decline in per capita living standards or in general well-being. The most common index of living standards, real income per capita, rose over the period. Asset formation always lags behind the flow of income.

TABLE 4.1   *The Current Value of Taxable Assets, 1850–90*

Year	Current Value $	Percent Increase %	Assets Per Capita Taxable Male $
1850	2,095,000	––	1,851
1860	3,249,000	55.1	2,272
1870	4,708,000	44.9	2,220
1880	5,110,000	8.5	1,731
1890	8,350,000	63.4	1,591

The current-value figures presented above reflect male asset holdings exclusively. Over the period, such holdings became a smaller and smaller proportion of all of the assets in the city. By 1890, there had been a very considerable increase in the frequency with which female heads of households held assets. It is not clear why this occurred. There had also been a sizable increase in the assets of corporations. These trends are reflected by the information that where all taxable assets were valued at $2,895,000 in 1850 (i.e., by $800,000 more than the holdings of taxable males), their value in 1890 was $15,211,000, or $6,861,000 greater than the holdings of taxable males.

All taxable males did not, needless to say, have equal claims upon the stock of wealth. The growing inequality in the distribution of assets, noted in Chapter I, as between 1822 and 1840, continued to 1890 with but one interruption. This occurred from 1850 through 1865, after which time the trend toward greater inequality was restored. What caused this short-lived reversal is not known. In any event, most of the inequality that was to arise had already occurred by 1850. A comparison of the 1850 and 1890 distributions of wealth indicates very little change at the top of the wealth distribution. The smallest asset-holders became fewer and held fewer assets, while the proportion of men without assets rose. It was the decline in small asset-holders that swelled the ranks of those without assets.

Contrary to the data presented, it is altogether possible—if not probable—that between 1850 and 1890 the distribution of assets did not become more inequitable at the bottom, and that it did become more inequitable at the top. Those with the fewest assets ($1–$999) and those with the most assets were the two tax groups most likely to have produced the observed distribution of assets by evading taxes.

The lowest asset group was likely to have held its assets in the form of personal estate rather than real estate. In 1890, very few houses and house lots were assessed at less than $1,000. The highest asset group was also likely to have held considerable assets in the form of personal estate. Personal estate taxes, it will be recalled, were based upon taxpayer declarations, a basis which provided ample opportunity for tax evasion. In contrast, real estate taxes were based upon publicly made assessments that could not be evaded.

Comparisons of the values of assessed real estate with the values of declared personal estates over time suggest the possibility that there was an increase in tax evasion over the period. This imputation is made in the absence of any known changes in taxing procedures. The proportions of the value of personal estates to the value of real estate were as follows:

1840	61.3%
1850	65.2
1860	67.1
1870	48.7
1880	35.4
1890	30.1

Almost all of the relative decline in personal estates between 1860 and 1870 took place after 1865. It is possible that a portion of this change was the result of valuations of real estate at current, inflated prices in 1870, while declarations of personal estates were made at purchase prices. No evidence of a change in assessment methods was found. Eighteen-seventy may therefore mark the beginning of widespread under-reports and non-reports of personal estates.

The increase in the value of real estate from $1.7 million in 1850 to $11.6 million in 1890 was accounted for by the growth of the stock of houses and by the appreciation of houses and lots that resulted from more dense settlement. Why the value of personal estates increased from $1.1 million to only $3.6 million over the same period is not clear, unless tax evasion is introduced as a possibility. It is true that homeownership appears to have been the most highly prized form of asset holding and that such a preference would result in high levels of assets being held in real estate. But the very same preference might also be expected to produce numbers of men who had some assets but not yet enough for the purchase of a home. These are the men most conspicuously absent from the 1890 distribution of assets.

Why taxpayers might have wished to minimize their tax burdens is readily understandable. Apart from a simple reluctance to part with funds, there was also the fact that so many men were so new to Waltham that they must have felt they owed it little, just as they expected to receive little benefit from its public activities. Moreover, personal estate taxes could be avoided without any threat of discovery and punishment. The ease of evasion thus bears upon the apparent willingness of the local government to turn its back to such behavior.

As Waltham grew in size, very little was done to alter the practices of tax administration. The number of tax assessors was increased from three to five, but these men were so taken up with the administration of a much enlarged real-estate tax base that they could not attempt to verify declarations of personal estate. Not only was there no staff for such an undertaking, there was also no precedent for it. Declarations for tax purposes had always depended upon the conscience of taxpayers. Since the volume of taxable real estate grew continuously, and since levies upon real estate could not be evaded, it was easier on all counts to depend upon this source for revenue. In time (after 1890) personal estate taxation was stopped altogether, presumably because it had been reduced to such a sham.

If there was tax evasion, then the 1890 distribution of assets presented in Table 4.2 probably overstates the proportion of men with no assets, and understates the proportion of men with some but less than $1,000 in assets. The proportion of assets held by the latter group and by the $10,000 plus group are also likely to be understated. Hence the assumption that tax evasion increased after 1865 suggests a reduction of inequality at the bottom of the distribution but an increase in over-all inequality by implying that the richest men were richer than indicated by the tax rolls. The main difficulty with this assumption is that its acceptance throws open to question all subsequent analyses of trends in asset holding. For example, we shall see that, over time, it became more difficult for persisting heads of households to amass assets for the first time or to add to assets already held. If personal estate taxes were increasingly evaded, neither of these conclusions holds true.

The easiest course to follow would be to take the tax data at face value and forget about the possibility of evasion. The only difficulty which such a course presents is the one of explaining why the change in the distribution of assets between 1850 and 1890 was so small. As will be indicated, it seems to be easier to explain why the distribution should have become more inequitable than to explain its relative stability.

Even if there were more direct evidence of tax evasion, the available data could not be corrected to take this into account. There would still be

TABLE 4.2 The Distribution of Assets among Males 1822–90

Assets $	1822		1840		1850		1860		1865		1870		1880		1890	
	Men Taxed %	Assets Held %	Men Taxed %	Assets Held %	Men Taxed %	Assets Held %	Men Taxed %	Assets Held %	Men Taxed %	Assets Held %	Men Taxed %	Assets Held %	Men Taxed %	Assets Held %	Men Taxed %	Assets Held %
Zero	48.6	0	58.5	0	62.5	0	56.1	0	56.3	0	63.0	0	67.2	0	69.8	0
1–999	26.3	8.1	13.7	4.7	11.9	5.0	13.7	4.5	12.0	3.1	7.0	2.0	8.0	2.7	6.7	1.7
1000–4999	22.5	50.5	20.0	37.6	17.3	25.5	19.1	22.2	21.6	24.1	20.2	24.2	16.9	25.6	16.1	27.8
5000–9999	1.6	10.7	6.3	30.0	4.9	19.1	5.8	17.5	6.1	19.6	5.4	16.9	4.5	18.0	4.3	18.5
10,000 & up	0.8	30.7	1.5	27.7	3.4	50.4	5.3	55.8	4.1	53.2	4.4	56.9	3.3	53.7	3.1	52.0

no way of knowing how much evasion there was and whose assets were understated. The data, therefore, must be taken at face value, but the implications of tax evasion for all findings must be borne in mind. In the following pages, the data will be employed without reservation up to the point where the conclusions they suggest are considered.

The value of all male assets quadrupled between 1850 and 1890, and the number of male asset holders grew almost as rapidly. Since the observed increase in inequality fell most heavily upon the smallest asset-holders, the men with assets in 1890 were not much wealthier on the average than their 1850 counterparts had been. The average holding in 1850 had amounted to $4,929, while in 1890 the average stood at $5,271. In absolute numbers, more men had more assets in 1890—1,584 men held $8.4 million as against 425 men with $2.1 million—but the largest change was that many more men still were altogether without assets. The men without assets in 1850 numbered 707, while in 1890 3,663 reported that they had no assets.

As was the case in previous considerations of the distribution of assets, the data in Table 4.2 are of much less value once considerations of age, kinship, household status, and physical mobility are introduced. The largest proportion of the men without assets was at all times composed of single men, many of them young, and some of them the sons of fathers present with assets. To many of these men the fact that they were without assets was neither a signal of failure nor a cause for grave concern. Most of them were only starting in to try to accumulate assets in Waltham. Moreover, most of the men without assets, the single and the married, the young and the old alike, were physically mobile into and out of the city. Waltham was but one of many places in which success was pursued.

The large, physically mobile population of men without assets does not and, in the nature of things, cannot enter into the calculation of asset mobility. (We are talking here about 60 to 70 percent of the adult males ever present without assets.) It would be erroneous, however, to neglect the contributions which these transients made to the growth in the stock of wealth. For these men were unquestionably responsible for some part of the increases in output and income that made asset accumulation possible. The same is true of the hosts of female workers who toiled in the textile mill and the watch factory. Without them, Waltham's growth could not have taken place.

These migrants cannot in any sense be taken to have formed an underclass. They were, most often, people in eager pursuit of their own material advantage who, during their stay, made a contribution to output, perhaps saved a little money or learned a skill (or perhaps did neither) and then moved on. What it was that prompted some, with or without assets, to settle down in this place and what it was that prompted out-migration cannot be known in every case with equal certainty. But success in the form of asset accumulation was, as we shall see, more likely to promote persistence than out-migration. The opposite was true for those without assets.

The examination of asset holding among heads of households and among persisters restricts the analysis of such holdings to men with family responsibilities and to men among whom temporal comparisons are possible. The persisting population is the only one whose asset mobility can be measured. The head-of-household population is the one which best reflects the distribution of assets in its most consequential form.

The distribution of assets among heads of households, when computed simply on the basis of some assets versus none, was consistently more equitable than it was among the entire adult male population. In 1850, when 62.5 percent of all adult males were without assets, 44 percent of the male household heads were assetless. In 1880, when the former proportion had risen to 67.2 percent, the latter had risen to approximately 59 percent. Thus, while consistently more equitable over all, the distribution of assets among household heads also became less equitable over time.

In Table 4.3 an effort has been made to trace the asset position of male household heads within the persisting male population. Taking each census population as a cohort, the cohort by cohort persistence of heads of households, their asset positions, and the contribution of each cohort to every other cohort's totals are indicated. The result is a serial picture of the mobility and asset history of Waltham's family heads. To illustrate: examine the record for the men of the fifties. In 1850, the number of household heads with assets (425) exceeded the number of those without (334). The rate of losses due to death and out-migration during the fifties was greatest among those without assets (208 of 334). Conversely the rate of persistence was greater among those with assets (202 of 425). Over the decade a number of family heads acquired assets, as did a number of single men who also became household heads. Hence, in 1860, there were more asset holders present (307) and fewer assetless (106) among the men of the fifties. Then, over the sixties, death and out-migration took their tolls once more, resulting in the disproportionate persistence of family heads with assets. The ranks of household heads were again supplemented by family formations among previously single persisters. More men acquired assets. By 1870, these forces combined to produce 238 men with assets, as against 85 men without assets. Once more came the cycle of death, out-migration, family formation, and asset accumulation. By 1890, 143 heads of households remained from the 1850 population. The ratio of asset holders to non-holders among these family heads was 4 to 1, whereas in 1850 it had stood at 1.3 to 1.

Among the men of the fifties who survived and remained in Waltham, the accumulation of some assets was a common phenomenon. In all, there were 515 men of the fifties who were household heads at some point over

TABLE 4.3 Asset Holding among Persisting Heads of Households, 1850–90

Year	Household Heads	Men of the 1850's w/assets	w/o	Men of the 1860's w/assets	w/o	Men of the 1870's w/assets	w/o	Men of the 1880's w/assets	w/o	Total w/assets	w/o
1850	Total No.*	425	334							425	334
	Died or Departed	223	208							202	126
	Persisted	202	126							202	126
1860	Total No.	307	106	283	428					590	534
	Died	49	16 }	172	294						
	Out-migrated	48	34 }								
	Persisted	210	56	111	134					321	190
1870	Total No.	238	85	192	127	334	685			764	897
	Died	54	13	21	8 }	177	442				
	Out-migrated	30	17	38	52 }						
	Persisted	154	55	133	67	151	243			444	365
1880	Total No.	171	62	156	96	268	242	329	751	924	1,151
	Died	47	15	31	12	46	34 }	165	357		
	Out-migrated	13	15	16	22	32	63 }				
	Persisted	111	32	109	62	190	145	164	394	574	633
1890	Total No.**	115	28	124	47	216	119	290	268		

*The number of asset holders in the first year of each cohort is overstated by the inclusion of a small number of single men with assets.

**In the absence of 1890 census returns, computations for 1880–1890 do not include additions to the numbers of heads of households occasioned by new family formations.

a decade of persistence. Of these, at least 416 held assets at some point or other during the years 1850, 1860, 1870, and 1880. The experience of the men of the fifties is biased, however. This cohort alone includes all of the long-term Waltham families. Even so, the record of the men of the sixties indicates that they too came to hold assets, and the same is suggested for the men of the seventies. Asset holding and persistence among household heads were strongly and positively associated. Since computations of social mobility which include asset holding as one component can only be made for the persisting population, we can expect to find that, in terms of assets alone, most family heads were upwardly mobile.

At any one time, most of the non-asset holders among household heads were recent in-migrants. In 1860, for example, 80 percent of the assetless family heads (428 out of 534) were men who were making their first appearance in the Waltham census. The comparable proportions for 1870 and 1880 were 76 percent and 65 percent. Most of these assetless newcomers did not remain in the city for a decade. Up to 1880, almost 2 out of every 3 of them either died or out-migrated before they could be included in a second enumeration. In contrast, among newcomers with assets, up to 1880, only about 1 out of every 2 disappeared within a decade. And after a decade of persistence, those still without assets were even more likely to out-migrate than those with assets. As Table 4.3 reveals, most of the men who disappeared after a decade of residence did so through out-migration if they were without assets and did so because of death if they had assets. This was a reflection of age differences; men without assets were likely to be young and physically mobile, while men with assets were likely to be older and have their persistence terminated by death.

The fact that the longer a man persisted, the more likely he was to possess assets, points to an important conclusion. Those men most likely to know one another and to be known in the community by virtue of their length of residence were also most likely to be those whose assets marked them as successful men of substance. These physically immobile men, to the extent that they provided a relatively stable point of reference in the midst of substantial population movement, were the standard bearers of positive material achievement.

The combination of greatly increased assets in the aggregate, of declining proportions of asset holders, and of the positive association between asset holding and persistence logically suggests that there must have been very considerable amounts of upward asset mobility among persisting family heads. Not only did many of these men come to possess assets for the first time, but many were also able to increase their holdings from decade to decade.

Table 4.4 indicates that what was true of all males generally was equally true of household heads: over time, progressively more men persisted without assets. But almost two-thirds of those who stayed for at least

TABLE 4.4 Asset Mobility among Persisting Heads of Households, 1850–90

Decade	Men of the	Started Decade		Asset Changes (%)			
		W/Assets	W/O	Added %	Lost %	Acquired %	Remained W/O %
1850–60	1850's	199	122	87.4	12.5	62.3	37.7
1860–70	1850's	210	54	89.5	10.5	37.0	63.0
	1860's	111	129	87.4	12.6	44.2	55.8
1870–80	1850's	150	52	60.7	39.3	40.4	59.6
	1860's	130	65	63.8	36.2	38.5	61.5
	1870's	151	238	62.9	37.1	40.3	59.7
1880–90	1850's	111	32	53.2	46.8	34.4	65.6
	1860's	109	62	68.8	31.2	35.5	64.5
	1870's	190	145	65.3	34.7	34.5	65.5
	1880's	164	394	60.4	39.6	37.6	62.4

a decade and had no assets were new to the city. Among long-term persisters, anywhere from one half to two-thirds were asset holders, on the average.

Most persisters improved their holdings in each and every decade, although the proportions varied considerably before and after 1870. It is possible that the very high proportions of those adding to their assets over 1860-70 are the result of inflated prices in 1870. No such possibility attaches to the 1850-60 figure (87.4), however. It therefore seems reasonable to infer that at some time around 1870 it became harder to add to assets than it had been previously. The timing of this change coincides so well with the presumed onset of tax evasion that perhaps evasion is what we see at work.

Alternatively, wide differences between 1860-70 and 1870-80 are to be expected because of the economic depression during the latter decade. However, if economic conditions were responsible, they should also have promoted differences between 1870-80 and 1880-90. These two decades are very similar.

It appears to have become slightly harder over time to acquire first assets. The proportion of new holders during the 1850-60 decade is inexplicably higher than at any other time. Why, when 9 out of 10 asset holders were able to improve their position during 1860-70, only 4 out of 10 of the unassetted were able to acquire assets, is not clear.

The average age at which assets were first acquired has been found to be thirty-four. If most men married in their twenties, no more than half of them could have been expected to have accumulated assets during their first decade as household heads. An analysis of the asset status of newly married men indicates that 36 percent who started the decade without assets ended it with some. Over time, the proportion of men setting up households without assets rose.

In summarizing, it appears that although over the entire period more persisting family heads were able to improve their asset positions than were not, the rates at which they were able to add or acquire assets declined. If we assume growing tax evasion, this conclusion is open to question. It might not have become progressively more difficult to accumulate first assets or to add to assets already held. A survey of the sources of asset accumulation tends to support this conjecture.

The primary evidence which suggests that it should not have become increasingly difficult to accumulate assets for the first time is the trend in real incomes. Between 1850-60, real wages at Boston Manufacturing appear to have risen slightly. Since there was unemployment in 1860, it is possible that real incomes had not risen. For the remaining decades, real wages at Waltham Watch showed a rise between 1860 and 1870, a decline over the following decade, and a rise between 1880 and 1890. Since 1870, 1880, and 1890 were years of high employment, it may be inferred that real-wage trends accurately reflect trends in real income. In light of these trends, it is not at all clear why it should have become more difficult to accumulate first assets, particularly over the decade 1880–90 when real wages rose by almost 35 percent. Either the population developed a decidedly lower propensity to save out of earnings, or it was under-reporting personal estates for tax purposes.

Assuming for the moment that there was tax evasion and that numbers of men who signified that they had no assets did have some, the result would be a more equitable distribution of assets in 1890. On the same assumption, however, the data under-record additions to assets already held. Such additions, in turn, would serve to increase inequality. The following discussion bears on why the 1890 distribution of assets might have been expected to display more inequality than it does.

As has been noted, most of Waltham's asset holders owned their own homes and little else. Assets in this form represented a species of consumption rather than investment. If there were returns, their most important embodiment was not so much economic as social. Homeownership was a testament to success; it signaled material accomplishment and security. As such, homeownership was a foremost ambition of many families.

The assets of the remaining minority of men were invested both in housing and in businesses. The latter investments yielded different kinds of returns and had significantly different economic and social consequences. Some men invested their assets in self-employing enterprises. The returns to these men took the forms of profit and the social esteem associated with being one's own boss. Other asset holders made investments in stocks, bonds, and real estate. The returns upon these assets might be expected to have resulted in an increasingly inequitable distribution of wealth. For such was the dynamic of industrial capitalism, that men whose current incomes exceeded their current consumption desires felt obliged to invest their otherwise idle funds. They thus acted in a way most likely to increase their future income and assets still further. Their assets brought in income in addition to the income received from the factor service they provided. This should have resulted in a faster rate of asset accumulation than was possible among men who lived on wage earnings alone. The blue-collar worker had only his labor to sell, while a professional man, for example, had his services to sell and his income-earning assets as well.

In addition, there is reason to believe that occupational income differences were widening in the favor of the higher occupational rankings. At Waltham Watch, the wages of foremen increased relative to those of skilled workmen, and the salary of the owner manager increased greatly over the earnings of foremen. Those with large asset holdings were thus doubly advantaged. Their incomes rose more rapidly over the period, and they had incomes from their invested assets as well. The case histories of two highly successful men can serve to illustrate two of the major sources of wealth.

When he first appeared upon the town tax rolls in 1840, Francis Buttrick was a young man of twenty-five, single, and without assets. Since he was listed as a carpenter in the 1850 census, it may be assumed that the housing boom of the forties had redounded to his advantage. By 1850, Mr. Buttrick had wed, owned his own home, and had total assets valued at $3,400. (We cannot say how important his marriage settlement had been in promoting his emergence as a householder.) Ten years later, he was listed in the census as a lumber dealer, an occupational listing which was never to change. His fortune in the space of a decade had increased ten-fold to $39,000, most of it in the form of rental property. The end of the Civil War found him with $75,000 in assets. He was, by 1870, the largest single non-corporate property owner in town, with total assets of $110,000. Ten years later, despite the depression, he had more than doubled his assets, and was worth a quarter of a million dollars. In 1890, when he was 75 years old and the city's virtual landlord, his assets totalled $396,000. While his total assets increased between 1870 and 1890, his declarations of personal property declined from $52,000 in 1872 to $30,000 in 1890.

Francis Buttrick's rise was conditioned most largely by his investments and reinvestments in real property. As such, his wealth was a product of Waltham's urbanization. Not only was there a direct incentive to invest in housing, but, in addition, the city's growth served to increase the value of properties already owned. In the terms of Henry George, Mr. Buttrick reaped the windfall of unearned increments to land values generated by urban development. Nor was he alone in this. Investment in real estate was regarded as sound practice to the point that many of Waltham's wealthier men held some of their assets in this form.

But the quickest route to riches lay not where Henry George thought, but where Marx thought, in industrial enterprise. The experience of Royal E. Robbins, the owner-manager of Waltham Watch, provides evidence on this point. Robbins never resided in Waltham and hence never appeared as an individual upon its tax rolls. But other sources of information can be used to illustrate his financial success. For example, in 1865, for federal tax purposes, Robbins declared an income of $377,000. He earned in that one year almost as much as Francis Buttrick accumulated in fifty. (Even if Mr. Buttrick is assumed to have earned a 15 percent return upon his investments in 1865, this would have yielded just $11,000 in income.) In 1865, Robbins drew a salary of $6,000 at Waltham Watch; in the early 1880's, he drew $15,000 for his services. This latter salary was at the time three times higher than that of his highest paid supervisor, roughly ten times the average income of a skilled employee, and roughly twenty times the average income of an unskilled employee. In addition to his salary, of course, Robbins also received sizeable returns upon his majority holdings in Waltham Watch and from his many other investments.

The inferences which may be drawn from these two illustrations are, first, that investments in industrial enterprise paid-off far more handsomely to the successful than did the fairly common and relatively riskless investments in real estate; second, that for those with invested assets and high occupational standings, incomes and assets rose exponentially in relation to those of blue-collar workingmen. The experiences of Buttrick and Robbins are illustrative of why it is to be expected that the rich grew richer over the period and why, for numbers of men, it should not have become more difficult to add to their assets.

Yet another factor that should have contributed to the growing inequality of the distribution of wealth was inheritance. The ability of some men to lay claims upon the past accumulations of their forebears and then to make additions in their own right should over time have produced greater degrees of disparity in wealth. Not only were inherited assets of importance in their own right, but to the extent that their possession by parents was associated with the conferring of occupational and income advantages upon sons, inheriting sons were all the more likely to be able to add to their legacies. To be sure, some sons were probably weakened by parental wealth in that things had come too easily to them. There were, similarly, men who failed in business where Robbins and Buttrick had succeeded. But, as we shall see, inter-generational failures were as rare as intra-generational collapses from high levels of asset holding appear to have been.

In summary, the analysis of asset holding among persisting heads of households indicates that most men experienced an improvement in their asset position, and that the longer they persisted, the more likely this was to have been the case. Fifty-five percent of all asset changes were improvements, 14 percent were declines, and 31 percent was the proportion of men with no change from zero assets over each decade. Most of the men in this latter group were young men, many of them newly wed and spending their first decade in Waltham. The assumption of increasing tax evasion over time, if valid, would suggest that the tallies from tax records understate the amount of upward mobility and overstate both downward mobility and immobility at the zero assets level.

Turning now to occupational mobility, we have already seen that, among adult persisters, immobility was the norm. The individual cases of Messrs. Buttrick and Robbins may have been untypical in the degree of asset mobility they suggest, but they are much more typical of the relative infrequency of occupational mobility among persisters. Had Robbins been included in the Waltham census, he would never have registered an occupational change. Francis Buttrick registered one change from 1840 to 1890. Most occupationally mobile men were young. We can expect therefore that such mobility was more important among inter-generational persisters than it was among persisters during their own lifetimes.

The remaining facets of social status: power, social leadership roles, familial origin, and religion are of a different order from assets and occupations and require different treatment. The latter two, for example, are not dimensions of status along which mobility is either likely or possible. The former two do afford opportunities for mobility, but they are by nature difficult to assess and to measure.

In absolute terms, there is little question but that the opportunities for exercising power over men or material resources and for occupying social leadership roles increased over the period. There were, for example, larger numbers of employing firms and, within firms, more men charged with supervisory and decision-making authority. This was as true of the public sector as it was of the private one; the town government expanded in terms of the diversity of its activities, and in terms of personnel and budgets. Similarly, voluntary associations multiplied and created new opportunities for social leadership. But whether these increases in absolute numbers were associated with increasing or decreasing opportunities for exercising power and leadership is a much harder question to answer. In the realm of power, the evidence provided by Waltham Watch and Boston Manufacturing, the largest private organizations in town, suggests that the opportunities to wield power underwent a relative decline.

At the watch factory in 1865, twenty-two men exercised authority at one level or another over 475 employees and an investment of approximately $200,000. In 1890, thirty-five men directed a work force of 2,800 and an investment of roughly three-quarters of a million dollars. Gauged either in relation to employment or to investment, the power wielded increased much more rapidly than did the number of power wielders. The same was true at Boston Manufacturing and, as we shall see at a later point, a similar trend prevailed in the public sector.

To offset the relative decline in the opportunities for exercising power within the three largest organizations in Waltham, there would have to have been a large increase in the number of new firms of size and consequence. New firms there were, but not in sufficient numbers or of sufficient scale to have increased the over-all proportion of power wielders in the population. In all likelihood, the distribution of power became, over time, even more inequitable than the distribution of wealth.

The opportunities for mobility associated with filling positions of social leadership do not appear to have undergone a similar relative decline. However, the use of such positions as a measure of social standing, and hence the view of them as potential channels for mobility, is much more ambiguous than all previous measures. This ambiguity deserves some elaboration, even though it was impossible in practice to make allowances for it in the actual mobility tallies.

In some voluntary associations, such as churches, for example, election or appointment to office was most often a *confirmation* of an individual's social standing. A man of age and means was not made mobile by being appointed a church warden. His appointment or election was premised upon his already achieved social status. In contrast, a man elected to office in the Masons, for example, had leadership status *conferred* upon him and may be taken as having been mobile in this regard.

The essential point of difference between these two examples turns upon the composition of each organizations' membership. Where the membership was heterogeneous with regard to age, wealth, occupational standing, and the like, the men chosen as leaders tended to be drawn from the status elite. Where the membership was relatively homogeneous, leadership positions tended to be filled by men whose interest and activities within the organization provided the basis for their selection. In the former organizations, leadership confirmed a previously high social standing in the city at large. In organizations in which men were pretty similar to one another as a condition of membership, leaders had to emerge by differentiating themselves on the basis of individual capabilities and interests. Only leadership positions of the latter sort can be associated with opportunities for mobility.

For mobility opportunities to have expanded in this sphere, it would have been necessary for the number of voluntary associations with relatively homogeneous memberships to have grown faster than the adult male population (that is, by a factor in excess of 4.4). There were, in 1890, approximately 45 such organizations in operation. The best estimate of the situation in 1850 is that there were approximately eight similar associations in working order. These figures suggest that opportunities for mobility in the form of occupying social leadership roles increased slightly over the period. This is not to say that mobility increased, however, for actual mobility depended upon how many men filled such positions. As might be expected, actual mobility was reduced by the fact that many of the men who led one organization led others as well. And many of the same men held leadership posts at different times. There were, in other words, some social lions who absorbed a disproportionate share of the available leadership roles.

Of the two remaining components of social status, familial origin and religion, neither by itself provided a basis for social mobility. Rising young men of old family stock had a relative advantage in their lineage, but only where their families provided endowments of more than lineage alone. A young man with nothing to his credit but colonial forebears would have been well advised to hide that fact, for most people would have held him suspect; his family here so long and he so poorly fixed. On the other hand, a young man of Irish Catholic descent was likely to be discriminated against. Familial origins couldn't help much but they could hinder a man.

In the nature of the situation, one had almost to advertise one's lineage if it was to count for anything at all. In a nation of immigrants, and in a village brought to city size by wholesale physical mobility, the fact that one man's forebears had arrived earlier than another's was without much weight unless it had assets or occupational prestige and a modicum of advertising to help it along. This probably accounts for some portion of the rage for biographical and genealogical compendia which marked the era. The publication of biographical sketches and family trees permitted men to broadcast what was otherwise a purely personal and often little known matter.

Religion could provide a basis for mobility only when it involved conversion, that is, when a Catholic became a Protestant or vice versa. Since few such conversions appear to have taken place, and since inter-faith marriages were also exceedingly rare, there is little reason for supposing that changes in religion were at all significant in generating mobility.

Up to this point, mobility has been discussed in terms of aggregate possibilities and aggregate movements. We now turn to the measurement of intra-generational mobility. This involves tracing the careers of individual men over time and evaluating any changes in their social standing as reflected by their asset holdings, their occupation rankings, their power, and their social roles.

It is important to note that there is one sense in which any measurement of intra-generational mobility in Waltham must be inadequate. So few men spent their entire adult lives in Waltham and, consequently, so few left records of their entire careers to be observed within the terminal dates of this study, that the numbers of men involved is very small. What measurement can be made, will be made. But one of the single most important conclusions of this study is that virtually no one who lived in Waltham from 1850 to 1890 could have known enough about completed careers in Waltham to have made more than an impressionistic judgment about the rate of social mobility. In the absence of information about pre- and post-Waltham careers, most men saw only what we shall see in more detail—bits and pieces of other men's lifetimes.

If this is so, then contemporary estimates of how much or how little social mobility the American social system afforded must have been based upon other evidence. This "other evidence" certainly owed more to personal experience and observation then it did to systematic analysis. America was young and growing. New lands were being occupied. Population was increasing. Output was expanding and, in the wake of technological advances, was becoming both more variegated and more scientifically wondrous. Society was getting richer. Change—positive, progressive change— was everywhere to be seen; and individual opportunity beckoned the ambitious and hard-working. In private lives, real incomes were most often rising. The goods and services which could be purchased meant more and better clothing, home furnishings, and amusements. It was important in itself, as a fuel for optimism, that there were so many new things to consume.

Those who were not noticeably successful in any one set of terms could almost always look to another set in which they did succeed, most often to their own standards of living. And almost everyone knew someone—a friend, relative, or acquaintance—whose advance had been truly remarkable in their eyes. Casual observation affirmed and personal experience most often reaffirmed that America was the land of opportunity in which material success was an act of rather common glory.

It was noted previously that when this study was begun, the decision was made to study the entire male population rather than a population sample, so that there would be a large enough group of persisters to provide evidence about social mobility and so that all portions of the male population would be adequately represented. As has been demonstrated, there was so much physical mobility that the number of persisters was remarkably small. Only 3,674 males persisted for a decade; 1,550 of these males remained for two decades, 533 for three decades, and 167 for four decades.

In deriving the figures presented in Table 4.5, steps were taken to increase by as much as possible the number of men included. The persistence data were re-examined, and men whose persistence was not continuous but involved an absence from only one intervening census were added. Practically, for example, this procedure resulted in 214 forty-year (1850–90) persisters instead of the 167 produced when continuous persistence was required.

On the other hand, numbers of persisters were either too young or too old at the start of their persistence to have left career records of value for the study of mobility. For example, a twenty-year persister who was four years old at the start would have left a record which ended at age twenty-four. Since such a record is an inadequate reflection of a lifetime career, it had to be excluded lest it distort the measurement of mobility. In practice, the preparation of Table 4.5 employed the following age cut-offs: All twenty-year persisters were included, provided they were at least twenty and under sixty years of age at the start of their stay; all thirty-year persisters were included, provided they were at least ten years old at the start; and all forty-year persisters were included regardless of their ages at the start.

The inclusion of non-continuous persisters, coupled with the exclusion of selected age groups, resulted in a study population composed of 476 twenty-year persisters, 273 thirty-year persisters, and 214 forty-year persisters—a total of 963 men.

The career records of each of these men was examined in turn. Asset changes were registered by comparing, where possible, assets held at the end of persistence with those held when the individual's record was closest to his thirtieth year. Where this was not possible (e.g., in the case of a man whose record began at age forty), the trend in asset holding was employed as a mobility indicator. Occupational mobility was registered in line with the occupational categories employed in the previous chapter. For the 1870–80 cohort alone, the occupational computation also involved the use of watch company payroll data to clarify skill differences and skill-level

TABLE 4.5 Upward Mobility among Long-Term Persisters, 1850–90

Decades	Persisters		Assets		Occupation		Roles		Power		Home Own.		Death	
	No.	%	No.	%	No.	%	No.	%	No.	%	No.	%	No.	%
1850–70	93	—	72	77.4	22	23.7	25	26.9	9	9.7	64	68.8	64	68.8
1850–80	93	—	58	62.4	18	19.4	36	38.7	11	11.8	53	57.0	70	75.3
1850–90	214	—	156	72.9	64	29.9	76	35.5	54	25.2	145	67.8	n.a.	n.a.
1860–80	66	—	42	63.6	11	16.7	12	18.2	3	4.5	42	63.6	41	62.1
1860–90	180	—	126	70.0	57	31.7	53	29.4	16	8.9	124	68.9	n.a.	n.a.
1870–90	317	—	196	61.8	77	24.3	120	37.9	14	4.4	190	59.9	n.a.	n.a.
All Cohorts	963	—	650	67.5	249	25.9	322	33.5	107	11.1	618	64.1	—	—
By Origins														
Old family	82	8.5	72	87.8	18	22.0	29	35.4	17	20.7	69	84.1	—	—
Waltham born	57	5.9	37	64.9	15	26.3	28	49.1	16	28.1	33	57.9	—	—
Native born	554	57.5	368	66.4	155	28.0	212	38.3	66	11.9	342	61.7	—	—
Foreign born	270	28.0	173	64.1	61	22.6	53	19.6	8	3.0	174	64.4	—	—
By Religion														
Protestant	720	74.8	495	68.8	193	26.8	276	38.3	100	13.9	461	64.0	—	—
Catholic	243	25.2	155	63.8	56	23.0	46	18.9	7	2.9	157	64.6	—	—

n.a. = No attempt was made to compute deaths after 1890.

changes. For this reason, the occupational mobility count for this cohort is potentially (but not actually) greater than that for any other cohort.

Credit for social leadership roles was given regardless of the number of roles filled, their nature, or the time in any career when they were filled. Such roles are underestimated in the 1850's for want of data. The same is probably true for the 1880 decade, though to a lesser extent and for the opposite reason, namely, the superabundance of data. Power was registered either on the basis of known occupational roles (e.g., factory foreman) or on the basis of known political-social roles (e.g., selectman). Ages, nativity, and religion were derived from the censuses; deaths from the mortality rolls; and home ownership from the tax rolls. Table 4.5 presents the basic findings for those persisters who were *upward* mobile in any dimension of their socio-economic standing.

The "All Cohorts" row in Table 4.5 tells us that two-thirds of all of the men who persisted in Waltham for twenty years or more improved their asset position during their stay. For almost the same proportion of men, asset holding included the ownership of a house and lot. One-third of all persisters served as leaders of voluntary associations at some time. One-quarter improved their occupational standing. And slightly better than one out of every ten persisters wielded power in one form or another.

If social mobility in Waltham was taken to be any positive change in lifetime material circumstance, then at least two-thirds of the persisting males were socially mobile upward. Lifetime improvement was most concretely manifested in home ownership, a facet of social standing which connoted physical stability, taxpaying responsibility, and economic security in one fell swoop. If, alternatively, social mobility was perceived as a multi-dimensional phenomenon involving all facets of social status simultaneously, then the number of upward social mobility experiences would have been substantially smaller. It should be noted that, if the former definition of social mobility is employed, the two-thirds figure becomes a minimum estimate. One reason for this is that some of the persisters without assets or asset improvements probably improved their material condition in consequence of rising real incomes. Another is that the existence of tax evasion would imply underestimates in asset mobility tallies.

Over-all, the "old family" persisters out-performed all of the origin groups, while the "foreign born" fared least well. The only surprise in this is that the foreign born fared as well as they did. They improved their assets almost with the same frequency as did all persisters, and owned homes at a rate equal to the average. They were, however, at a distinct disadvantage when it came to filling social leadership roles and power positions within the city. For example, they constituted 28 percent of the persisters, but individually wielded power at a rate of 3 percent of their number. Since many of the foreign born were Catholics, the differences in mobility associated with religious groupings are very similar to those associated with origins groupings.

Protestants out-performed Catholics along every dimension except home ownership. Catholics, like the foreign born, were significantly under-represented in social leadership roles and in positions of power. They did almost as well as Protestants in the frequencies with which they improved their assets and were occupationally mobile. These frequency tabulations, however, do not take into account several of the qualitative differences between Protestant and Catholic asset and occupational mobility.

Catholic persisters came to own homes as often as Protestant per-sisters, but on the average their homes were lower in value. The same was true of assets generally; Catholic asset holders held smaller amounts of wealth than their Protestant counterparts. Catholics were also almost as frequently mobile as Protestants in occupational terms. Among both groups, a majority of the upwardly mobile rose into self-employment. Among the remainder, the Protestants significantly outdistanced Catho-lics. They rose to become employers, professionals, or white-collar workers, while Catholics became skilled blue-collar workers and white-collar workers.

In summarizing, it must be concluded that, if social mobility was de-fined as any positive change in lifetime material circumstance, the vast majority of the long-term persisters were upwardly mobile. The "old family" men were over all the most successful, a result strongly conditioned by the fact that this group was the most likely to be advantaged by inheri-tance. Nativity and religious differences limited the number of dimensions along which social standings could be improved and also produced quali-tatively different mobility results. It must be recognized, though, that foreign-born and even native-born Catholics had not started their careers from positions equal to those of Protestants. Their relative success and the frequency of their upward improvements are all the more impressive for this reason.

Inter-generational comparisons of the positions of fathers and sons at approximately the same ages could only be made in 273 cases. This is the number of fathers and sons, out of the aggregate male population, who satisfied the following criteria: (a) records for both the father and the son included at least two census enumerations; (b) the sons' age at the time of comparison was at least thirty; (c) there could be no more than a ten-year difference between the ages of fathers and sons at the time of compari-son. Comparisons were always made at the most advanced age of the son, within the limitation imposed by item (c).

Table 4.6 presents the results of these inter-generational compari-sons. Sons and fathers were compared in terms of assets, occupations, social leadership roles, and power. In Measures I and II, sons are regis-tered as asset mobile if at the age of comparison their asset holdings were greater than those of their fathers. Occupational mobility was registered in Measure I if the son's occupational ranking was higher than his father's, at the same age. In Measure II, occupational mobility was expanded to include sons whose occupations were identical with their fathers, but only where these occupations were in the top three occupational ranks (i.e., large-scale employer, professional-technical, self-employed). The rationale behind this adjustment stems from the assumption that the sons of occupationally high-ranked fathers were relatively successful if they managed to follow in their father's footsteps. Most obviously in the case of self-employed farmers and shopkeepers, sons who equalled their fathers in occupational terms had very strong incentives to do just that, and their success in this regard *was* a species of success rather than a form of retrogression or failure.

In Measure I, sons were taken to be upward mobile in terms of social leadership roles and power wielding if they entered into such roles at an earlier age than their fathers or if their fathers had never occupied such positions. In Measure II, sons were included if, by the age of comparison, they equaled their fathers in leadership roles or power wielding. The justification for such inclusion is very similar to that employed in the case of occupations. Sons who equaled their fathers in leadership roles and in the possession of power were successful in these regards even if, as was sometimes the case, their roles or power were inherited from their fathers. Sons of fathers already established in social organizations and in situations associated with discretionary power, were successes if they as much as matched their fathers' achievements. To have required that they have bested their fathers before they could be classed as upward mobile would

TABLE 4.6   *Upward Inter-Generational Mobility*

Son's Age at Time of Comparison	Assets		Occupation		Roles		Power	
	No.	%	No.	%	No.	%	No.	%
PROTESTANTS								
Measure I								
30's (N=88)	22	25.0	30	34.0	14	15.9	1	1.1
40's (N=76)	36	47.4	19	25.0	18	23.7	8	10.5
50's (N=32)	19	59.4	7	21.9	15	46.9	4	12.5
60's (N=16)	12	75.0	2	18.8	––	––	––	––
Measure II								
30's (N=88)	22	25.0	39	44.3	25	28.4	2	2.3
40's (N=76)	36	47.4	38	50.0	31	40.8	13	17.1
50's (N=32)	19	59.4	20	62.5	17	53.1	5	15.6
60's (N=16)	12	75.0	11	68.8	––	––	––	––
CATHOLICS								
Measure I								
30's (N=50)	10	20.0	23	46.0	9	18.0	1	2.0
40's (N=8)	1	12.5	2	25.0	1	12.5	1	12.5
50's (N=3)	2	66.7	1	33.3	2	66.7	1	33.3
60's (N=0)	0	––	0	––	0	––	0	––

automatically have served to reduce the amount of mobility registered. In mobility terms, sons of fathers already at the top of a role or power hierarchy had nowhere to go but down. Hence their preservation of their fathers' roles or power represented a real accomplishment.

With the foregoing points in mind, the figures in Table 4.6 suggest the following conclusions: Most sons were upward-mobile vis-à-vis their fathers in terms of assets. The later the age of comparison, the greater the proportion of upward-mobile sons. The relationship between age of comparison and occupational mobility was inverse when upward moves through the occupational ranking were used exclusively (Measure I), but direct when allowance was made for sons who occupied the identical and high ranking occupations of their fathers (Measure II). Majority proportions of sons were upward-mobile in terms of social leadership roles among the sons who were oldest (in their fifties) at the time of comparison. (Comparisons of sons and fathers in their sixties could not be made because too few role and power data were available for the fathers. However, judging on the basis of those cases for which data were available, it seems unlikely that the sons in their sixties could have been more mobile in roles and power than were the sons in their fifties.) The proportion of sons upward-mobile or equal to their fathers in the realm of power was significant given the rather limited absolute number of power positions.

In essence, Table 4.6 suggests that the rates of inter-generational mobility in Waltham were at least as high as the rates of intra-generational mobility among long-term persisters. (Compare Measure II, men in their fifties, with the all cohort row in Table 4.5.) Unfortunately, this conclusion holds only for the Protestant population. Most comparisons of fathers and sons among the Catholic population took place when the sons were in their thirties. These sons were proportionately less mobile in assets but more mobile in occupations and roles than were their Protestant counterparts. Catholic rates of occupational mobility by Measure I would have to have been higher if they were to match the experience of Protestant sons in Measure II. This is so because there was a smaller proportion of Catholic fathers in high-ranking occupations who could be replaced by their sons. The occupational mobility among Catholic sons in their thirties was the same in Measure II as it was in Measure I. Measure II for the Catholic population is not presented because in every dimension it does not differ materially from Measure I.

In making the comparisons required for Table 4.6, a number of interesting facets of inter-generational mobility came to light. One of these was the relationship between a father's asset-homeownership position and his son's out-migration or persistence. It appears that sons were most likely to persist if they were in line to inherit their father's business or farm or if their fathers were altogether without assets. Presumably, the former group of sons remained to collect their inheritance while the latter remained to help their parents. Those sons most likely to out-migrate were those whose fathers possessed assets, usually in the form of a home, but whose occupations did not signify the possible inheritance of a shop, farm, or profession by sons.

One consequence of these patterns of persistence and out-migration is made manifest by the differences in occupational mobility as registered by Measure I and by Measure II. Sons of fathers in the top three occupational rankings were very likely to persist and to follow in their father's occupational footsteps. Sons who persisted but whose fathers were without assets appear to have contributed their earnings toward the eventual purchase of a home by their fathers. This seems to have been much more common among Catholic sons. It may explain the slightly higher rate of home-ownership among long-term persisting Catholics on the one hand (Table 4.5) and their over-all lower rate of asset improvement on the other. Catholic fathers tended to end up as home owners, but as a consequence, their persisting sons ended up with no asset holdings of their own.

Another point which emerged from the analysis of inter-generational mobility was that sons of fathers who had filled social leadership roles were themselves very likely to become similarly engaged. The opposite was also the case: inactive fathers tended to have sons who were also inactive. The power of example, plus the factor of role or power inheritance, plus longevity in Waltham help to explain the disproportionate representation of Waltham-born men in the associational and power structures of the city in spite of their lower representation among asset improvers and homeowners.

The mobility tallies presented in Tables 4.5 and 4.6 do not lend support to the inference that discrete social classes existed. Waltham society was certainly stratified, but except for the limitations imposed upon Catholic entry into social leadership roles and positions of power, there were few barriers to mobility. Most of the men who remained in Waltham for twenty years or more were able to realize three of the most widely esteemed ambitions: asset accumulation, homeownership, and self-employment. Nor were the physically mobile dispossessed and downtrodden. They were, more often than not, the young and ambitious, questing for their place in the sun. There was still too little permanency in men's physical, occupational, and social placements to permit the definition of social classes.

In many ways, however, the trends we have seen in the various dimensions of social standing suggest that it was becoming progressively more difficult to experience mobility. Occupational entry was becoming structured on the basis of formal education or job-specific training. Over the period, increasing amounts of assets were required for setting up a business. The number of power positions and of social leadership roles either declined or increased slightly, relative to the growth of the population. The trends in asset formation and asset improvements are unfortunately shrouded from our view by the likelihood of growing tax evasion.

Only the rising trend of real incomes appears to have stood in the way of a long-term worsening of mobility chances.

* * *

SUMMARY   In the absence of a widely accepted methodology applicable to the measurement and analysis of social mobility, each social-status attribute was examined independently. Taxable assets increased five-fold between 1850 and 1890. Unexpectedly, however, there was no significant change in the distribution of taxable assets over the same period. A discussion of the sources of asset disparity suggested why greater inequality should have come to prevail. A variety of considerations lent credence to the possibility that tax evasion became important at about 1870 and colored most readings of asset structure and mobility.

Among household heads, those with assets were more likely to persist than those without, and the longer men persisted, the more likely they were to come to hold assets. Most of the men who persisted for twenty years or more possessed assets, added to their assets, owned their own homes, and were self-employed. Thus, the men most likely to know one another and to be known in their neighborhoods were men whose assets, homeownership, and occupational independence marked them as the relatively successful.

As a group, the old-family persisters out-performed all others in the various dimensions of social standing. The mobility rates of Catholics were very creditable, but these reflected different absolute values. While Catholics came to own homes as frequently as Protestants did, for example, their homes were more modest on the average.

Inter-generational mobility appears to have occurred with about the same frequency as intra-generational mobility. Persisting sons routinely advanced their positions over those of their persisting fathers or preserved the already high position of their fathers. Sons appear to have been more likely to remain in Waltham when their inheritances were considerable or when their fathers were altogether without assets. Given the small numbers of very long-term persisters and father-son persisters, it seems clear that whatever the popular estimates of mobility during the period, they must have been highly impressionistic.

V · Government
and Power

The past three chapters have been concerned with mobility in the lives of individual men. In this chapter and the next, developments in local government, in voluntary associations, and in residence patterns will be examined with two goals in mind. The first of these will be to trace the developments through which the town of 1850 was transformed into the city of 1890. The second one will be to attempt the identification of sources of change and to suggest some of the major contributions of mobility to the process of change.

These two objectives are quite distinct in that the first one requires for its realization a body of empirical evidence, much of which is available in existing records. Annual reports of the local government, for example, provide data on public receipts and expenditures, the structure of government, and the names of office holders. From this information it has been fairly easy to portray trends in the activities, structure, and personnel of local government. But was there, over the period, a significant shift in popular attitudes toward government which influenced these trends? This important question and many others bearing upon why many of the observed changes took place are questions for which no comparable body of solid evidence exists. Sometimes the record provides statements which make attitudes explicit; but we must always remain dubious about the authority of such statements when they are made by one or two men. More often, the record provides no direct expressions of sentiments or attitudes.

The safest course to follow might have been to avoid discussions of attitudes altogether. In practice, this has proved to be impossible, for shifting attitudes were often felt to lie at the heart of the changes which produced the Waltham of 1890. To avoid drawing inferences about attitudes would have reduced the effort to understand the city's political and social development to the narrowest sort of empiricism. Inferences are clearly designated as such in the following pages.

In its most secure definition, Waltham must be viewed as a geographically distinct political unit. This unit had initially been created so that its inhabitants might exercise as much control as possible over the conduct of their own affairs. No additional reason for the city's existence

104

was ever put forward and none was needed. Waltham, like most cities, was in this sense neither more nor less than a fairly arbitrary unit of collective decision-making. The institution of local government was simultaneously an expression of the city's purpose and the means of its realization. Local government embodied the legislative intent to maintain Waltham as a distinct political entity. The offices of local government were the agencies through which residents could make decisions which affected them collectively. From one point of view, local government was an expression of freedom, the freedom of those most affected by political decisions to participate in making them and the prior judgments as to which issues were to be considered. From another viewpoint, local government was also an instrument of power. It meant taxes and ordinances and enforced compliance.

The people of Waltham built their city. They added schools, provided pure water, street lighting, a public library, and many more things which improved the conditions under which they lived. But there was neither joy nor fulfillment in the process. They regarded their opportunities to build as problems rather than as opportunities, and they begrudged the expense of each new public concern and every new public venture. Public progress was, like a merchant's distress sale, a painful way to remain solvent.

Many of the issues which arose to challenge Waltham's polity were created by population growth. The scale of public undertakings in such traditional areas as fire protection, road and street maintenance, public education, and the care of the indigent had to be increased rapidly. Because the city quadrupled in size between 1850 and 1890, from 4,464 to 18,707 persons, and at rates of increase as high as 60 percent in any one decade, just keeping pace in these spheres of public activity would have been challenge enough. The public authority was obliged, however, to assume many new commitments as well. The state legislature added some obligations by requiring municipalities to provide certain services once they reached a specified size. Waltham, for example, was compelled to provide evening classes for adults and vocational training classes in consequence of such laws. New-found knowledge about the relationship between dirt and disease added weight to scale-created concerns over refuse disposal, sewage, drainage, and water supply. The changing character of the population raised new issues in the areas of law enforcement and street lighting. Zoning, building standards, milk inspection, the public library, cemeteries, domesticated and back-yard animals, all arose as new sources of public concern.

In addition to these issues, the management of public affairs itself became problematic. Questions of authority, budgeting, borrowing, and fiscal accountability emerged. And, over-arching the entire array of public issues and concerns, a heated dispute developed over the representativeness of the local government. Waltham's Irish Catholic population demanded a role in public affairs. This was perhaps *the* political issue of the era, and the passions it aroused obscured questions about public purposes and practices that might otherwise have been raised.

In the following pages, those elements of the city's public life which lend themselves to quantitative analysis will be examined first. These include: budgets, tables of organization, the characteristics of office holders, and voting patterns. Following this, such issues as the dispute over Irish Catholic representation, the changing definition of public service, the quality of public services, and the question of actual versus ostensible power will be considered.

Viewed simply as a matter of budgets, the men who managed Waltham's public affairs made very considerable accommodations to the city's growth. Municipal receipts increased eighteenfold, expenditures sixteen and one-half fold, and the municipal debt by more than one hundred fold (Table 5.1). These increases must be reduced slightly if allowance is made for the ten-percent difference in prices between 1850 and 1890; but even so, the city's fiscal growth far outstripped its increase in population.

TABLE 5.1   *Fiscal Trends, 1850–90*

	Valuation of Real & Personal Property	Tax Rate	Public Receipts	Public Expenditures[a]	Public Debt
1850	$2,795,325	$5.00/1,000	$25,165	$23,556	$ 7,367
1860	4,692,500	6.80/1,000	36,330	31,999	45,186
1870	6,898,400	14.50/1,000	132,653	109,601	142,234
1880	8,827,150	15.50/1,000	191,542	184,691	413.466[b]
1890	15,210,714	14.00/1,000	452,619	382,506	793,936[b]

[a] Net of taxes paid to other jurisdictions.
[b] Includes the bonded debt of capital projects.

The larger 1890 population was also a much richer population. The total valuation of all real and personal property rose from $2.8 million in 1850 to $15.2 million in 1890. This increase in wealth was not sufficient in itself, however, to provide the added revenue required by government. Tax rates had to be increased, and they were. The rate in 1850 had been $5 per $1,000 of assessed valuation. It stood at $14 per $1,000 in 1890.[1]

The men of Waltham may have been as strongly committed to the doctrine of laissez-faire as most Americans, but their needs for local services clearly were not sacrificed to ideological scruples. The same was true of the much-vaunted Protestant distaste for borrowing. However, popular attitudes toward public expenditures, taxes, and borrowing may have held these to a bare minimum. In other words, the exponential in-

[1]All fiscal data were compiled from *Town Reports*, 1850–84, and *Waltham City Documents*, 1885–90, both series published annually by the local government.

TABLE 5.2   *Municipal Budgets, 1850 and 1890*

Object of Expenditure	1850 $	1850 %	1890 $	1890 %
Current Operating Expenditures:	17,833	75.7	319,485	83.5
Ash Collection*			1,196	0.4
Bath House*			340	–
Board of Health*			1,199	0.4
Cemeteries*			5,333	1.7
Fire Department	2,102	11.8	10,630	3.3
Hydrant Service*			4,041	1.3
Library*			3,241	1.0
Notes & Interest	3,676	20.6	53,291	16.7
Printing & Stationery			1,892	0.6
Prior Bills			2,231	0.7
Public Assistance	302	1.7	12,253	3.8
Public Buildings			16,051	5.0
Salaries (n.e.c.)[1]	750	4.2	10,498	3.3
Schools	4,698	26.3	51,986	16.3
Streets & Roads	2,579	14.5	72,659	22.7
Swill Collection*			2,797	0.9
Watch & Police			13,674	4.3
Water Works*			50,777	15.9
Miscellaneous	3,726	20.9	5,396	1.7
Capital Expenditures	5,723	24.3	63,021	16.5
TOTAL EXPENDITURES	23,556		382,506	

[1]Not elsewhere classified.
*1890 activities which had no counterpart in 1850 are starred.

creases that occurred might have been greater still in the absence of such attitudes. Few frills of any sorts were provided from public expenditures. Department heads continued to 1890 to strive to return some portion of their appropriations back to the treasury, which suggests that they continued to view their frugality rather than their spending as a test of their efficiency.[2] Public projects were undertaken only after much delay and almost always with a sense of painful reluctance.

A comparison of the 1850 and 1890 municipal budgets provides a summary view of some of the new responsibilities assumed by the public authority over the period. It also reveals some of the changes in the priorities of the body politic, assuming that public expenditures fairly reflected the desires of the voting population. Some of the expenditure categories listed in 1890 also existed in 1850, but they were then such small items that they were not recorded separately. This distinction has been signified by starring those activities of 1890 which had no counterpart in 1850.

The data in Table 5.2 indicate that the wholly new activities of government absorbed slightly more than one-fifth of the 1890 budget. Most

[2]*Waltham City Documents*, 1890.

of these expenditures, in turn, were devoted to a single activity, the public water system. The remaining new services—ash and swill collection, the bath house, the Board of Health, cemeteries, and the public library—absorbed less than 5 percent of the current operating expenditures in 1890. Except for the water system, then, it would appear that the assumption of new responsibilities was not a major factor in the growth of the public authority. The 1890 budget is deceptive on this count, however, for some portion of the expenditures in the long-established categories of expenditure were also devoted to new functions. The Highway Department, for example, was now spending funds to provide street lighting and sidewalks. The Board of Education was now providing evening classes and vocational training classes. If these sorts of expenditures are added to those of entirely new activities, the proportion of the budget going to recently introduced programs and services may have been as high as 40 percent of total operating expenditures. ·

In dollar terms, each of the more traditional categories of public expenditures was expanded considerably by 1890. There were shifts in the relative importance of these various categories, and these, rather than the absolute dollar changes, reflected changes in the priorities attached to public functions. The most significant shifts were those away from the fire department and the school system in the favor of public assistance, streets and roads, and the police department. It is also quite likely that, over-all, the proportion of the budget going to wages and salaries was greater in 1890 than it had been in 1850.

A number of interpretations of these changes in budgetary priorities is possible. For example, the relative decline in public-school expenditures may have resulted because a larger portion of the population valued education less. Or the decline might have come about because school expenditures were mainly influenced by size considerations, whereas the highway department, for example, had to contend with technological changes and with changing standards of function and performance as well as with size-related problems. These arguments deserve some elaboration, for they hold an important clue to the dynamics of Waltham's public life.

In 1890, the public schools were doing pretty much the same things and in pretty much the same ways as had been true in 1850. There were more schools, more teachers, and more students, but the educational process itself had not changed much. Apart from offering some classes for adults and introducing music and art into the curriculum, the only change of substance had been the addition of a commercial curriculum in the high school. The only "problem" in the schools was truancy, and that problem was thought to be resolved by the appointment of a truant officer.[3] The extremely high drop-out rates in the high school were not recognized as a

---

[3]*Town Reports*, 1869. That this problem continued is indicated in the *Waltham Free Press*, 10/5/77, and *Waltham City Documents*, 1882.

problem. In the early 1880's, anywhere from one-half to three-quarters of those entering the school failed to graduate.[4]

In consequence of so little change, school appropriations had only to reflect changes in the numbers of buildings, teachers and students. There appears to be little warrant for the argument that the increase in the proportion of Catholic voters may have reduced the pressure favoring school appropriations. School boards continued until 1890 to be Protestant dominated. These boards would have had the same incentive to promote schools in the 1880's as they had had in the 1850's. In addition, by 1880 most of the grammar-school teachers and a majority of their pupils were Catholics.[5] Catholic voters, therefore, had a very real stake in the quality of the school system. The relative decline in school expenditures thus seems more likely to have occurred because school boards had too few urgent problems to solve and too few changes to introduce. Even when an opportunity arose to introduce something new, school boards were slow to seize the initiative. The 1863 school board, for example, had visited the neighboring city of Newton to inspect its newly established kindergartens, but decided against their adoption. The 1890 school board was still deferring the introduction of kindergartens on the ground that they were still in the experimental stage.[6] The only major innovation associated with the schools was a political one. The first woman to hold public office was elected to the school board in 1885.[7]

In contrast, in the area of streets and roads, appropriations were required to keep pace with the city's growth *and* to take advantage of technological innovations *and* to respond to changing conceptions of what services were to be provided and how. Experiments with various road surfaces, alterations in drainage patterns, demands for well-lit streets and paved sidewalks, all added to highway expenditures above and beyond the need for new streets and street maintenance. Because the substance and methods of its functions were changing, the highway department was able to lay claim to an increasing share of the municipal budget.

This process may be seen at work in detail by examining the single issue of street lighting. In 1850, there were few street lights in the town and many of these had been installed by private individuals at their own expense. As the city grew, complaints were made to the effect that the streets were no longer safe after dark (here is one of the sources of the growth of the police department). More street lights were demanded along with more use of them—it was the practice until at least 1875 not to light the lamps when the moon shone brightly. In response, the municipal gov-

[4]*Town Reports*, 1881.

[5]*Ibid.*, 1880.

[6]*Town Reports*, 1863, and *Waltham City Documents*, 1890.

[7]*Ibid.*, 1885.

ernment assumed the full burden of providing and maintaining a network of street lights. This function was reflected as an addition to the appropriation for streets and roads.[8]

Public funds thus tended to flow to those problem areas the public wished to treat and away from those areas where problems were either non-existent or ignored. As an increase in traffic led to a more frequent watering-down of streets, so for example, an increase in crime and drunkenness led to an enlarged watch and police.

The growing public debt of the city indicates that the willingness to spend was not matched by a willingness to tax at levels which obviated borrowing. One plausible explanation for this discrepancy may be that, to the extent that the debt was incurred for capital improvements in the form of buildings and equipment, the burdens of the debt were thought to be equitably distributed only if they were spread over the lifetime of those assets. Why should the taxpayers of any one year absorb the entire expense of building a new police station if that station, like other capital improvements, would redound to the benefit of future taxpayers as well? Equity required that future benefitors bear a portion of the costs of such improvements. Between 1850 and 1890 the city went from a position where it owned 13 school buildings and $493 worth of road maintenance equipment to one where it had $1,388,420 invested in land, buildings, and equipment.[9]

When the municipal debt approached the ceiling imposed by the state legislature (in 1890 this ceiling was set at 2½ percent of a municipality's assessed valuation), the need to raise funds was met by floating special-purpose bonds which were not affected by the debt limit. The water works and the sewerage system were funded in this manner and between them accounted for more than half of the 1890 debt.

Needless to say, the increasing scale and variety of public services required the reorganization of the institution of local government itself. In 1884 Waltham sought and was granted a charter of incorporation as a city. By this act, the annual town meeting with its executive board of selectmen was replaced by a mayor and board of aldermen. Even before incorporation, steps had been taken to rationalize the administration of public affairs. Activities had been divided and re-divided. Progressively, full-time "professionals" were introduced as heads of departments, as in the cases of the supervisor of highways (1857), the school superintendent (1879), and the chief of police (1883). These full-time administrators now had full-time staffs working under their supervision, in place of either an exclusive reliance upon volunteers (fire companies) or part-time men (highways). The city government, in consequence, became an employer of some importance in the community.

[8]*Town Reports*, 1852, 1871, 1876, and *Waltham Free Press* 9/24/75.
[9]*Town Reports*, 1850, and *Waltham City Documents*, 1890.

TABLE 5.3   *Municipal Offices, 1890*

*Auditor
*Board of Aldermen
 Board of Assessors
 Board of Fire Engineers
*Board of Health
 Board of Overseers of the Poor
 Board of Street Commissioners
*Board of Water Commissioners
 City Clerk
*City Engineer & Inspector of Buildings
*City Physician
*City Messenger
*City Solicitor
*Commissioners of Public Buildings & Grounds
*Commissioners of Drainage & Sewage
*Commissioners of the Sinking Fund
*Inspector of Milk & Vinegar
*Keeper of the Pound
*License Commissioners
*Managers of Public Cemeteries
 Mayor
 Measurers of Grain
 Measurers of Wood & Bark
*Police Department
 Registrars of Voters
 School Board
*Sealer of Weights & Measures
*Superintendent of the Bath House
 Superintendent of the Hay Scales
 Surveyors of Lumber
 Treasurer & Collector of Taxes
*Trustees of the Leland Charity Fund
*Weighers of Coal

*Offices existing in 1890 with no counterpart in 1850.

Table 5.3 presents a list of the offices of government in 1890. Those offices for which no functional equivalent existed in 1850 have been marked with an asterisk.

In spite of the increasing specialization and professionalization that occurred in government, the policy makers in the public sector were, throughout the period, part-time public servants. Whether elected or appointed, the boards of selectmen, the school boards, the mayors, the aldermen, and the various commissioners assumed their public duties on top of full-time private occupational pursuits. The monetary returns for their public service were purely token. The members of the last Board of Selectmen in 1884, for example, received $200 per annum. The mayor in 1890 received $500 for his services, and the aldermen received no payment at all.[10] Thus, side by side with the increasing reliance upon full-time,

[10]*Town Reports*, 1884, and *Waltham City Documents*, 1890.

salaried heads of departments, the effective control over the public authority continued to be entrusted into the hands of men whose commitments of time and energy were necessarily quite limited. Presumably, the popular distrust for professional politicians, and for government per se, fostered the preference for casual government by ordinary citizens.

Who were the men who held office in Waltham? Were they "ordinary" citizens, and was the power they appeared to wield truly theirs? In an effort to answer these questions, an analysis of the men who served in elective offices has been prepared. Table 5.4 provides a comparison of the assets and occupational standings of all elected officials for the 1850's and for the period 1880 through 1884. This comparison indicates that there was no significant change in the kinds of men elected at the beginning and at the end of the period 1850–84.

For purposes of comparison, each category of asset holding and occupational standing has been associated with a rank-order index number. To compute the index average for assets among 1850–59 officials, 8×1, 15×2, 14×3, 1×4, and 5×5 were added and then divided by the whole number of officials, which was 43. This procedure yielded an index average of 2.5. The comparable average for officials of the 1880's was 2.7. These index averages indicate that both groups of men had slightly less than $5,000 in assets on the average, and that the men of the eighties were slightly less wealthy than their earlier counterparts. The index of average occupational standings was 3.1 for the men of the fifties and 3.0 for the men of the eighties. In both periods, most officials were either small-scale businessmen or self-employed professionals.

When selectmen alone are considered—and selectmen were the most important public officers between 1850 and 1884—it is clear that they were, as a group, wealthier than the generality of office holders and more concentrated in the small businessmen occupational category.

Using the same criteria and measurement technique as employed in Table 5.4, a comparison of selectmen of 1850–59 and 1880–84 with the aldermen who served between 1885 and 1890 reveals that the change in the form of government had a direct influence upon the kinds of men elected to public office (Table 5.6). For the eleven selectmen who served during the fifties, the asset and occupational index averages were 2.4 and 2.6 respectively. For the six selectmen of the eighties, the comparable index averages were 2.0 and 2.7 respectively. In contrast, the sixty men who served as aldermen after 1884 were, on the average, both less wealthy and lower in the occupational hierarchy. Their asset and occupational index averages were 3.0 and 4.0 respectively. When we note in addition that seventeen of the aldermen were Catholic whereas out of all previous selectmen only one had been a Catholic, it becomes clearer still that the act of incorporating as a city made for wider representation in public office.

Prior to 1885, the absolute numbers of men who held public office was quite small. In the 1850's, for example, 47 different men occupied the 131

TABLE 5.4   *Assets and Occupations of Public Officials*[a]

Index	Assets $	No. of Officials		Occupation	No. of Officials	
		1850–59	1880–84		1850–59	1880–84
1	10,000 or more	8	6	Large-Scale Businessman	3	1
2	5,000–9,999	15	11	Professional	10	9
3	1,000–4,999	14	12	Small-Scale Businessman	20	11
4	1– 999	1	1	White Collar	3	7
5	None	5	4	Skilled	4	3
6				Unskilled	2	0
				Not in Labor Force	0	3
				Unknown	1	0
Index averages		2.5	2.7		3.1[b]	3.0[b]

[a]Data could not be obtained for 1850–59 on 4 officials and for 1880–84 on 5 officials.
[b]Those not in the labor force or whose occupations were unknown were excluded from the computation of the index average.

TABLE 5.5 *Characteristics of Selectmen, 1850–84*

Assets $	No. of Selectmen	Occupations	No. of Selectmen	Persistence	No. of Selectmen
10,000 or more	19	Large-Scale Businessmen	6	Waltham born	10
5,000–9,999	16	Professional	3	30 years +	7
1,000–4,999	10	Small-Scale Businessmen	29[a]	20–29 years	11
1– 999	0	White Collar	4	10–19 years	9
None	1	Skilled	2	1–9 years	9
		Unskilled	0		
		Not in Labor Force	2		

[a] Of the small-scale businessmen, there were 17 in retail trade, 6 farmers, 4 manufacturers, and 2 in the construction business.

possible offices available over the decade. In the 1860's, 40 different men occupied an unchanged number of possible offices. The election of such small numbers reflected a tendency to re-elect incumbents rather than the existence of a tightly-knit ruling clique. The failure of the number of elective offices to grow between 1850 and 1870, in addition to other evidence, lends support to this contention. As yet the institution of local government was unvexed by population-growth pains. This, in turn, implies a lack of disputation over the conduct of government. In the absence of divisive problems, it was all the easier to re-elect incumbents.

This tendency to re-elect the same men was also reinforced by the limitations which physical mobility imposed upon leadership choices. As indicated in Table 5.5, long-term persistence was virtually a pre-requisite to office holding. Since persistence, the possession of assets, and a comfortably high occupational standing all went hand in hand among middle-aged men, Waltham's officialdom tended to form a quite homogeneous grouping. Those most often and repeatedly chosen for public office were those who stayed in the community, who were known to it, and who had important stakes in it.

The creation of a city government in 1884 promoted a wider diversity among elected officials. Elections to the office of mayor were conducted on a city-wide basis, but those for aldermen were based upon newly constituted wards. The result was an increase in Catholic representation and a broadened asset-occupation mix among aldermen. The new arrangement also resulted in an increase in the turnover of office holders. Between 1885 and 1890 the city had three different mayors (two of them lawyers and the third a foreman at Waltham Watch) and 60 different aldermen out of 6 and 126 possibilities respectively. The increasing representativeness of government thus also increased the extent to which public decisions were made by part-time novices.

The most striking consequence of the governmental reorganization of 1884 was that Waltham renounced the traditional leadership of shop-keepers and farmers for that of the skilled and supervisory elite among industrial workers. In 1890, the mayor and five of the twenty-one aldermen were watch company employees. Two additional aldermen were Boston Manufacturing employees, one a foreman and the other a bookkeeper. The city clerk, the postmaster, the city's representative to the state legislature, and the editor of the local newspaper were all former Waltham Watch employees.

During most of the period under consideration here, however, small businessmen clearly predominated among the highest ranking public officials. Their dominance suggests why one of the major goals of public policy was to keep tax rates as low as possible. It was not only politically expedient to minimize the tax burden, it also served the private interests of the sorts of men who conducted public affairs. Shopkeepers, farmers, and professionals were among the city's major taxpayers.

TABLE 5.6 Assets and Occupations of Selectmen and Aldermen

Category	Assets			Category	Occupations		
	Selectmen 1850–59	Selectmen 1880–84	Aldermen 1885–90		Selectmen 1850–59	Selectmen 1880–84	Aldermen 1885–90
$10,000 +	3	1	11	Lg. Scale Business	2	1	0
5,000–9,999	3	4	13	Professional	2	0	4
1,000–4,999	4	1	17	Small Business	6	5	22
1– 999	0	0	1	White Collar	0	0	13
None	1	0	16	Skilled	1	0	13
Unknown	0	0	2	Unskilled	0	0	4
				Not in Labor Force	0	0	3
				Unknown	0	0	1
Index Averages	2.4	2.0	3.0	Index Averages	2.6	2.7	4.0

Small-business leadership also meant that little in the way of imagination or daring was brought to the conduct of government. The very qualities that must have recommended such men for offices—their demonstrated business acumen (on a small scale), their stake in the community, their hard-headed practicality—augured against experimentation or extravagance. Innovation and creative leadership were not only likely to be expensive, they also required degrees of objectivity and imagination which shopkeepers were unlikely to possess in abundance. The popular preference for "solid citizens" in leadership positions assured the election of men most wedded to the social (but not necessarily the personal) status quo.

In an effort to discern whether public officials were truly "solid" and independent or whether instead they acted out roles prescribed for them by the city's major business interests, two different sorts of tests were conducted. The first of these involved an analysis of the men who sat upon a number of committees charged with making important community decisions. It was hypothesized that, if these men either held elective office at one time or another or, failing this, were drawn from different constituencies for each decision, then it could be concluded that decision-making was an open, above-the-table process. Election to office would indicate that decision-makers had wide community support. The representation of various constituencies would indicate an effort to entertain the views of diverse interest groups. The second test of openness involved an examination of the relationships between the city's two most powerful private interests, Boston Manufacturing and Waltham Watch, and its public authority. To the extent that these relationships revealed disagreement or discord, they would signify that the public authority was not subservient to private interests.

The points of decision investigated included: the organization of the Waltham Improvement Company in 1853; the sponsorship of the citizen's rally at the outbreak of the Civil War in 1861; the general committee to arrange the Waltham Fair in 1872; and the committee to petition the state legislature for a city charter in 1883. In each case it was found that the men who served on these committees were, in majority proportions, the same men who served in elective office. The remaining participants were drawn from diverse groups, although old-family farmers and factory foremen appear to have been given a modicum of special recognition. Since, as we shall see, these latter two groups figured importantly in voluntary associations, this may account for their consistent inclusion in the decision-making process. Later in the period there was also an obvious effort made to include representatives from the Irish community on public and quasi-public committees. This evidence, on the whole, suggests the conclusions that the powers of decision-making in Waltham were openly held and wielded, and that such powers came increasingly into the hands of diverse groupings within the population.

A survey of the relations between the local government and the city's two largest business firms lends further support to the first of these conclusions. Neither company was able to have the town do its bidding.

The men who served as resident agents for Boston Manufacturing were not viewed as other than equals by publicly involved townsmen. They sometimes served in public office and were frequently called upon as appointees to an extent that suggests that they were good citizens rather than behind-the-scenes manipulators. Because of their positions as hired managers, their limited assets, and their newness to the town none of them were granted untoward deference. They were, to the contrary, so unprivileged that, at least in one instance, one of their number was chided about child-labor practices at a semi-public meeting. In another instance, when the town undertook to divert water from the Charles River for its water system, Boston Manufacturing was so far unable to influence town officers that it was obliged to go to court in an attempt to block their action.[11]

On the other hand, Royal E. Robbins, as owner-manager of Waltham Watch, with bountiful assets and an acquaintance with the town dating from 1858, chose not to reside in Waltham, but in Boston. This must have diminished his influence somewhat. Although Robbins was undoubtedly kept abreast of local developments by his assistants, a number of whom were active in town affairs, he appears to have taken little direct interest in local matters. For all the informal power he may have commanded as the town's largest employer, even he could not have his way for the asking. When he requested that the town build a bridge across the Charles near his factory, the town refused to comply. Robbins had plans drawn at his own expense, but there was an eighteen-year lapse between his request and its fulfillment. And Robbins was quite capable of stepping on local toes when it served his purpose: the street railway he organized between Newton and Waltham in 1865 took the route he preferred over that preferred by town officers. Since it was a matter of Robbin's investment and choice of routes or no street cars at all, the town leadership acquiesced in his plan.[12]

The foregoing instances of town and company disagreement have been cited in support of the view that the two largest economic interests in the town did not hold sway over the formal political power structure and, in consequence, did not constitute a hidden, private power structure independent of the elected public officials. It would be a mistake to place more weight upon such disagreements than this, for while Waltham may not have been a company town, neither was it hostile to its major enterprises. Much more frequently than not, relations between the town and the companies were friendly and mutually accommodating.

[11]*Waltham Free Press* 12/16/70, 12/23/70, and 12/11/74.
[12]*Town Reports*, 1870 and 1865; *Waltham City Documents*, 1888.

Over the forty years from 1850 to 1890, the Waltham political scene moved from a condition of confusion and change to one of party regularity and straight party-line voting. This trend is perhaps best reflected in the political career of the town's most eminent son, Nathaniel Banks. Born in Waltham in 1816, Banks attended the local school, worked for a time at Boston Manufacturing as a bobbin boy (his father was an overseer), and undertook to prepare himself for a political career. After repeated attempts, he was finally returned to the state legislature in 1849, as a Democrat. Re-elected, he went on to win state-wide recognition for his role as presiding officer of the state constitutional convention of 1853. Following this, he was elected to Congress, as a Democrat and Free Soiler. He won a second term on the Know-Nothing ticket, and a third one as a Republican. During his second term, he was elected Speaker of the House and played an active part in the organization of the Republican Party. In 1857, he accepted the Republican Party's nomination for governor. His victory at the polls was repeated in 1858 and 1859. Henceforth, with the exception of a breach precipitated by a quarrel with Ulysses S. Grant, Banks was always a Republican Party regular. It should be noted that Banks was one of the few local men who, within the space of a little more than a decade, moved from a position of nativism to a position of positive rapport with Waltham's Irish population. From 1865 onward, he regularly honored Irish clubs and societies by appearing at their social functions.[13]

The shifts in political affiliation which marked Banks' career in the 1850's reflected similar shifts among many political activists. Until the war, men who participated in one party caucus could often be found in the opposing caucus the following year. By the war's end, such shifting appears to have stopped. From this time onward, Waltham had a fairly solid Republican majority which lost only when the state as a whole went Democratic or when there were sharp fluctuations in the numbers of votes cast. After 1860, Waltham's gubernatorial pluralities went to Republicans twenty-four times and to Democrats six times. The state elected Democratic governors twice.

Voting tallies after 1860 indicate that most voters cast straight tickets in most elections. So strong were party attachments that they almost always overpowered any tendency to favor local sons. If a townsman ran for Congress or the state senate as a Democrat, he was very unlikely to carry Waltham. A clear example of party regularity is provided by the tallies in the state and local elections of 1880, presented in Table 5.7.[14]

Between two-fifths and three-fourths of the men who paid poll taxes and were old enough to vote cast ballots in state and local elections. Many poll taxpayers were disqualified from voting because they had not regis-

[13]Fred H. Harrington, *Fighting Politician; Major General N. P. Banks* (Philadelphia: University of Pennsylvania Press, 1948); and *Waltham Free Press* 9/4/68 and 3/24/71.

[14]*Town Reports*, 1881.

TABLE 5.7   *Election Returns, November 1880*

Candidates	No. of Votes
Governor:	
J. L. Long	1,115
C. P. Thompson	727
H. B. Sargent	271
Lt. Governor:	
B. Weston	1,122
A. E. Thompson	728
Secretary:	
H. B. Pierce	1,124
M. T. Donahoe	722
Treasurer:	
D. A. Gleason	1,123
F. J. Parker	726
Auditor:	
C. R. Ladd	1,123
C. R. Field	726
Attorney General:	
G. Marston	1,124
P. A. Collins	721

tered. In 1890, a third of the poll taxpayers were unregistered. One factor which accounts for this was the failure of foreign-born adults to become naturalized citizens. It was estimated in 1874 that better than half of the foreign-born males of voting age lacked citizenship.[15]

TABLE 5.8   *Poll Tax Payers and Voters, 1860–90*

	Poll Tax Payers	Votes Cast	Percent of Payers Who Voted
1860	1,403	856	61.0
1870	2,121	947	44.6
1875	2,594	1,893	73.1
1880	2,967	1,848	62.3
1890	5,247	2,875	54.8

Elections for town officers were ostensibly non-partisan. But since there were local Democratic and Republican party caucuses actively at work, and since many of the men who participated in these also stood for local office, there may have been more partisanship than can be discerned. The Irish, it should be noted, had affiliated with the Democratic caucus at an early date. This undoubtedly resulted in the introduction of an added element of partisanship into the controversy over Irish representation in town offices. All Republicans may not have been anti-Irish, but they were anti-Democrat, and most Irishmen fell into the Democratic camp.

[15]*Waltham Sentinel* 2/27/74.

For all the claims of their non-partisan nature, elections for town officers did become both more hotly contested and more divisive. This was particularly true after 1870, when ethnic-religious differences bred rivalry and animus into what had been a ritual of consensus.[16] The heart of the matter was that this "consensus" had until now excluded the Irish. Starting about 1870, the Irish began to intensify their demands for an active participating role in community affairs.

That it was the question of Irish representation which so affected town affairs must, in the first instance, be inferred. The local press, after the style of the day, was oblique to the point of obscurity when it came to discussing what issues were producing disharmony.

In 1872, a committee charged with preparing a set of bylaws for the town recommended that school-board members henceforth receive $100 per annum for their services. This represented a $50 reduction from the current stipend. When the town meeting approved this change, four of the six incumbent members of the board resigned in view of what they took to be a slur upon their conduct of office. They did so in spite of a public acknowledgment by the bylaws committee that the fee had been reduced to insure that no one would be tempted to seek office for the salary involved.[17]

In the eyes of the Yankee bylaws committee and the town's Protestant majority, only the Irish could have been construed as a danger. By virtue of their recent arrival, the Irish were thought to be the least wedded to American traditions of public service. Many had failed to become naturalized citizens, which suggested a reluctance to accept American institutions. Finally, the Irish were known to be the lowest-income group in the community. Since a day laborer at the time could probably not have earned much more than $375 per annum—computed as 250 working days at $1.50 per day—an additional $150 of income was not an inconsiderable amount. These were among the sorts of fears which very likely motivated the bylaws committee and other townsmen.

Another and not unrelated symptom of change took the form of rivalry for public office. In the 1876 town elections, for example, as many as thirteen factions were reported to be working in support of various slates of office seekers.[18] This development may well have signaled the emergence of a wholly new perspective upon the meaning of public service.

Waltham, like most towns and villages of the era, was heir to a long-standing tradition of public service by those able to afford the luxury of office holding. We have seen that, in practice, this tradition obliged public

---

[16]An exception to this was the town meeting of 1861, described in the *Sentinel* of March 8, 1861 as a "spectacle." Presumably tempers flared over differences of opinion about secession and union.

[17]*Ibid.*, 6/7/72 and 6/14/72.

[18]*Waltham Free Press* 3/10/76.

officials to satisfy four criteria. Their occupational pursuits had to be such as to afford them the time to serve. Their persistence was required both as a testament of their commitment to the community and as a prerequisite for their being known within it. Their assets, although most often directly associated with occupational status and age, independently provided assurance of their disinterested handling of public monies. Taken together, these attributes connoted decision-making talents, mature judgment, and responsible demeanor. Since the men who satisfied these criteria were not compelled to serve the public—and some consistently refused to serve— those who stood for office probably did so as much out of a sense of duty as for the honor involved.[19]

The emergence of rival town factions created a wholly new set of possibilities. It now became possible to believe that some men might seek office for no better reason than to win, for victory at the polls had become the means for vindicating factions and partisanship. The contest and victory themselves could now be construed as the objects of political involvement. The service which victory obliged would, in such a scheme of things, have been reduced in importance. And who might not, from such an altered perspective, believe that some (Irish) men might even be so retrograde as to seek office for the money involved?

The ultimate irony in this was that Yankee fears were entirely misplaced. When, for example, the Irish won a seat on the board of selectmen, the man they elected was in every way a carbon copy of the sorts of men usually elected except, of course, that he was a Catholic. Waltham-born, educated in local public schools, a homeowner, and a grocer by trade, Timothy Leary posed no threat to the existing order of things. The same was true of the Catholic businessmen and professionals who served on the school board, the board of health, and as directors of the public library in the 1870's and 1880's. The Irish supported the same petit-bourgeois types for election as did the Yankees.

The practical accommodation of the Irish in public life came about in the following way. In 1874, in response to the growing burdens of public administration, the number of selectmen was increased from three to five. The various political factions in the town laid plans to capture the two new seats.

Several leaders of the Irish community called a meeting to organize the Waltham Naturalization Association. The stated object of both the

---

[19]Jonathan B. Bright was among those who refused to stand for public office. Scion of a family that had arrived in Watertown in 1630 and removed to Waltham in 1776, Bright had become a cotton broker in New York City. When he returned to Waltham in 1849, at the age of 49, he possessed a fortune that enabled him to retire. He spent the remaining thirty years of his life in Waltham. He travelled widely and centered much of his life around his Boston club. At his death, he bequeathed $50,000 to Harvard University, although he had not attended. His diaries, mainly taken up with daily weather reports, are held by the Waltham Historical Society.

meeting and the Association was to encourage Irishmen to become naturalized citizens and registered voters. The press, however, viewed the
meeting as an effort to solidify the Irish vote in the up-coming elections.
Although this was vociferously denied, one of the main speakers at the
meeting did argue that Irishmen had to stand together to combat the
"know-nothingism" which he thought prevailed in the town. Timothy
Leary, on the other hand, spoke to the effect that Waltham was a "model
town" and that it was up to the Irish to vote as they thought best for the
town.[20]

After the election, in which no Irishman was elected, a correspondent
noted in *The Sentinel* that the Irish had demanded only to name one
selectman and to have the town employ one Irish policeman. Having
failed on both counts, he bitterly concluded: "There is no town office ob-
tainable here for an Irish-American unless getting enrolled in the pick-
and-shovel brigade."[21] Just one year later, however, in 1875, an Irish selectman was elected, and the first Irish policeman was hired. Henceforth, for
as long as Waltham retained the town-meeting form of government, an
Irishman served as selectman. It was always the same man who served,
Timothy Leary. He occupied what became in effect the Irish seat on the
board.

In a few years' time, a sprinkling of Irishmen were elected to other
public offices and, as has been indicated, important committees came to
include Catholic representatives. The opponents of Irish representation
did not give up their fight, but enough Yankees supported Leary to insure
his re-election year after year and to add to the numbers of Irishmen in
public office. When, in 1885, Leary stood as a candidate in Waltham's first
mayoralty election, he made a very respectable showing but was defeated
1,278 to 1,019.[22] Waltham was not to have a Catholic mayor until 1904.

On the face of it, Catholic representation in public offices occurred
only when the numbers of Catholic businessmen and professionals had
risen to a point where such men could be called upon for public service.
Whether the Protestant majority delayed representation up to this point,
or whether the existence of a pool of eligible men catalyzed Irish demands
for representation, cannot be known with any certainty. There is a sense in
which both explanations may apply. The Irish population may have become more militant (as it did) because the availability of the "right" kinds
of men among them may have made the lack of representation seem more
arbitrary than ever. On the other hand, the Catholic minority won representation only with the votes of some Protestants. These votes may have
been the more readily forthcoming now that Irish candidates could satisfy
the traditional social standards set for office holders.

[20]*Waltham Sentinel* 2/27/74.

[21]*Ibid.*, 3/13/74.

[22]*Waltham City Documents*, 1885.

An alternative possibility is that discrimination in office holding had to give way as soon as it was challenged because it contradicted the beliefs of the discriminating majority. This argument rests upon the following interpretation: The famine immigrants had had little energy to devote to questions of status or representation. They had been unknowing strangers in a wholly new environment. Their primary burdens had been to survive, to get by, and to win what security and comfort they could. Their children, in comparison, were both less pressured by survival considerations and more knowledgeable about the society of which they were members. One of the lessons they had been obliged to learn was that all men were believed to be equal. The Yankees were so proud of their egalitarian commitment that they insisted upon its repeated pronouncement in the schools, in newspapers, and from public platforms.

Of all the institutions in society, political institutions were most vulnerable to attack on this score. Discrimination in private employment, in voluntary associations, and in real-estate transfers was sanctioned by the freedom of contract and/or by personal preferences. Discrimination in public life, in contrast, was wholly without sanction and, further, made a mockery of the professed commitment to political equality. When the Irish became cognizant of this discrepancy, they moved against it. The appearance among them of men who could meet the traditional socio-economic standards for office holding, probably heightened their sensitivity to the discriminatory practices they faced. Some Protestants probably felt compelled to support them in honor of their own attachment to equality.[23]

The growth of the city was itself a factor of very considerable importance in the entry of the Irish into public life. They might have protested over their lack of representation to no avail had it not been that growth compelled governmental reorganization. And reorganization, in turn, made it that much easier for Yankees to make concessions without losing face. As the "Irish seat" upon the board of selectmen came into existence only after the board's expansion, so too, as we have seen, the reorganization into a mayoral form of government increased the number of Irish representatives by easing their election to the aldermanic council. In at least one instance, an ethnic-religious dispute itself provided an incentive for reorganization. Hostility between Catholic and Protestant volunteer fire companies rose to such a level in the early 1870's that the town's fire-fighting efficiency was jeopardized. This prompted the reorganization of the fire department under one central authority in 1875.[24]

[23]The fact that the Irish became office holders throughout the state at about the same time lends support to the notion that timing and the turnover of generations were of some importance. Barbara Solomon, in *Ancestors and Immigrants* (Cambridge: Harvard University Press, 1956), p. 48, indicates that by 1890 the Irish dominated the governments of 68 Massachusetts cities and towns.

[24]*Waltham Sentinel* 12/2/73; *Town Reports*, 1875; and *Waltham Free Press* 12/24/75.

The 1870's thus saw the Irish-Yankee animus rise to near fever pitch only gradually to subside with the accession of Irish representatives to public office. What role the general economic depression played in exacerbating ethnic-religious tensions and what role it played in influencing the accommodation that was made cannot be said. That the depression, which began late in 1873, did add to such tensions, was borne out in at least one instance by a complaint voiced in the letters-to-the-editor column of the *Free Press*. Noting that jobs as town laborers were being given to those most likely to become public charges, the correspondent wanted to know what was to become of the *temperate*, respectable, taxpaying homeowners who needed work.[25] On the other hand, it is just possible that the extraordinary setting of the economic crisis made the notion of change more acceptable than would have been the case under normal conditions.

The complainant about town employment policies was by no means alone in holding the view that public expenditures ought in the first instance benefit those who bore the tax burden. An 1889 newspaper editorial argued the same point more explicitly. Having heard the president of the Board of Aldermen speak to the effect that "in the distribution of offices, old residents of this city, men who have paid taxes here and the children of such men had the first claim to recognition, " the editor went on to decry the appointment of a clerk who had been a resident for only two months and had never paid a dollar in taxes.[26] This sentiment was as old as the town itself, for, it will be recalled, a dispute over equity in the disbursement of public funds had figured in Waltham's separation from Watertown in 1738. That the issue of tax payments versus benefits should arise *within* the city, however, was something new.

Any explanation of this development must necessarily be speculative since the record provides no basis for a clear and unambiguous understanding. The following argument attempts to provide one of a number of plausible explanations.

The issue of fairness in the disbursement of public funds and offices was the other side of the coin from the issue of taxation. Just as many men with assets had an interest in keeping their tax payments to a minimum, so they had an equivalent interest in deriving the maximum benefit—personal for some, social for others—from public expenditures. It was perhaps only natural, then, that some taxpayers should have been concerned about "free riders," i.e., about those who received benefits without having made a contribution of tax dollars. In the eyes of those who shared this concern, men were equal as beneficiaries only when they bore the burden of taxation.

In 1850, Waltham was still a relatively small town, with a preponderantly native-born Yankee population. It was still possible to believe that,

---

[25]*Waltham Free Press* 2/11/76; italics appear in the original.

[26]*Daily Free Press* 1/16/89.

for all of the in- and out-migration taking place, there remained a large core of permanent residents who were peers. Even of the newer and often assetless Yankee residents it could be believed that they lacked assets and reputations because of their youthfulness rather than because of any distinct debility. Given time and perseverance, these men too would acquire a standing in the town, would settle down, raise families, and make their contributions to the public purse.

As for the newly arriving numbers of Irish families, it seems that no one knew what to make of them. What they would do for a living and how long they would remain in town was not known. Many townsmen probably expected them to depart in the near future, for demonstrably they were not wanted here, and making ends meet was a struggle for them. The wish was father to the thought, and for most public purposes the new Irish element was largely ignored. For political purposes, however, the Irish were kept very much in the forefront. Their presence was exploited as a threat, to the advantage of nativist politicians.

Effectively viewing their public as one people, as permanent residents, and as peers, it is readily understandable that public officials should earnestly have desired to make their town as good as they possibly could. Because their public mattered, the quality of public affairs did, too.

By the 1870's, the Waltham public must have seemed a very different thing to public officials. Growth had produced a situation in which many more inhabitants, whether permanent residents or not, were forever strangers to one another and to their public representatives. Nor could it any longer be assumed that many residents were permanently fixed in Waltham. The absolute size of the mobile population was too large to sustain such an assumption. The public was now composed of many diverse groups. It no longer made sense to suppose that most of the men present at any one time would ever make a return to the city for the benefits they received. The absolute numbers of men without assets, and hence without tax burdens, was large, and many of these men would probably move on. The Irish Catholic element, by now an unmistakably permanent population group, was distinctly poorer and either paid no taxes or fewer tax dollars on the average than did the Protestant majority.

For a public so conceived, city leaders perhaps thought that whatever they provided from the public purse was sufficient if they adjudged it so. From their point of view, as responsible members of the taxpaying community, they may have felt that they were conferring the beneficence of taxpayers upon barely deserving elements: upon strangers, upon persons unlikely ever to pay their fair share, upon persons different in background, heritage, and behavior. It was enough in such circumstances to be beneficent. This had to be, if only to meet the legitimate demands of those who were peers. But there was no imperative that such largesse bear the burdens of affection and excellence as well. The public was no longer one but many; no longer a society of equals but a heterogeneous mass in which some men mattered more than others. Public leadership from such a perspective could no longer be a duty of service. It was instead a patronizing charity rendered by men as often resentful as respectful of the body politic.

The one major public body which existed over the entire forty year period and made detailed annual reports of its activities was the School Board. For these reasons, public school management affords the best context in which to explore the shifting attitudes of public officials toward their functions and their public.

During the mid-1850's, the Reverend Thomas Hill served as the chairman of the Board. Along with his local standing as the leading minister of the town, Reverend Hill enjoyed regional prominence as a co-worker with Horace Mann in the field of education. When he left Waltham, it was to succeed Mann in the presidency of Antioch College. He later served for a time as the president of Harvard College.

By virtue of his standing and interests, Reverend Hill was free to lead the community in school matters. He could strive to make the Waltham, schools among the best of the day. When he thought townsmen remiss in their duties toward the schools, he was able to say so and to exhort them to greater efforts. During his tenure of office, in 1856, the local paper reported with considerable pride that out of 331 Massachusetts towns and cities only 25 appropriated more funds per student than Waltham.[27]

So far had matters changed by the 1870's that the school boards then and henceforth sought public approval for their stewardship by reporting that Waltham's per capita pupil expenditures were *lower* than those of almost all neighboring towns and cities. School boards by this time construed their roles so differently that—far from being able to criticize the public in any way except for timorous asides to the effect that teachers' salaries might be too low—their reports smacked of boosterism. They were full of self-praise and assertions of the more than satisfactory state of school affairs.[28]

It might be argued that these changes resulted from differences in personnel alone. Reverend Hill had been an exceptionally able leader. Without an equivalent replacement, the school system was bound to deteriorate somewhat. For whatever the kernel of truth in this, it remains that similar changes occurred in other public activity areas as well. The notions that public officials were literally servants of the people and that their stewardship made them responsible both to the public and for the public's interest gradually gave way to the view that election to office was a personal triumph which gave testimony to leadership capabilities. It was no longer as necessary to lead, but merely to tend the public's business. Leadership,

---

[27]*Town Reports*, 1854; *Waltham Sentinel* 4/3/56.
[28]*Town Reports*, 1875, 1877.

in at least one sense, became dangerous, for it almost always involved criticism of what existed and expenditures on something new. The respect that had made criticism and public ambition possible had been weakened by growth, by mobility, and by the heterogeneity of the population.

The leadership functions abnegated by elected officials were not assumed by the "professionals" who were hired by them. These professionals were usually men up from the ranks, whose primary virtue was that they "knew the ropes" rather than that they brought fresh ideas to their various functions. The chief of police in 1890 had been an unsuccessful businessman and then a Boston patrolman, prior to his appointment. The school superintendent had previously been a teacher in Newton. There was nothing at all unusual about appointing administrators on the basis of their practical experience since it was often impossible to find men with professional training in the modern sense. But this administrative corps in Waltham was not composed of notably able men, perhaps because the pay was so low.

The ambivalence with which townsmen demanded more and more public services on the one hand and were reluctant to pay for them on the other hand made for government on the cheap. Most elected officials received only token payments for their services. The school superintendent, salaried at $2,200 per annum in 1890, received less than most of the foremen at Waltham Watch.

The growing disparity between private and public monetary rewards could be rationalized and probably was rationalized by the belief that the public service was somehow higher or more noble than private enterprise. But the truth of the matter seems to be that the esteem of public service diminished at the same time that the monetary gap widened. When, with the increase in representativeness in 1884, elections became little more than popularity contests, the men who won had no duty which they owed the public and the public owed them no homage in return. Local government became an instrumentality of "politicians" (as state government did at an earlier date), the implication of the term being that the governed and the governing were no longer one and the same.

Where in the 1850's inadequate city budgets had prompted private citizens to organize fund-raising drives to help the poor, the city spent much more on public assistance by 1890. But by 1890 the poor had also to swallow a dose of cant with their relief. The prescription in this instance was provided by the city physician:

> Knowing that the idea of pauperism and dependence may be gradually acquired I have in several instances, the past year, discouraged persons from taking the first step in this way . . . I have said, "You do not wish if you can avoid it, to become the recipient of public charity. I will come and take care of your sick ones, but not as City Physician." Thus braced up and stimulated to self-respect and exertion, a number of families have been prevented from

helping to swell the list of dependents, while the apparent record of service of the City Physician has been diminished.[29]

Where in the 1850's public officials could directly address themselves to questions about the beauty of their town and make even extravagant expenditures upon beautification projects, the men of the 1880's were too practical and hard-headed for such concerns. Questions of physical amenity were rarely raised on their own merits. They had to be brought before the public in the guise of some more pragmatic issue. Thus no public official asked whether the practice of keeping backyard pigs was esthetically offensive, perhaps because the animals served simultaneously as garbage disposal units and as a source of food. But when in 1884 the board of health found almost 1,000 pigs domiciled within a one mile radius of town common, the issue could be and was raised on public health grounds. The same was often true of sewage and drainage problems.[30]

Physical amenity did not entirely disappear as a public concern, but town officers became reluctant to initiate this class of expenditures. For example, a group of private citizens organized the "Town Improvement Society" in 1881 for the purpose of planting trees in the center of the town. The Society conducted a private subscription drive and then asked the city for additional funds. Only at this point were town officers prepared to allocate funds for plantings.[31]

The issue of the separation of private and public activities which might potentially have arisen in this example (the public monies were given to the Society for disbursement) had not yet been resolved. In another area, the government continued without objection to allocate $350 annually to the local post of the Grand Army of the Republic in support of that organization's activities on Memorial Day. The only dispute which did occur dated from 1875, when the town auditor refused to honor the bill of the band that had been hired to play at the high school commencement exercises. The auditor held that the commencement ceremony was a private rather than a public event because it was of interest only to the small number of graduates and their families.[32]

The related issue of conflict of interest was never broached during the period. Since many public officials were businessmen, it was not uncommon for the government to make some purchases from firms owned by town officers. But, presumably because such purchases were usually small, no objections were ever made to this practice.

It was also the case that modern notions of fiduciary clarity and responsibility just did not exist. Men who were duty-bound to serve the

[29]*Waltham City Documents*, 1890.
[30]*Town Reports*, 1884.
[31]*Minute Book*, Town Improvement Society, Waltham Public Library.
[32]*Waltham Free Press* 9/24/75.

public could be and were trusted to conduct public affairs honorably. Indicative of the casual sloppiness which marked public administration at the start of the period was the budget mix-up of 1854. In that year the selectmen spent $3,800—an amount equal to approximately 10 percent of the total budget—for which there had been no authorized appropriation. The selectmen publicly acknowledged and apologized for their error, and the matter was dropped.[33] The town did not move to create an auditor's office until 1872, but even then the post was created to rationalize accountability rather than as a safeguard against malfeasance. When the auditor, in 1875, created a stir by refusing to pay the band bill, some men had second thoughts about the wisdom of having established the office.[34]

The Board of Health, as has been intimated, came to occupy a strategic position in decisions affecting public improvements. From its inception in 1880, the Board was often able to spark public action on grounds of health when no other grounds were sufficient, in the eyes of public officials, to justify expenditures or action. The Board prepared reports on a number of topics, such as the causes of mortality and the incidence of disease, and related these to demographic characteristics, sanitary practices, and public policy. As we shall see, the reports of the Board not only indicated the extent to which prevailing practices conflicted with current medical standards, they also revealed that those who stood most in need of health assistance and guidance were least likely to be served by public water, sewage, and drainage policies. Alone among all of the agencies of government, the Board was able, on this factual basis, to level criticism at the population and at the public authority for their shortcomings in the areas of health and sanitation. Presumably, it was their monopoly of scientific expertise that gave the doctors on the Board such license.

In conclusion, it would be erroneous to infer from what has been said that the men of the 1850's were somehow superior to the men of 1870's and 1880's. If their view of public service and their concern for such matters as physical amenity strike us as preferable to the views of their successors, it must be remembered that the men of the fifties were themselves neither paragons of virtue nor the bearers of the same burdens of growth and change that was the lot of the men of the eighties. They, for example, were quite capable of spending large sums on planting and fencing the town common to the public neglect of the needs of many recent famine immigrants. The men of the fifties were not superior, only different.

What is most regrettable is that the democratization of political life, which was partially a response to growth and to population heterogeneity, was over-weighted by "free rider" and xenophobic concerns. These concerns made city-building a rancorous rather than an ennobling process. In

---

[33]*Town Reports*, 1854.

[34]*Waltham Free Press* 10/29/75.

the microcosm of Waltham, we can gain some sense of how cities became problem centers for society while at the same time they flourished as opportunity centers for individuals.

VI · Neighborhoods
and Social Life

Sparked by the growth and development of population and industry, the tempo of Waltham's social life increased steadily after 1850. During a fairly typical week in the winter of 1870, a list of publicized events included: two dances, a free lecture on geology, an exhibit (of undetermined nature), a choral concert, a meeting of the Farmer's Club, and prayer meetings on almost every evening at one church or another. The number and variety of these activities suggests something of the growing cosmopolitan atmosphere of Waltham. But perhaps "cosmopolitan" is too strong a word, for at the time the town's population just exceeded nine thousand, and the proximity of Boston probably provided much too high a standard for favorable comparison. The English novelist George Gissing, for one, could not bring himself to remain for more than a few months in 1877. Although he needed the income he derived from teaching in the high school and although he enjoyed his pupils, he found the town too dull to suit his tastes.[1] Nonetheless, among men unacquainted with Boston society, the growing variety of community life gave credence to the view that Waltham was becoming a city in more ways than numbers alone.

In this chapter, two major aspects of the life of the city will be examined: residence patterns, and social life as organized through voluntary associations. These two facets of Waltham have been singled out for attention because they can tell us so much about the emergent social order of the city.

The earliest pattern of residence location had developed by 1830 as a reflection of Waltham's three distinct economic activities. Families that were engaged in agriculture occupied homesteads scattered thinly throughout the town. Shopkeepers, merchants, craftsmen, and their employees lived in the row of houses that lined the high road. Mill operatives lived in fairly cramped quarters surrounding the cotton mill and the bleachery, in housing provided by Boston Manufacturing. For as long as men and women were obliged to walk to work, the location of economic activity dictated the location of residences.

[1]See Mabel Collins Donnelly, *George Gissing, Grave Comedian* (Cambridge: Harvard University Press, 1954), p. 28.

The housing boom of the 1840's had involved single-family and two-family constructions centered around the town common. By 1850 this area of densest settlement was approximately a mile and a half long and two blocks deep on either side of Main Street (see Figure 6.1).

When the Waltham Watch Company arrived in 1854, it found itself in much the same position as had Boston Manufacturing in 1815. The existing stock of housing was inadequate to its needs. The company had to begin building immediately. The first company houses were constructed at the same time that the factory building was raised.

It has already been noted that Aaron Dennison, the guiding spirit of the firm, had hoped to create an integrated living-working community upon the company's 100-acre tract of land. He had occupied a house there, and had encouraged employees to think first of this area as the place to reside. But there was not enough housing available. Numbers of men were obliged to live across the river, in the older part of town. The long walk to work which this entailed prompted some men to purchase boats, "so that a flotilla of boats of various sizes made their periodical voyages across the river."[2] When the river froze, these men walked to work across the ice.

Dennison's successor, Royal E. Robbins, was less concerned about building a homogeneous community than with meeting the housing requirements of his expanded workforce. By offering company land at low prices, he attempted to attract building speculators who would create a housing supply. When speculators failed to appear, he had no choice but to invest company funds. This he did time and again, in response to the company's sustained employment growth. By the end of the Civil War, almost $100,000 had been invested in dwelling units, compared to $140,000 in the manufacturing plant. As late as 1882, Robbins was still bemoaning the shortage of housing:

> Rapidly as this quarter of town is being built up there is the greatest need for more tenements. Hundreds of our employees are living in discomfort for want of small houses and good boarding places. In time no doubt the village will grow so as to supply the want which is now so severely felt but meantime the factory is growing rapid[ly] too in the number of its operatives. The question is a serious one where all these people are to live. We already have a large investment in tenement property and naturally prefer to keep our capital strictly in the manufacturing operations. But unless outside money is drawn hither by the prospect of getting fair returns from investment in such property we shall be compelled to invest and upon a large scale ourselves.[3]

Employees were encouraged by the company to build their own homes. Loans were extended for this purpose, and easy credit terms were arranged to encourage the purchase of company land. At the same time,

[2]*History [of the Waltham Watch Company]*. Anonymously prepared manuscript, dated 1921. Waltham Watch Company Collection, Baker Library, Harvard University.

[3]Treasurer's Reports 1859–87, Waltham Watch Company Collection.

however, company rental fees were so low that they offered little incentive toward homeownership. In 1860, when the average monthly earnings of day-rated males was $45.86, a single-family cottage rented for $3.50 per month. In 1885, the company's master mechanic, on contract at $5,000 per annum, rented a company house for $20 per month. Still, by 1888, one estimate has it that slightly better than one-quarter of all the married male employees owned their own homes.[4]

Settlement in the area surrounding the watch factory was orderly and attractive. The entire company tract had been surveyed at the time of purchase. Streets had been laid out, and division made into house lots. A variety of modest houses were built, many of them two-storied doubles accommodating two families each. The company also built and maintained two large boarding houses, one for men and the other for women. It also assumed the responsibility for planting the area, and maintained a park in the blocks immediately in front of the factory.

What was true for Boston Manufacturing and Waltham Watch held for smaller companies as well. Newton Chemical, the Davis and Farnum Iron Foundry, and Robert's Paper Mill, were all obliged to build quarters for their employees. It appears that it was not until 1890, when the Thompson Screw factory opened, that a firm of some size was able to locate in Waltham without having to invest in employee housing.

As a direct consequence of the importance of company housing, housing conditions in Waltham reflected the economic situation of employing firms to a degree. Those firms which paid relatively high wages built small units and took care to provide fair-sized lots and high levels of maintenance. Those firms which had mainly unskilled, low-wage work forces built larger units and worried less about physical amenity and maintenance. The exceptions to this, as for example in the case of the Robert's Paper Mill, occurred where the firm was situated away from the center of town. When space was abundant and relatively cheap, even low-wage workers were relatively well-housed.

Waltham had a housing reformer in its midst during the seventies and eighties in the person of Robert Treat Paine. But Paine's experiments in financing the construction of low-cost housing for workers were carried out in Boston rather than Waltham. Whether this reflected his sense that local workers' housing was adequate or his greater concern for the problems of Boston is not clear.[5]

As the following map indicates, the major area of the expansion of residential settlement after 1850 lay to the south of the Charles River. Most of this expansion was associated with the growth of Waltham Watch

---

[4]John Swinton, *A Model Factory in a Model City: A Social Study* (New York, 1888), Waltham Public Library.

[5]*See* Sam B. Warner Jr., *Streetcar Suburbs*, (Cambridge: Harvard and M.I.T. University Presses, 1962) pp. 101–5.

FIGURE 6.1 *Settlement Patterns, 1854, 1874, and 1890*

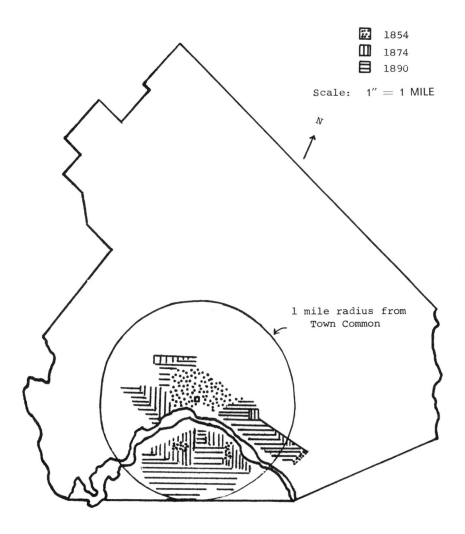

1854
1874
1890

Scale: 1″ = 1 MILE

N

1 mile radius from
Town Common

and Newton Chemical. The zone in between these two distinct residence areas was converted to housing only after the dissolution of the latter company in 1872. Except for the development of the south bank and a neighborhood to the west of the town common, along the river, most of the city's population growth to 1890 was achieved at the expense of an increasing density of settlement within the old village area. This may be seen most clearly from a comparison of the housing stock in 1872 and 1890 in the light of the residence map.

Excluding company housing, most of the housing stock was composed of single-family frame units as late as 1872. In that year, the stock included 1,058 single units, 7 doubles, 29 tenements (i.e., multiple occupancies) plus 161 company houses of various types. By 1890, single-family units still predominated, but the numbers of doubles and tenements had increased very much more rapidly. As against 1,645 singles, there were now 595 doubles and 252 tenements.[6] The degree of congestion was increasing.

What makes this increasingly dense settlement all the more surprising is that transportation developments had progressively weakened the bonds between place of work and place of residence. The introduction of trolleys, an additional bridge over the Charles, improved roadways, and the appearance of the bicycle might have been expected to result in greater population dispersion. This had happened among long-distance commuters, for many more men trained to work in Boston in 1890 than had been true in 1870. It was not until the advent of the automobile, however, that all of Waltham was to be opened to intensive residential settlement.

The arrival of substantial numbers of Irish Catholics in the late 1840's and early 1850's had had the initial and necessary consequence of making neighborhoods more heterogeneous. There were, in 1854, distinct concentrations of Irish in "Chemistry," the south-bank neighborhood adjacent to the Newton Chemical Company, and in the area northwest of the town common, a block or two off the high road, near St. Mary's. These concentrations, however, were not sufficiently large or homogeneous to warrant classification as neighborhoods. The same streets and blocks occupied by the Irish also had Yankee residents. Numbers of Irish families were also to be found residing in preponderantly Yankee neighborhoods.

By 1874, the initial areas of concentrated Irish settlement had become more homogeneous. The Chemistry district was now a distinctly Irish neighborhood, as was the settlement bordering on the church. In addition, new concentrations had emerged in the area immediately west of the common along the river and, to the east, in the vicinity of the bleachery and the iron foundry. Three of these four areas were situated within walking distance of the major Irish employment centers: Chemistry adjacent to Newton Chemical and Boston Manufacturing; Bleachery adjacent to the

[6]Compiled from tax rolls.

bleachery and iron foundry; and the Felton Street neighborhood adjacent to the coal and lumber yards and the small workshops that lined the river to the west of the common. The neighborhood around St. Mary's had no similar employment center, but its residents were within walking distance of Boston Manufacturing, the stores and stables along Main Street, and the railroad depot, all of which offered employment opportunities.

In their choice of residence locations the Irish were constrained, as were Yankees, by work sites and by their incomes. The Irish, however, faced the additional constraint of discrimination. Until 1884, for example, all of the land sales made by the Waltham Watch Company included covenants which restricted purchasers to resell only to native-born persons.[7] It is not clear whether the company enforced such covenants against its own English employees as well as Irishmen. Nor is it clear whether the company discontinued its practice because it no longer wished to discriminate or because the form of its restrictive covenant was no longer effective given the increasing numbers of native-born Catholics. It may also have been the case that the company could now count upon its land purchasers to enforce its preferences of their own free will.

The over-all increase in residential segregation suggests that Waltham Watch was not alone in practicing discrimination. Presumably other real-estate transfers were also made with an eye to keeping the Irish out of certain neighborhoods. In spite of any such tacit agreement to discriminate, a small number of Irish families in 1874 did reside outside the Irish neighborhoods. Several families had even taken up residence in the farmsteads that dotted the countryside.

Some portion of the residential segregation which took place undoubtedly reflected Catholic preferences as well as Yankee discrimination. In view of the sharp differences which divided the two groups, Catholics were probably as unlikely to want to live near Protestants as Protestants were to want Catholics for neighbors. Even so, the fact that so much of Waltham's population growth was accommodated within so small a physical area insured that the two groups were never far away from one another.

An 1885 survey of sanitary conditions, conducted by the Board of Health, provides an excellent opportunity to examine some of the differences in living conditions which prevailed between Catholics and Protestants. In this survey, groups were identified on the basis of nationality. Since this term was not defined, it is not clear whether native-born persons of Irish descent were classed as Irish or American. Given the degree of residential segregation, I have assumed that those health districts which had large numbers of Irish also had large numbers of native-

---

[7]Minutes, Board of Directors Meetings, Waltham Improvement Company, April 26, 1882, February 26, 1884 and August 21, 1886. Held by the Newall Company, Waltham, Massachusetts.

born men of Irish descent, however classified. The comparisons presented below were drawn between the three health districts in which the Irish clearly predominated and the three in which they formed the smallest proportion of the population.[8]

Demographically, the Irish health districts were distinct in that they had higher ratios of children per household and lower ratios of adults per household. Thus the Irish had larger families and they tended more often to live in nuclear families and/or to take in fewer boarders. In five of the six districts under consideration, the heads of families had predominantly blue-collar occupations. The three Irish districts had disproportionately fewer representatives among the professional and mercantile occupations

Dwelling units in the Irish districts were the least likely to have indoor plumbing and the most likely to depend upon impure water supplies. Fifty percent or more of the units in all of the Irish districts had "general surroundings" which were classified as fair or poor (as opposed to good). In contrast, in the worst of the three Yankee districts, 38 percent of the units were fair or poor, while in the best district only 6 percent were so classed. The predominantly Irish districts were also more likely to dispose of their garbage by feeding it to pigs. Presumably these differences in living conditions, coupled with the comparatively poorer diets that went along with lower incomes, accounted for the distinctly higher mortality rates in two of the three Irish health districts. The mortality rate in the highest Irish district was almost three times that in the lowest Protestant district.

The Irish may have been as greatly disadvantaged by their lack of information about good health practices as by their low incomes. Had they become as aware as many Yankees were of the relationship between health and pure water supplies and personal hygiene habits, they might have responded more quickly to the availability of indoor plumbing despite its expense. To the extent that they were not knowledgeable, they may have regarded running water (which was purer than most well water) and such appurtenances as bathtubs and water closets as mere conveniences whose adoption could be delayed until easily afforded.

Even within the Yankee population, modern ideas about the transmission of disease were fairly new. For example, the use of the town pump necessitated drinking from a common ladle into the 1870's. The Irish, because of their background and their lack of knowledge about new medical theories, may be presumed to have been further still from such an understanding.

That Yankees rapidly adopted indoor plumbing and its associated fixtures is attested to by the tabulations of water users published by the Water Commission. In 1875, three years after the town began providing

[8]*Waltham City Documents*, 1885.

FIGURE 6.2 *Residences of the Irish, 1854, 1874, and 1890*

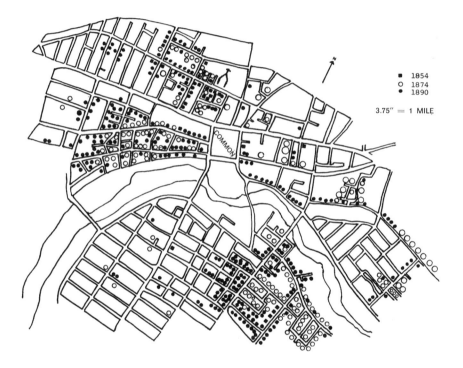

■ 1854
○ 1874
● 1890

3.75″ = 1 MILE

water to the public, Waltham had a grand total of 51 running-water bathtubs and 74 water closets. By 1890, there were, among 3,855 families, 797 bathtubs and 1,274 water closets. A public bathhouse was first provided in 1877. (This facility, incidentally, was the continual object of youthful pranks. Every so often townsmen would awake to find that during the night the shell of the house had been moved from its position abreast of the river to an open field or into someone's yard.)

When Waltham was reorganized as a city, its ward lines were drawn in accordance with the pattern of residential segregation which prevailed. In 1890, wards 1, 3, 4, and 7 contained the bulk of the Catholic population. Ward 2, distinctly smaller than all of the others in population, was composed mainly of the wealthier Yankee families. Wards 5 and 6 were the almost exclusive provinces of Protestant watch workers.

Ward 7, the most unambiguously Catholic ward (the Chemistry district) had the lowest average tax payment in 1890, $41 as compared to $145 for Ward 2. The other wards with substantial Catholic populations paid taxes which averaged from $71 to $80. These compared favorably with the averages of $63 and $54 for wards 5 and 6. The differences in wealth indicated by average tax payments suggests that ward lines also reflected the economic as well as the religious dimension of residence patterns.

Not only were Protestants on the average wealthier than Catholics, and not only was this difference expressed in residence patterns, but among Protestants and among Catholics there were also economic differences which affected residential patterns. Wards 5 and 6 were composed primarily of Protestant blue-collar working men, while Ward 2 was predominantly Protestant but managerial, professional, and entrepreneurial. Ward 7 contained the poorest element of the Catholic population, while Ward 3 Catholics more nearly comprised the "lace-curtain" Irish. The distribution of adult males without assets varied in conformity with the size of average tax payments, except that the preponderantly Protestant wards had consistently fewer men without assets.

To the extent that the residential distribution of the 1890 population reflected differences in religion, wealth, and, to a degree, occupational-income groupings, it might seem plausible to conclude that this distribution signaled the emergence of discrete social classes. It could be maintained that the differences between men had now become large enough and/or important enough to result in residential patterns which brought similar men together and at the same time placed them apart from dissimilar men. Socio-economic differences would be expressed in and confirmed by residence location decisions.

But whether social classes can truly be said to have emerged cannot be inferred from residence patterns alone. Classes are something more than categories of locational and material differentiation. They are, ultimately, expressions of values and attitudes toward life within a social system. Before developing this argument any further, however, it will be necessary to consider another facet of city life, namely, the organization and activities of voluntary associations.

In 1850 churches were still the centers of much of the organized social life of the community. Apart from their regular devotional services, churches sponsored bazaars and sewing and literary circles. Church congregations very often assumed the burden of philanthropy over and above the then meager efforts of the public authority. Ministers were likely to be called upon for leadership support in community-wide activities, whether it was the organization of a town fair, the dissemination of religious tracts, or temperance agitation.

By 1850, a number of voluntary associations existed which bore no direct relation to the churches. Rumford Institute, which at its inception had been guided by a clergyman, was now directed by an elected board of its members. A debating club, a musical association, a Masonic lodge, a militia troop, and a firemen's club rounded out the organized and secular social life of the town. In the political sphere, active Whig and Democratic caucuses worked to nominate and elect candidates for state and national offices.

Progressively, more and more of the social activity of the community was sponsored by voluntary associations which had no church connections. The churches continued to flourish as social as well as religious centers, but they declined in relative importance in the former function as purely secular clubs and associations developed. Over the 1850's, at least eleven new associations of one sort or another were organized. In the following decade, at least twenty-seven new organizations appeared. Seventeen new associations came into existence during the first half of the 1870's.

Was the proliferation of voluntary associations a by-product of the declining importance of religion and hence of the declining dependence upon churches as focal points for community organization? Did men progressively organize outside of churches because the interests around which they organized themselves seemed more and more unrelated to religious concerns? Or was this development an independent consequence of the organizational needs and desires of a growing, mobile, and heterogeneous population? An examination of Waltham's religious institutions over this period may help provide an answer to these questions.

Six new churches were established in the forty years after 1850: two of them Baptist, one Swedenborgian, one Universalist, one Methodist, and one Episcopalian. These, added to the previous five organized after 1820, made for a total of eleven new congregations organized in the short space of 70 years. In the previous 184 years of the town's existence there had been but one church and one congregation. Except for St. Mary's, all of the churches were Protestant. St. Mary's was to remain the only Catholic church until the founding of St. Joseph's in 1894.

Main Street at the Common (c. 1888)

Eastern Main Street (c. 1888)

Waltham Watch Company (c. 1888)

Boston Manufacturing Company seen across the Charles River (c. 1888)

St. Mary's Catholic Church and Rectory (c. 1888)

A Residence Area near "The Chemistry District" (c. 1888)

North Grammar School (c. 1888)

West End of Main Street (c. 1888)

Leaving aside the fundamental differences between Catholics and Protestants for the time being, a number of interpretations can be placed upon the development of sects within Waltham's Protestant population. From one point of view it can be said that sectarian differences were simply a by-product of the growth and growing diversity of the population. Given the mixing of men that took place, it was only natural that the various population groupings would organize churches which reflected their diverse backgrounds. Sectarianism in this sense was imported by settling migrants.

From another point of view it can be held that sectarian division also testified to the importance attached to religious sentiments. The men of Waltham were prepared to seek out like-minded men, organize congregations, build churches, and retain clergymen; all this, so that they might give expression to their religious beliefs.

At the very same time, however, the division into sects can be taken to symbolize the breakdown of the one institution and the one ideological rooting ground which had long served as a major source of social unity and coherence. This was true in the most obvious sense, for the city came to have many churches and creeds where once it had had only one. Moreover, while that one church had been a public matter, discussed in public, supported by public funds, and coterminous in membership with the body politic, the many churches of the late nineteenth century were exclusively private affairs. Religious affiliation and belief had become matters of individual choice and discretion.

In addition, there is evidence that the sectarian divisions among Protestants were inconsequential in several important regards. Had religious beliefs been important, it might have been expected that sectarian divisions would have isolated the members of one sect from the members of another. This did not occur among Waltham Protestants. It did occur between Protestants and Catholics, but Protestants in many spheres of action overlooked their sectarian differences. A survey of the marriage rolls indicates that sect lines were as frequently breached as honored in this one most significant of all forms of social interaction. The same was true of interactions in political clubs (even Catholic-Protestant barriers fell in party caucuses), in voluntary associations generally, and in business firms. Thus it was not simply that religion became a private matter, it also became a less important matter to the extent that it had less and less bearing upon other personal activities and decisions.

Among the many contributing factors to this very complex process of secularization, two stand out in the Waltham record. Protestant churches lost two of their prime functions, philanthropy and education, to the public authority. The churches continued to provide charity and religious education, but the burdens of poverty and indigency on the one hand and of providing literacy on the other hand were absorbed as primary functions of government. It is quite possible that the growing sectarian and economic diversity of the population contributed to the view that only an un-biased and tax-collecting public authority could properly meet these needs.

Simultaneously, the churches lost their standing as repositories of wisdom. The men and women who eagerly attended the Rumford Insti-tute lectures on Lyell's geologic theories and Darwin's theory of evolution, and the still larger numbers who in their daily lives encountered and adopted new tools, new ways of doing things, and new explanations of things, must by degrees have become more intrigued with science and with man's growing power over nature. The churches had little to tell such men about the new world in the making. The older world of the spirit was still to be considered, but it must have lost at least some of its interest in the face of the worldly optimism engendered by scientific discoveries and technological change. The waves of religious revivalism that swept through the town in the fifties, sixties, and seventies may, in this unkind light, be seen as frantic short-order searches for salvation.[9]

Progressively then, if men wanted to organize for some social or in-tellectual purpose, they no longer felt any need to turn to their churches. The churches and the creeds associated with them had become specialized in terms of their ideological and social legerdemain. Secular voluntary associations partially signaled this development and partially compen-sated for it.

A number of the voluntary associations organized between 1850 and 1877 proved to be transitory. This was particularly true of sports clubs, which tended to fall apart at the end of each season. Similarly, a number of the organizations founded as a result of the Civil War passed into ob-livion when that conflict ended. Some organizations lapsed only to be re-constituted at a later time. For example, from 1850 onwards, there were numerous temperance societies which flourished for a time, disbanded, and were then reorganized under a new name, often by some of the same men who had participated in the initial venture.

Most of the new organizations which appeared between 1850 and 1877 were created either to foster the self-improvement of members, or to provide self-help to a group, or to aid in the realization of one sort of social betterment or another. Typical of the self-improvement groups were the debating, literary, and musical clubs. Representative of the self-help organ-izations were the Watch Factory Relief Association and the St. Patrick's Relief Association. The Y.M.C.A. and the numerous temperance societies accounted for most of the social betterment organizations. Lesser numbers of voluntary associations were organized around sports activities (mainly baseball, cricket, and boating) and toward what might be termed pure

[9]As much as anyone, the clergy was swept along by the same rationalistic tides. Rev. Thomas Hill, for one, had an interest in botany that prompted him to accompany a scientific expedi-tion to Central America.

socializing (e.g., the Masons, Oddfellows, and Redmen), although many of these fraternal organizations had philanthropic objectives as well.

The number of self-improvement, social betterment, and sporting clubs and associations was as large as it was because, on balance, such organizations tended to be short-lived but recurring. In contrast, most of the self-help societies and most of the purely social organizations were able to remain in continuous operation over time.

What to make of these differences in organizational survival rates is highly problematic. One explanation might be that the physical mobility of the population made the maintenance of voluntary associations a very difficult task. This line of argument, however, fails to indicate why population turnover did not have an equal impact on all of the organizations. For example, the seasonality of most sports, coupled with physical mobility, might explain the continuous waxing and waning of athletic clubs, but these same factors do not explain why temperance societies tended to be unstable while fraternal organizations tended to be stable.

One explanation of the stability of self-help organizations is provided by the evidence that those associations which were anchored in on-going institutions flourished, while those without such an institutional base failed to survive. The long-lived Watch Factory and St. Patrick's Relief associations were organized within and supported by Waltham Watch and St. Mary's respectively. The Waltham Protective Association, a wartime retail cooperative venture organized by Watch workers, had no institutional support and proved to be unlasting. A similar fate met the Waltham Naturalization Association which also had no institutional base.

The recurrent failure of temperance societies, ironically, owed more to their effectiveness than to the physical mobility of the population. The issue of whether Waltham was to be "wet" or "dry" was repeatedly battled out at the polls during the period. Since votes were cast at the spring town meeting, the interest in the temperance issue was practically as seasonal as that in baseball. When the town voted to go dry, the incentive for temperance agitation was considerably reduced. When the town voted to permit the sale of alcoholic beverages, temperance agitation was almost certain to emerge during the following winter.

Save for the temperance issue, reformist sympathies of any sort were not a hallmark of the Waltham population. On the question of slavery, for example, the debates of the Everett Literary Association prove informative. This club was composed mainly of young Protestant men, some of whom were scions of old Waltham families and some of whom were comparative newcomers. In 1857, the club considered the question: "Which have been most abused, the Indians or Negroes?" and concluded that the Indians had suffered most at the hands of white men. This conclusion may or may not have been warranted by the facts then available, but it is suggestive of a lack of sympathy with the heated agitation for abolition then underway. In the following year the club debated the question: "Should the North interfere with the domestic institutions of the South?" and voted unanimously in favor of the negative.[10]

With the firing on Fort Sumter, most Waltham citizens lined up behind the Union cause. The only overt evidence of dissent was signaled by the establishment of a new weekly newspaper which, rumor had it, came into existence because of the lukewarm attitude of the editor of the existing paper.

Sparked by a new sense of patriotism, rallies were held, a Union Club formed, funds raised, and numbers of townsmen volunteered for military service. Some of the same young men who in the carefree debates of the Everett Literary Association had wanted to avoid conflict at all costs were soon to be found practicing military drills on the town common. Ladies of the town busily turned to sewing uniforms, only to discover that the grey material they had selected to use had been chosen by the rebels. So they began again, this time with Union blue.

As the war progressed, groups of townsmen organized for a variety of tasks. The Union Club continually raised funds to be used to induce military enlistments. The town ultimately provided upwards of 700 soldiers and sailors, 380 of whom were residents. A Soldier's Aid Society was organized to send packages to Waltham's fighting men and to assist their dependents. In 1864, a committee was formed to collect funds for the aid of freed slaves.

Any concern for the fate of the former slaves soon disappeared from post-war Waltham. Only the presence of disabled men and the Memorial Day services of the new Grand Army of the Republic encampment served as reminders of the past. Blacks in small numbers subsequently drifted through the town, but presumably found neither sufficient opportunity nor respect. None remained for as long as a decade.

The issue of labor reform also found little support in post-war Waltham. Ira Steward, the founder of the eight-hour movement, presented his theories on several occasions at Rumford Institute lectures. He won few adherents, however, and local workingmen let the eight-hour day campaigns of 1867 and 1886 pass by unnoticed. In 1870, Wendell Phillips garnered only 80 votes out of 1,001 in his campaign for governor on a labor-reform ticket.[11]

Apart from some organization of boot and shoe workers during the fifties and the later organization of some building-trades workers, unionism was neither a threat to Waltham employers nor, it would seem, a promise to employees. Some watch workers enlisted in the Knights of

---

[10]Manuscript minutes held at the Waltham Public Library.

[11]On Steward and Phillips, see David Montgomery, *Beyond Equality* (New York: Knopf, 1967). Phillips' vote was reported in *The Waltham Sentinel*, 11/11/70.

Labor in the mid-1880's, while a few had earlier formed a chapter of the Ancient Order of United Workmen. These appear to have been fraternal rather than collective-bargaining affiliations.

Cooperation was twice advocated and twice unsuccessful. A wartime venture at retail cooperation among watch workers lasted for only one year. During the seventies, a chapter of the Sovereigns of Industry was organized, but it disappeared without ever having established a working co-op.

The issue of child-labor reform attracted little local attention, probably because the state legislature had taken the initiative as early as 1865.[12] When discussed at all, child labor was thought of in terms of the school truancy problem. That children worked was not a source of concern. What did matter was that some of those who worked were by law required to be in school. Boston Manufacturing, as the major employer of children, sought to avoid and successfully avoided public embarrassment on this score by policing the work permits of its minor employees.

Viewing Waltham in terms of the objectives for which its residents organized groups and associations, it seems clear that the population had no desire to alter in any fundamental way the existing order of society. Most social betterment, self-improvement, and self-help associations were directed toward modest improvements in the habits or conditions of individuals. They had no intent to restructure social or economic or political relationships between groups of men. The only exception to this was the movement for Irish political representation. Even here, however, it was not so much a question of altering the social system as of accommodating it to a change wholly consonant with the precept of political equality. The Irish themselves understood that all that they were asking for in representation was fairly due them. Their more radical sentiments were associated with Ireland's independence and found expression in forming sections of the Fenian Brotherhood and Sisterhood.

The single most prestigious voluntary association in the city was the Farmer's Club. Organized in 1857, when it was already quite clear that farming was a waning activity in the local economy, the club nonetheless flourished. It continued in working order through 1890. Oddly enough, many of its members were not farmers, but businessmen and professionals. The composition of the club's membership over the period provides the evidence of its prestige. It was also the only association whose minutes were regularly carried in full in the local press.

The Farmer's Club met weekly to discuss questions of farm management and agronomy. What possible interest the manager of the Boston Manufacturing Company, for instance, might have had in the techniques

---

[12]*See* Charles E. Persons, "The Early History of Factory Legislation in Massachusetts" in Susan M. Kingsbury (ed.) *Labor Laws and Their Enforcement* (New York, 1911) pp. 94–97.

for increasing the yield from milk cows is obscure. And yet, week after week, year in and out, the non-farmers of the Farmer's Club exposed themselves to technical lessons on farming. Only on rare occasions were non-farm issues discussed, and then with rather peculiar results. For example, in the winter of 1870, the subject of labor reform was discussed. The consensus of the group was that it was opposed both to the organization of workers for collective bargaining and to the reluctance of employers to treat their workers decently. This "a plague on both your houses" attitude suggests that the employer members of the club even spoke like farmers during meetings.[13]

The incongruity of the club's membership did not go unnoticed. In conjunction with a fair sponsored by the club in 1870, a town paper spoke caustically about "many of our mechanics and professionals [who] like to . . . palm themselves off for farmers."[14] At another point (in 1875), a club member defended it in the following terms: "In very many towns only the older families will associate, leaving the newcomers to make their own association together, or bear isolation. Here the new families come into speedy and harmonious acquaintance, and into a most useful element."[15] But another member rejoined that the club "is not sufficiently democratic and entails too much expense on those who wish to entertain. It does not benefit those intended to be benefitted. The meetings should be held in a public hall. The farm laborers should be members . . . Though reports of the discussions are published, they are but little read. . . ."[16]

The composition of the Farmer's Club makes a bit more sense when it is recalled that among many men of means, land ownership was a common form of asset holding. It may be presumed that holding land was considered to be safe and profitable, and highly respectable as well. Perhaps one of the main functions of the club then, for its non-farming members at any rate, was to bolster their identification as men of wealth and landed substance. If this was so, then the existence and perpetuation of the club may be evidence that industrial and commercial employments were not yet so highly valued that they could be made to stand on their own for purposes of prestige and social status. A man still had to have some connection with the land to be truly respected.

A defender of the Farmer's Club, quoted above, made an explicit reference to the integrative functions of voluntary associations in the face of population turnover. Was it true that associations brought older and newer residents together? And if it was, was this an objective of associational life or merely a by-product of it? In the purely social clubs, such as the

[13]*The Waltham Sentinel*, 12/16/70.

[14]*Ibid.*, 1/14/70.

[15]*Waltham Free Press*, 4/2/75.

[16]*Ibid.*, 12/24/75.

fraternal orders, it would appear that the primary objective of their existence was to provide the opportunity for comparative strangers to come
together and socialize with men most like themselves. To the extent that
this was so, the members of social clubs should have been fairly homoge-
nous with regard to wealth and occupation, but fairly diverse as regards
the timing of their arrival in Waltham.

An analysis of the officers of a group of social associations in 1880
provided the following information. In Waltham's two Masonic lodges, an
officer in either one was more the occupational and asset peer of his fellow
officers than of the officers of the other lodge. Monitor Lodge was led by
five businessmen, all of whom possessed assets. Isaac Parker Lodge was
officered by four watch workers and a store clerk, none of whom had
assets. Except for Monitor Lodge and the Farmer's Club, the other clubs
examined were all led by blue-collar workers of fairly comparable economic standing. These included the Isaac Parker Lodge, the Sons of Temperance, the Waltham Reform Club (temperance), and the Odd Fellows.
All six organizations had leaders whose dates of arrival in Waltham differed widely. Hence, it can be concluded that social clubs did serve to
integrate new and old residents and that they did so within clear limits of
economic-occupational similarity. They also reinforced religious distinctions. None of the associations had a Catholic officer, and at least three
of them had no Catholic members.

The evidence available on the asset and occupational standings of lay
church leaders indicates that the Protestant churches were quite as stratified as most voluntary associations appear to have been. The deacons of
Christ Episcopal were consistently men of wealth and high occupational
standing. In contrast, the deacons of Ascension Episcopal were watch
workers. Similarly, the lay leaders of the First Baptist and the First Methodist Churches were generally wealthier and higher in the occupational
scale than their counterparts at Beth Eden Baptist and the Second Methodist Church. As between sects, a rank ordering of the general pattern of
lay leadership asset and occupational characteristics produces the following result:

> First Parish (Unitarian) and Christ Episcopal
> First Methodist and New Jerusalem (Swedenborgian)
> First Baptist and Trinitarian
> Universalist, Ascension Episcopal, Beth Eden Baptist, and Second Methodist

The leaderships of the last four named churches were predominantly blue-
collar workmen.

The inordinately active role of blue-collar workers in town life can only
be explained by understanding the position of Waltham Watch in the town
and that company's employment policies. The blue-collar activists in voluntary associations, in churches, in political caucuses, and in town government were, for the most part, watch workers.

By the standards of the day, Waltham Watch was a technological wonder. That so delicate and precise an instrument as a watch could be produced in mass quantities was simply amazing. It is not to be denied that the ability of the company to consistently earn profits also added to its luster. Both its technological and its economic accomplishments were taken as manifestations of American ingenuity and exceptionalism. The company consciously played upon such chauvinistic sentiments in developing its national market and its local reputation. The name of the company through most of the period was the American Waltham Watch Company. Its work force was composed largely of native-born men and women. Here was an American company, producing watches made by Americans, for Americans. Once this point had been gotten across during the Civil War years in connection with the sale of low-priced watches, the company was economically secure.

The watch factory, like the textile mill before it, became a showcase, a model of its type. As noted previously, visitors—and there were many, from the King of Hawaii to convention delegates from the Brotherhood of Locomotive Engineers to President Ulysses S. Grant—never failed to be impressed with the company's technological achievements and with the quality of its work force. Royal Robbins, a man not given to vain boasting, was moved to report to the stockholders in his 1883 report that the factory "is even now a true Palace of Industry of which you may well be proud."[17] Many of his employees shared this view, as did many townsmen. The triumph of company products at the Centennial Exposition of 1876 was just another piece of evidence confirming the excellence of the company.

Throughout the period, the company workforce was composed mainly of young men and women, most of whom were native-born New Englanders. Company hiring policies favored the young because they could be introduced into the factory and trained on the job. They favored the native-born out of prejudice and in support of the company's image. (A contingent of immigrant English watchmakers was almost always present, but was too small and too highly regarded—for being English—to attract adverse notice.) Many of the males were highly skilled, and many of the semi-skilled had the prospect of becoming skilled and, hence, highly paid. The company was a decidedly attractive place to work, both in terms of wages and the conditions of the work place.

The combined effects of the company's attributes and the characteristics of its work force were to win for it local esteem and a strong sense of group solidarity among its employees. These, in turn, enabled and prompted watch workers to engage in group activities within the company and in the town at large.

[17]Treasurers Reports 1859–87, Waltham Watch Company Collection.

Among the earliest organizational efforts of the watch workers were the Watch Factory Soldier's Aid Society and the Watch Factory Brass Band. The first of these organizations raised funds within and without the factory to aid Civil War combatants and their dependents. The Brass Band was composed of employees who hired an instructor, and purchased instruments and uniforms with only token assistance from the company. The Band provided free concerts on the town common during the summer months, represented Waltham at parades in the Boston area, and provided accompaniment when employees marched to the polls on election day.

In 1866 the most lasting of all employee associations was organized. This was the Watch Factory Relief Association, a mutual-aid society open to all employees and officered by them. The objects of the Association were to provide financial and moral support to members in case of sickness, and to their families in case of death.

In time, the watch workers, foremen, and rank-and-file workers alike, branched out from company-oriented activities to a wide range of community activities. They underwrote the establishment of several churches, staffed the town's first cricket team (on the initiative of the English workers), composed the bulk of the users of Rumford Institute, and joined many of the voluntary associations. As early as 1870, watch workers were represented in or controlled the management of the following activities: Isaac Parker Masonic Lodge, the Y.M.C.A., the Waltham Fire Club, Waltham Constabulary, the Choral Union, Rumford Institute, the Knights Templar, the Musical Association, the Waltham Military Band, and the Republican and Democratic Party caucuses. By the late 1880's watch workers were a power in city government. At the time, the factory workforce of 2,450 formed 16 percent of the city's population.

Apart from membership and/or leadership in local organizations, the watch workers appear to have dominated the social life of the town from an early date. They were primarily responsible for organizing and populating the picnics, boat rides, dances, and strawberry festivals in the summer, and the sleigh rides, skating parties, lectures, and musicales in the winter. They made a leisure-time life for themselves that was at once both varied and expressive of their self-confidence. Their status as young, skilled, and highly paid Yankees made them eminently acceptable to one another and to townsmen as peers of the realm. The watch workers may not have been able to penetrate some of the organizations of Waltham's income-occupational elite, but they were, even by this group, respected and admired.

One of the factors which undoubtedly affected the level of their participation in community life was the comparative permanence of the watch workers in the city. Because the terms and conditions of employment at Waltham Watch were consistently good, many men came and stayed for long periods. This cadre of long-service employees gave continuity to employee activities both within and outside the company. The following length of service tallies were prepared from payroll records.

TABLE 6.1   *Length of Service at Waltham Watch Co., 1860–90*[a]

| | Number of Men According to Length of Service Number of Years | | | | | | Males with 5 or More Years of Service |
	5	10	15	20	25	30	%
1865	51						26
1870	96	38					65
1875	69	49	21				40
1880	167	50	49	19			40
1885	304	123	45	45	16		42
1890	366	214	105	39	33	12	59
Weighted average							48

[a]To provide uniformity, 1885 is employed. Data for 1884 were actually used.

[b]The number of years of service is understated to the extent that (a) some of the 1860–65 persisters had joined the company prior to 1860, and (b) many workers may have joined the company prior to a quinquennial date. The number is overstated to the extent that service between quinquennial dates was not continuous.

In spite of turnover, Table 6.1 indicates that there was always present a substantial pool of persisting watch workers. Clearly, turnover by itself was not a barrier to trade union organization here. Nor, in view of their many other activities, did turnover, promotions, or social mobility rob the employees of potential trade-union leaders. On the contrary, the evidence suggests that the watch workers simply had no desire to form a union. Those who remained with the company were apparently satisfied with their terms and conditions of employment and those who were not, for whatever reason, departed. Physical departure may thus be seen as having been a preferred means of responding to grievances for some and a necessary act for others whose occupational and social status aspirations could not be realized within the company.

Waltham's Catholic population had a wholly different experience with regard to voluntary associations and to town social life in general. With few exceptions, Catholics and Protestants did not commingle in voluntary associations. Catholics were not without organizations; they instead developed their own, many of which paralleled the Protestant clubs and societies. In addition, the Catholic population was and remained more cohesive, and centered more of their activities around their church.

In contrast to the proliferation of Protestant churches, Catholics were all parishioners of St. Mary's. Many social activities were either sponsored by the church or sought and received its sanction. Hence, at the same time that Protestant churches were losing their dominance as centers for the organization of social life, the Catholic church continued to play this role for its communicants. The position of the church has a bearing upon any understanding of the Catholic population.

As happened elsewhere, the Catholic population of Waltham lavishly endowed its church. Fund-raising fairs consistently provided sums of money which seem out of all proportion to the wealth of the parish. For example, in the spring of 1876, in the midst of a major business depression, a church fair netted an estimated $20,000. Sizeable sums came from the very benefit societies which might have been expected to be most hard-pressed for funds in a period of high unemployment. Yet the St. Patrick's Mutual Relief Society contributed $3,500, the Waltham Mutual Relief Society $1,900, and the Ancient Order of Hibernians $2,600.[18]

The monies so raised were often used to support the church establishment. Over the years, St. Mary's was expanded and its interior redecorated and made more elaborate. As early as 1867, a local paper touted it as the most beautiful and expensive church outside of Boston.[19] Nor did the largesse of parishioners stop there. When, for example, Rev. Bernard Flood returned from a seven-month visit to the old country (a trip underwritten in part by gifts), he was presented with $200 in cash and the locally ubiquitous gift of a Waltham watch.

Presumably, the maintenance of an elaborate church establishment was of great importance to Waltham Catholics. In this they were not alone, for similar efforts were made by Catholics throughout the country. To argue, as has been done, that in this manner the church drained away resources that might have been put to better use by its communicants is to ignore the obvious: endowing the church was one of the best uses to which many Catholics thought to put their funds. That, comparatively speaking, Catholics sacrificed higher personal consumption or savings levels, or kept their children at work, or that in so doing they may have disadvantaged themselves and their children relative to Protestants is, if not wholly incorrect, beside the point. For the church, in its doctrines and in the elegance of its trappings provided a haven from the world. To strive to maintain it was at once a symbolic act of resignation to the unalterable baseness of life and a testament of triumph over despair. The church was a memorial of the dead to the living, an act of immortality which transcended the mortality of the flesh.

From this point of view, the church was not a leech feeding upon a poor and unwilling population. It was an active assertion of that population's view of life. That that view was in great measure other-worldly and fatalistic, and hence often inconsistent with the optimism and yet still cautious materialism of the Protestant population, in no way reduced its validity or integrity. If Catholics did, by so liberally supporting their church, reduce their chances for material success relative to Protestants, it was only because the church mattered more to them. Most important, however, is that little support can be mustered to demonstrate that gifts to the church actually impaired Catholic chances in the race to success. Contributions to St. Mary's may have been large in the aggregate, but they

[18]*Waltham Free Press*, 3/17/76.
[19]*Waltham Sentinel*, 2/1/67.

were undoubtedly small in terms of the donations of individual families. It would be unreasonable to suppose that individual families gave up opportunities to go into business or that they were obliged to keep their children at work merely that they might endow the church. It would be equally unreasonable to suppose that the aggregate flow of gifts might have been diverted in some way that would have enhanced the economic position of Catholics. No other agency or institution could have attracted such funds.

Catholic persisters, as has been shown, fared rather well in Waltham. In considerable proportion they became homeowners and occupationally more diversified and skilled. The church as an institution did not demonstrably impair their material achievements. And the unswerving dedication of Catholics to the church may, in the long run, have worked as much in their favor as it contributed in the short run to nativism and discrimination. For it manifested a capacity for self-sacrifice and respect which Protestants could not continue to ignore and which eventually compelled the acceptance of Catholicism as a fact of community life consistent with American ideals.

Waltham had been unprepared to receive and make welcome large numbers of Catholics and the record of snubs and slights was a painfully long one. True, Protestants did donate $1,000 toward the construction of a new Catholic church in the 1850's, but this act did not balance well against the widespread (but unsubstantiated) belief that two earlier church buildings had been destroyed by arsonists.

Throughout the period, there was always present a group of men (their names and numbers unknown) who were fervidly anti-Catholic. In the heyday of overt nativism in the 1850's, the Everett Literary Association went on record deploring the efforts of Boston Catholics to ban Bible reading in the public schools. The same group favored the adoption of a ten-year residence prerequisite for enfranchisement. But such cuts were undoubtedly easier to bear than the town's nativist vote, and the unthinking actions of Protestant townsmen.

Symbolic of the latter was an event associated with Waltham's first agricultural and industrial fair in 1857. The opening act of the fair was a mass march to the Congregational Church where the Reverend Hill bestowed his blessing. The implication here is that as yet the Yankees had no sense that they might have to modify their behavior lest they give offense to the new immigrants. At the fair, the active participation of Catholics was signified only by their sweep of the spading contests. Protestants took all of the awards in the more genteel competitions.

On another not so unthinking an occasion one of the town's churches opened its pulpit to an apostate French Canadian priest who proceeded to condemn that which he so recently cherished.

Along with its ardent anti-Catholics, Waltham also had men who actively sought to win the acceptance of Catholics by the community. This division was openly acknowledged in and by the town's two newspapers

from 1861 through 1875. The editor of the *Sentinel*, Josiah Hastings, regularly reported news of interest to Catholics and endeavored to provide
Protestants with an understanding of Catholicism by explaining the significance of holy days and the mass. His paper was open to Catholic cor-
respondents. On numerous occasions his editorials praised the Irish as
hard workers and respectable citizens. Hastings' commitment went so far
that, on one occasion, he editorially apologized for having reprinted an
item from *Harper's Magazine* which contained anti-Catholic overtones.[20]
In contrast, the editor of the *Free Press* left one guessing as to the existence of a Catholic population. Too often it was only when reporting crimes
or arrests that his columns signified an Irish presence.

That the Irish did come to the attention of Protestants as drunkards
and criminals was not so much a distortion on the part of one newspaper
as it was a reflection of the unprecedented problem of public order which
growth thrust upon the town. As the *Sentinel* noted in reporting the theft
of the pocketbook of the postmaster's wife, "we are becoming quite citi-
fied."[21]

Prior to the arrival of the Irish, there had been no problem of maintaining public order. Crimes and arrests were few and far between and
most often involved locking up vagrants for the night and hustling them
out of town in the morning. Fly-by-night businessmen were not uncommon, but they were rarely apprehended. At the start of the period, in 1850,
the town had one part-time constable. The following year it was thought
wise to employ a man to serve as night watch.

By 1872, when the first police records became available, the volume
of arrests had risen to almost 500 per year, more than half of them on
charges of drunkenness. The second most numerous group of arrests was
for assault. Most of those arrested were Irish.

As appears to be true of most minority groups in American society, the
felonies of the Irish were almost always committed at the expense of fellow
Irishmen. In the very few cases of murder, both the culprits and the vic-
tims were Irish. The same was true of participants in brawls. But this did
not absolve the Irish or reduce the fear in which they were held by many
Protestants. The courts, in the few cases reported in the press, were almost
always disposed to mete out maximum punishments to Irish offenders by
way of setting "examples." And ladies had their menfolk address letters
to the newspapers deploring the jeopardy in which a woman placed her-
self when passing a corner occupied by numbers of Irish youths.

Most of the public disturbances of the Irish and probably most of the
fear which they engendered was associated with drunkenness. In this area
it appears that temperance societies realized their objective when they
succeeded in banning the sale of alcoholic beverages. In dry years the

[20]*Ibid.,* 10/16/74.
[21]*Ibid.,* 12/7/60.

TABLE 6.2   *Arrests, 1872–90*

Year	Arrests	Arrests Involving Drunkenness
1872	487	275
73	587	379
74	557	336
75	531	307
76	387	217
77	324	170
78	426	198
79	445	258
1880	431	238
81	347	199
82	255	107
83	376	158
84	314	227
85	349	178
86	467	267
87	444	254
88	504	263
89	668	413
1890	907	605

number of drunk and drunk-and-disorderly arrests tended to be smaller than in wet years. But such arrests, which quite consistently accounted for more than half of all arrests every year, were also related to prevailing economic conditions. In years of prosperity, drunkenness arrests rose, while in years of high unemployment they fell. This suggests—if the arrest rate fairly reflected consumption patterns—that for most men drinking was a luxury rather than a means of escaping or forgetting their difficulties.

Between 1872 and 1890 there was no discernible trend in the numbers of arrests or of arrests for drunkenness. Since the population was growing, the stability of these numbers implies a decline in the rates of crime and drunkenness. It may also have been the case that police officers became more adept at dealing with drunks to the point that they saw them safely home without making an arrest. At the very end of the period, in the prosperity years of 1889 and 1890, the number of arrests for drunkenness suddenly rose to unprecedented heights. The previous peak of 379 arrests had occurred in 1873; in 1890 605 inebriates were booked. By the latter date, the police force had increased to thirteen officers and men.[22]

Since throughout the period most of the men ever arrested were Catholics, while most of the leading "dries" were Protestants, there may have been more than a touch of nativism involved in temperance agitation. This was undoubtedly the case to some extent. As was noted earlier, though,

[22]Arrest figures compiled from *Town Reports* and *Waltham City Documents*.

temperance societies were among the few voluntary associations which sometimes had religiously integrated memberships. At times Catholic and Protestant temperance groups carried on independently of one another, but on more than one occasion they combined forces.

Those Protestant voices which were raised in defense of Catholics argued that much of the anti-social behavior of some of the Irish was a product of the twin forces of discrimination and ignorance. These, Protestants were held duty-bound to correct. Josiah Hastings, among his many efforts on behalf of the Irish, roundly condemned discrimination in hiring as anti-Christian and anti-democratic. Daniel French, the town clerk during the 1860's, was so disturbed by the evidence he compiled on the mortality differences between the Irish and the native born, that he repeatedly called upon the community to act to relieve the situation. One of his pleas, incorporated in his report of 1865, is sufficiently eloquent to warrant quotation.

> The discrepancy in the average age of the native and foreign born [at death] is largely attributable to the number of deaths in infancy and early life in the latter class. The record is painful, and shows the necessity of an early corrective. There is no inherent reason why the average of life of such residents should be but half that of the native citizens. It shows a want of conformity to the laws of health, demanding investigation and change. The trials necessarily incident to human life are sufficient, and sufficiently hard to be borne, without a needless increase either in number or character. Life is too precious to be so treated. Nor is the calamity confined to the immediate sufferers. It reaches and must reach every interest, every feeling. Were the anguish attendant upon such suffering not equally painfully felt; were the sensibilities of the sufferers not equally acute, it were not an argument for inaction or indifference in the premises. Whatever affects injuriously any class or any individual, has an injurious effect upon the whole body politic. Hence the right of the community to demand such action as shall reduce the trials and sufferings of life to their minimum. Any argument other than this must resolve itself into the simple interrogatory. Am I my brother's keeper? Common in origin, in endowments, in aspirations, it becomes us to recognize the duties incident to the relations we sustain and so to meet them as best to subserve every interest vital to the general weal.[23]

But for all the good offices of the valiant group of Yankees who openly condemned discrimination and mistrust, the acceptance of Catholics—at best a grudging acceptance as late as 1890—appears to have been won largely by the Catholics themselves. As in increasing numbers they settled in and became taxpaying homeowners; as they acquired skills and established businesses; as they demonstrated reverence for their church and displayed interest and organizational skills in their own voluntary associa-

[23]*Ibid.*, 1865.

tions; and as they became voters and public officials, their permanency in and commitment to Waltham made them at one with it. There is considerable merit in the argument that the more like Protestants the Catholics became in so many ways, the harder it became to disapprove of them on grounds of difference.

The clash of cultures occasioned by the arrival of the Irish had its effects upon them as well as upon the Yankee population. In the last chapter, an effort was made to suggest some of the ways in which this clash affected many Yankees. At this juncture it must be added that it would be wholly unrealistic to have expected the Protestant population to have greeted the Catholics with open arms. This is not said by way of ignoring or minimizing the Protestant abuse of Catholics, but by way of attempting to understand it. Little but our own sense of rectitude can be served by making gratuitous judgments of right and wrong and letting the matter rest there.

Many facets of Irish behavior, including those most likely to repel Yankees, were directly traceable to peasant origins and conditions at the time of arrival. Very frequently the "peasantization of the city" can be traced in dietary differences, property care and decoration, and health habits.[24] In the instance of the Irish this cannot be done because they had neither distinct dietary preferences to preserve nor any housing styles worthy of imitation in their new setting. As to health habits, it is impossible to distinguish between those bred of peasant origins and those resulting from low incomes. But peasant origins and poverty can help to explain that which in the most general terms distressed the Yankees: the Irish propensity to respond to persons and situations directly and emotionally, without interposing elements of self-control. The drinking and brawling, the criminality, the large families, the rowdiness of children, the illiteracy, and the lack of occupational skills and discipline were, to Protestants, signs of an absolute perversity. For, if the Protestant tradition may be faulted for the sin of pride, that pride was vested in precisely the quality of self-control which the Irish seemed so completely to lack.

Many of the aspects of Irish behavior that were deplored proved in time to be less the irremediable consequences of Celtic genes or Catholicism than the temporal effects of peasant origins and destitution. As over time the famine immigrants died off and as segments of the Catholic population improved their economic situation, much of this intemperate behavior disappeared. It was perpetuated to some extent by new immigrant arrivals and by new, poor, in-migrants. To the degree that Waltham Protestants were aware of the distinction between new and old, they would have had grounds for optimism about the ultimate arrival of Catholics as

---

[24]Joel M. Halpern, *The Changing Village Community* (Englewood Cliffs, N.J.: Prentice-Hall, 1967), pp. 34f.

peers. To the extent that they viewed the Irish as an undifferentiated mass, they could perpetuate their anti-Irish stereotypes.

The Irish themselves changed in their new surroundings in response to discrimination and to economic opportunity. Illustrative of the lengths to which discrimination compelled adjustment is the change in naming practices. In the federal and state censuses from 1850 to 1865, Irish females were most likely to bear the names: Mary, Margaret, Catherine, or Bridget, while males were named: James, John, Michael, Patrick, Peter, or Thomas. These ten names were borne by at least eighty percent (roughly estimated) of all the Irish. In subsequent censuses, the range of names given to children became much broader, a fact which suggests a willingness to conform to American naming practices. But one name, Bridget, almost completely disappeared.

At the time, Irish males were collectively and pejoratively referred to as Micks (whether from the frequency of Michaels or the Mc surname prefaces is not clear) or, in the singular, as Paddy (from Patrick; leading to paddy-wagon?). Female domestic servants were, in the same vein, referred to as Bridgets. The names Michael and Patrick continued to have high currency among the Irish, while Bridget lost favor. One possible explanation for this is that the association of Bridget with menial service to Protestants served to discredit the name. Slanders against men either didn't matter as much because unassociated with menial service or because the custom of naming sons after their fathers was too strong to give way.

St. Patrick's Day may also be seen to have undergone change in the new setting. An old-country religious feast day, it came to bear the added significance of demonstrating ethnic-religious solidarity. By the early 1870's, the Boston Manufacturing Company felt obliged to close down for the day, and after 1876 Waltham witnessed an annual parade. St. Patrick's Day became a day when all Irishmen were expected to stand up and be counted.

There is, in the Waltham record, a clearer and perhaps more significant example of the change which took place among the Irish. Thomas Eaton, a young man of Irish birth, returned to Ireland in 1870 to study law. Eaton had grown up in Waltham and subsequently returned to open his law practice. During his sojourn in Ireland, he sent to a local paper articles depicting the condition of the peasantry. These articles painted a picture of abject poverty, ignorance, and suffering. The response of the Waltham Irish community was one of disbelief. Surely, it was argued, Eaton's descriptions were gross misrepresentations of the true state of affairs and could only serve to defame the Irish. In self-defense, Eaton had the rector of his university attest to the accuracy of his reports.[25]

<hr />

[25]*Waltham Sentinel*, 9/23/70.

By this time then, in so short a time after the famine migration, numbers of Waltham Irishmen could not or would not believe that they had sprung from so desolate a background. Either their own present situation made an impoverished Ireland impossible to identify with, or they were embarrassed to be associated with such an Ireland. Possibly both things were true. The point remains, though, that Waltham's Irish had by 1870 been so altered by their new environment that they could not accept the reality of their past. So strong was this feeling that in due time the "auld sod" would become a fictive isle of green rolling hills, quaint cottages, and bright-eyed lasses. Little, if any, memory would remain of rotting potatoes.

Or did that memory survive in some other form after all? Could it explain why the persisting Catholic population developed consistently lower horizons than those of the Yankee population? Catholics came to prize homeownership and assets and self-employment as much. Yet, though they owned homes as often, theirs were the cheaper ones. They may have confronted an equal proportion of occupational opportunities, but theirs were generally lower on the skill-prestige scales. Why then did they persist as often as Protestants? Had the shock of the famine reduced them to such straits that they were prepared to view any modest achievement as something grand? Or was it an aspect of their Catholicism that made them content with satisficing rather than with maximizing behavior?

It might be argued that Catholics adopted lower achievement horizons because of the discriminations enforced against them. Had this been the case, however, there would have been less reason for the convergence of physical mobility and persistence rates. Catholics would have had more reasons for moving and fewer reasons for remaining in Waltham. But remain they did, while in every dimension of social standing—assets, homes, occupations, incomes, roles, and power—they appear to have been prepared to settle for less. Why this was so we cannot say.

VII · Summary
and Conclusions

In view of the number and variety of the topics which have been examined in the preceding chapters, it may prove helpful to review briefly some salient findings. Following this, an attempt will be made to interpret many of the developments noted, first within the context of Waltham and then within the broader context of Waltham as an American case study.

Among the earliest sites of colonial settlement in North America, Waltham was formally established as a town in 1736. Its Puritan inhabitants worked the land and prospered. But even so, their numbers, whether through natural increase or through net in-migration, increased very slowly. By 1810, after 180 years of continuous settlement, the population stood at 1,014 men, women, and children.

The advent of the textile industry in the second decade of the nineteenth century propelled the town into the modern industrial era. From this time onward, industrial employment and population, income and wealth grew without substantial interruption and at rates which were probably distinctly higher than ever before. The Boston Manufacturing Company, the main agent of this initial growth, influenced the timing, the size, the rates, and the character of development. It attracted numbers of fairly transient young women and smaller numbers of almost equally transient young men to the town. Until 1830, its employment recruits were native-born Protestants drawn from rural Massachusetts and from the farmsteads of neighboring states. The company also introduced the first Irish Catholics into the town and, after 1845, provided a major source of employment to the Irish and to a smaller number of English immigrant textile workers.

In 1822, the year for which wealth data are first available, the distribution of assets in Waltham was more equitable than it was ever to be subsequently. It appears that much of the inequality that existed at the time was a reflection of the recent in-migration of young men in the Company's hire. Those men who had been resident for some time, and subsequently those in-migrants who persisted in Waltham for a time, were likely to possess assets or to come to possess assets. Those men without assets were most likely to be young, recent in-migrants, and those most likely to out-migrate were also likely to be young and without assets. Most in- and out-migrants were at all times, with the singular exception of the 1840's, young men without dependents.

During the 1840's the railroad came to Waltham, the town acquired a 600 acre tract of land from Newton, and large numbers of Irish immigrants and Yankee in-migrants arrived. Because the Irish, and the Yankees to a lesser extent, came as family units, the in-migrants of this decade differed demographically from the subsequent norm of predominantly young and single movers. The stock of housing was doubled within the decade, and new shops, the establishment of several boot and shoe producing firms, and the growth of Boston Manufacturing added to the levels of employment and of economic activity in general. By 1850 the population was already four times greater than it had been in 1810.

Of long-term consequence was the arrival of the Waltham Watch Company in 1854. In its sustained expansion, this company significantly augmented the demographic and economic growth and change which had been sparked by Boston Manufacturing. It attracted large numbers of native-born men and women to the town and it also recruited English and, later, British Canadian immigrants. Because it employed a much higher proportion of males and because it offered exemplary terms and conditions of employment, the people who were attracted by it to Waltham tended to settle in as residents to a greater degree than was true of the cotton-mill employees. In addition, the company's higher skill requirements resulted in a work force with higher average incomes and hence with increased possibilities for assets accumulation. Like its predecessor, the watch company was obliged to provide employee housing and a number of services which, by modern standards, were unrelated to production. Its employees organized a number of activities within the firm and were extremely active in the town's social and political life.

From 1850 through 1890, when the town of 4,464 people rose to become a city of 18,707, at least 10,987 and perhaps as many as 17,000 males in-migrated, and at least 6,158 and perhaps as many as 12,000 males out-migrated. On the average, 49 percent of the males present for any one census enumeration were not present ten years later, and 61 percent of the males present for any one enumeration had not been present ten years earlier. These proportions reflect physical migration exclusively. If population losses attributable to deaths are included, then on the average 57 percent of those enumerated once were not present in the succeeding census. And if population gains attributable to births are included (this computation covers only the period 1850–80), an average of 70 percent of the males enumerated once had not appeared in the preceding census.

Most male in-migrants were native-born and preponderantly Massachusetts born. Almost all native-born in-migrants born outside the state hailed from contiguous states. Among the foreign born, Irish Catholics predominated, followed by smaller numbers of British and British Canadian immigrants. One-fifth of both the in- and the out-migrants were dependent children. Two-fifths of the out-migrants and slightly more of the in-migrants were single men, and the respective remainders were composed of married men. The age groupings, household statuses, and asset positions of the in- and out-migrants were quite similar. Young men, single men, married men with young children, and men without assets, accounted for most of the movement which occurred.

Over the first three decades of the period, the rates at which males in-migrated declined. This trend was reversed in the final decade, 1880–90. The absolute numbers of in-migrants, however, consistently increased. The decennial rates of out-migration steadily declined. The absolute numbers of out-migrants rose just as steadily, at least until 1880. It seems likely that the number fell over the terminal decade, and this likelihood leads to the supposition that after 1880 the city had achieved a critical minimum size which reduced the propensity of men to look elsewhere for economic opportunities.

A major change brought about by the flow of population took the form of a rise in the numbers and proportions of Irish Catholic residents. From a mere handful in 1830, the Catholic population grew to a point where it constituted 44 percent of the population in 1870. The significance of this development lay in the very considerable differences between the Catholic and Protestant populations. In addition to their fundamental religious difference, the Catholic population was of more recent arrival in the country, poorer, less well educated, less skilled, given to higher birth rates, and the victim of higher rates of mortality. The influx of so disparate a population grouping was in its own way of as much consequence for the developing social order as was the presence and expansion of local industry.

The opportunities for occupational mobility in Waltham appear to have increased steadily over time. Progressively larger portions of the labor-force requirements of the local economy involved skilled workers and white-collar workers. By 1890, educational attainment had just begun to emerge as a criterion for occupational entry. Experience garnered on the job was thus still the main and the most easily accessible route to advancement in many occupations. The capital requirements for entry into independent businesses rose over the period, but this does not appear to have dampened the desire of men to attempt going into business for themselves. Religious discrimination in hiring probably diminished with the passage of time, but the city's single largest firm did not moderate and may even have intensified its discrimination against Irish Catholics.

Most of the occupational mobility which took place could not be estimated. This was so because so large a portion of the labor force was composed of migrants for whom information on pre- and post-Waltham occupations was not available. Among those adult men who persisted for a decade or more, upwards of 70 percent were occupationally immobile. This, however, may have been among the reasons why they persisted. They may have found employments so congenial to their interests that they decided to remain in the city. When payroll data for the watch company were analyzed, they indicated that there was a considerable amount of occupational mobility among persisters which was obscured in census data. Much of this mobility involved relatively small changes in occupational standings.

Catholics, over most of the period, tended to compete with Protestants only in the blue-collar occupations and, among these, in the unskilled and semi-skilled job categories. Catholic men and boys constituted the bulk of the day laboring force and the operatives or "hands" in male textile-mill jobs, in the bleachery, the chemical works, the paper mill, and the iron foundry. The building trades, small business and shopkeeping, and to a lesser degree the professions formed the main channels for movement out of the very lowest occupation groupings. Catholic children, often to their life-long disadvantage, tended to enter the labor force early and, of necessity, were given simple-minded jobs on which little could be learned of what might be of use for future occupational advance. In consequence of low skills and the difficulty of acquiring skills in the face of discrimination on the one hand and early labor-force entry on the other hand, the Catholic population continued to be a population of comparatively low income earners.

In the aggregate, male asset holdings rose from $2 million in 1850 to $8.4 million in 1890. The rate of increase here was almost identical to that of total population growth. On the assumption that there was increasing tax evasion after 1870, the distribution of assets among males was slightly more inequitable in 1890 than it had been in 1850. After making allowances for such factors as age and marital standing, however, the distribution of wealth as a socio-economic indicator was perceptibly more equitable. Most of the men who persisted in Waltham were able to accumulate assets and/or to add to their holdings over time. This, undoubtedly, was a direct consequence of the rise in real incomes which marked the period over all.

Reckoning on the basis of appearances in successive censuses, only 167 males persisted from 1850 through 1890. An additional 533 males spent at least 30 years in the city, and 1,550 more remained for as long as 20 years. Out of the 17,938 males enumerated in the 1850, 1860, 1870, and 1880 censuses and in the 1890 tax rolls, 12,014 appeared only once. All of the remaining observations involved 3,674 persisters who remained for a decade or more. Since the persisting males were the only ones for whom intra- and inter-generational mobility tallies could be made, and since a large number of these persisters had to be excluded because of age or the length of their records, the requirement of appearing in successive censuses was relaxed. In making the mobility tallies, persisters who were absent from one intervening census enumeration were also included. For intra-generational analysis. this resulted in a study population of 963 men:

476 20-year persisters, 273 30-year persisters, and 214 40-year persisters. The records of only 273 pairs of fathers and sons could be employed for the inter-generational analysis.

The persisting population, Protestant and Catholic alike, was materially successful. Most persisting men and their persisting sons accumulated assets and added to them over time. Most of them owned their own homes. They predominated among the leaderships of voluntary associations, churches, and the local government. Some occupied positions of power over other men and resources, and many more of them were independent businessmen. Catholic persisters were in several regards (i.e., asset accumulation and home ownership) as frequently as successful as Protestants, but uniformly at lower levels of achievement. Their occupational standings were also distinctly lower. And except for their increasing role in local government, Catholics were quite unlikely to occupy positions of power.

The high degree of correspondence between persistence, asset accumulation, homeownership, and fairly high occupational standing, produced a situation in which those men most likely to know one another and to be known in the community were the materially successful. That these men were accepted as the standard for emulation is confirmed by the frequency with which they were elected to positions of political and social leadership. The Catholic population also drew its leaders from among men of this sort.

Inter-generational mobility tallies indicate that most persisting sons were more likely than not to achieve occupational standings equivalent to those of their fathers. This pattern was all the clearer the later the ages of fathers and sons at the time of comparison. Such occupational immobility, however, was largely a product of those factors which worked to select the fathers and sons whose records could be studied. Among these pairs, the fathers tended to have high occupational rankings. Hence, that their sons failed to surpass them was not reflective of failure, but of the inherent difficulty of surpassing when just equaling itself involved a high standing.

Sons who stood to inherit a farm, a business, or a large estate and sons of low-income fathers without assets appear to have persisted most frequently. Sons without such inheritance prospects and whose fathers were men of moderate means were more likely to out-migrate. The number of sons in a family probably also influenced the patterns of persistence and migration.

Let us turn now to a consideration of trends in the social structure of Waltham as reflected in residence patterns, voluntary associations, and the institution of local government. Our first objective will be to comprehend how and the extent to which these aspects of community life were influenced by population growth, mobility, and industrial development. Our second objective will be to estimate the consequences of such changes for the men and for the social order which they bred.

The emergence of fairly homogeneous residence areas and of distinct differences among the leadership groups of many voluntary associations suggests that socio-economic differences within the Waltham population grew increasingly important over time. Such developments imply that men and their families more often and more exclusively interacted with other men and their family members who were most like themselves in regard to religion, assets, and occupational and income levels. Further support for the contention that Waltham society became more markedly stratified can be mustered from the evidence that the capital prerequisites for self-employment ventures were rising and that formal educational attainment had begun to bear increasing weight as a rationing device for occupational opportunities. What men might do for a living and, hence, what incomes and living standards they might achieve were, by implication, increasingly dependent upon family accomplishments and attitudes in the past. Those parents, for example, who had both the means and the will to endow their children with more education or training conferred an advantage upon them relative to the children of parents who could not or would not provide such an endowment.

Developments such as these worked to broaden and clarify stratification patterns. They did *not* create a system of stratification where none had previously existed. Consider that, in 1840, it would have been possible to identify the following groups: a mass of assetless workers, many of whom were young, unskilled, single, and new to Waltham; a smaller group of assetted, more often skilled, older, and married workers; a corps of self-employed shopkeepers, tradesmen, and professionals; a group of old family freehold farmers; and a handful of very wealthy Boston-oriented men of commerce and finance. Practically the same groupings can be identified in the 1890 population. How, then, did it happen, that by 1890 differences within the population were more telling dimensions of social organization than they had been previously? What changes occurred that promoted socio-economic differentiation within the population?

At the very least, four major developments can be identified in this connection: the population grew in size, the population grew richer, the population became ethnically and religiously heterogeneous, and the population grew more diversified in terms of the occupational, institutional, and social activities of its members. These developments, in combination, produced a number of significant results. They increased the grounds upon which individuals and/or groups could be differentiated. They added to the imperative to differentiate. And they enhanced the ease with which differences could be given expression in behavior patterns. The accuracy or fruitfulness of these observations may be gauged by applying them to the stratification patterns known to have prevailed.

Where in 1850 village streets and neighborhoods were occupied by families of diverse backgrounds and socio-economic standings, there had emerged by 1890 fairly distinct Yankee and Irish neighborhoods, among and between which it was possible to discern occupational-income-wealth gradations as well. The clear implication of this is that religious and economic differences had increasingly become grounds for residential stratification. Population growth may be seen to have added to the imperative to segregate residentially not simply because of the well-known tendency of migrants to form enclaves, but also because growth had led to the physical expansion of residence areas and the stock of housing. This expansion, in combination with rising incomes, permitted more families to satisfy their preference for living in homogeneous neighborhoods.

Residence patterns shaped by choice tell us what the preferences of the choosers looked like. They do not, however, tell us much about the values or factors which created such preferences. Perhaps an answer will emerge as we proceed.

The growth of the population, its increasing wealth, and the diversity of ethnic-religious and occupational-income groups also combined to influence the stratification patterns discerned in the organization of churches and voluntary associations. Because in some instances there were too many people per church congregation, club, or association, and in other instances because the size and wealth of population groups from diverse backgrounds was sufficient to sustain independent activities, it became either necessary or possible to organize new churches and associations and to do so on the basis of socio-economic and/or ethnic-religious peer groups. History was clearly repetitious in this regard. As early as 1820, when the influx of textile workers had required the establishment of a second church, that church became a preponderantly blue-collar institution. In 1894, when the growth of the Catholic population required a similar division, the second church became a preponderantly French-Canadian institution.

Religious differences within the Waltham population both reinforced stratification patterns and overrode them. Had Catholics actively desired to live in integrated neighborhoods and to join numbers of voluntary associations, they would have been unable to do so in many instances because of discriminatory barriers. Such barriers would alone have accomplished— as they did in the occupational realm—the same result as was produced by the willful desire of most men to live near and interact with co-religionists.

Implicit in the very existence of religious discrimination was the presumption that two men with otherwise identical socio-economic characteristics could not be status peers if one was a Catholic and the other a Protestant. Hence religious affiliation was an independent force in status ordering, so that there developed not one but two status hierarchies, one composed of Catholics and the other of Protestants. Very low rates of inter-marriage both testified to this division and served to perpetuate it over time.

The increasing importance attached to educational attainment as a prerequisite to occupational entry may be regarded initially as a response to population scale. Excepting the professions, where formal schooling was directly associated with an expected occupational competence, most occupations had performance requirements for which, apart from providing literacy skills, public education was largely irrelevant. Thus it cannot have been the case that education attainment grew in importance because of its curricular content. It seems likely that this trend developed because years of schooling could be taken as a fair proxy for other characteristics of the educated, such as perseverance, discipline, and reliability. These attributes, admixed with the factor of age, provided an essentially impressionistic expectation of the personal traits that could be associated with educational attainment. The development of vocational programs and of commercial curricula may, in this light, be seen as affording more—but also more limited—occupational opportunities to those who, for a variety of reasons, could not or would not abide the classical curriculum and the classroom regimentation associated with it. Equipped with a degree of occupational competence, the students enrolled in programs of this sort could avoid occupational evaluation and placement in terms under which they were likely to lose out.

But the need to have any objective standard whatever by which to ration occupational opportunities probably flowed from the needs of employers to hire from a growing and mobile population. Hiring on the basis of personal references could no longer be depended upon to the extent that many job seekers were new to the city and unknown to hiring foremen. Nor could previous work experience be counted upon in industries which themselves were new or fast growing, or in a population whose mobile elements were predominantly young. Strangers and neophytes composed a large portion of the labor force. In these circumstances, educational attainment provided a ready-made impersonal standard upon which employment decisions could be made.

Was *this* standard increasingly relied upon because of an assumed relationship between education and the growing complexity of many occupations? For blue-collar industrial workers the answer would appear to be no, because the progressive division and redivision of occupational tasks implies that workers were obliged to be less rather than more knowledgeable insofar as their work was concerned. The opposite seems to have been the case in the white-collar occupations. But technological change and scientific advance were not limited to work alone. Most generations of industrial men appear to believe that their lives are more complex and challenging than those of their antecedents by virtue of the expansion of knowledge and changes in techniques. From such a perspective it is fairly simple to presume that education increases the likelihood of psychic and social mastery.

In a different vein, the question can be raised as to whether the educational attainment standard emerged because it was known to produce results consonant with existing religious and socio-economic differences.

If Catholics placed a low valuation upon secular education, and if to many Catholics and Protestants the opportunity costs of public education were relatively high, then the educational standard would insure that most Catholic sons would be consigned to the lower reaches of the occupational hierarchy and that, among Protestants, the occupational rankings of sons would be closely related to family income. Was the educational standard developed as a covert form of religious and socio-economic discrimination? Or did it serve simply to reinforce differences which existed for entirely unrelated reasons?

Had the educational standard been a product of existing population differences, the timing and spread of its adoption might have been expected to parallel stratification developments. This, however, did not happen. By 1890, the education standard had only begun to emerge. (Indeed, our very awareness of this trend has more largely been conditioned by our knowledge of subsequent developments than by the clarity of the trend in the Waltham record.) Actual performance and on the job training remained the predominant modes of access to occupational opportunities.

It seems that what we have here is an illustration of the tendency for those men who are freest in their options to express, and to express first, the preferences of their society when they exercise their options. If many men came to believe that education was necessary in the face of technological change, institutional growth and development, and scientific advance, then those most likely to respond first were those who first perceived this relationship and whose present circumstances afforded the greatest latitude in responding. The Waltham evidence indicates that the occupational need for education was felt first at the top of the occupational hierarchy. The professions, finance, and large-scale industrial management were pace-setters in this regard. The wealthy, many of whom had ties of one sort or another with these occupational strata, might be expected to have been made aware rather early of this development. They were also the social element that could most readily undertake to provide their children with high school and college educations. Hence the educational standard as it bore upon occupational choices would tend to follow and reinforce existing socio-economic differences.

Such a "trickle down" theory may explain the direction in which and the means by which behavior patterns were transmitted through society. It cannot, however, explain the origins of the preference systems which shaped behavior patterns. In the argument presented above, it was suggested that education came to be viewed as a species of investment. But there is an even greater likelihood that educational attainment became economically important as a by-product of the rising importance of education as a preferred form of consumption. As incomes rose and as children were less obliged to work and their entry into the labor force could be delayed, schooling became both an alternative to idleness and an expression of social standing. Employers could then utilize the educational attainment standard in hiring because it was now possible to do so. They might have wished to do so because this standard served as a proxy for the socio-economic characteristics and selected personality traits of potential employees.

A similar line of reasoning seems to apply to residential and associational preference formation. If this is so, three broad conclusions appear to be sustained. First, that those at the top of a socio-economic hierarchy were the primary agents in defining preferences. Second, that their preferences were less strongly shaped by the positive attributes of the things preferred than by the negative attributes of alternatives heretofore compelled by necessity. And third, that among the most positive values of expressed preferences was that they bore witness to a social standing which permitted choice away from necessity.

Long before the educational attainment standard had permeated the entire occupational hierarchy, sustained immigration and internal migration had created a heterogeneous labor force in Waltham. Overt religious discrimination, lack of capital, and recentness of arrival in the country, among other factors, served to channelize occupational opportunities in a variety of ways. And even though by 1890 it was probably the case that the men to be found at all occupational levels were more diverse in their backgrounds than was true of the men of 1850, there are still grounds for maintaining that the occupational hierarchy was also becoming more and more stratified.

The evidence of the relatively narrow range of employments in which Catholics were to be found in 1890, and, among Catholics, the high concentration of the most recent immigrants in the lowest day-laboring jobs are suggestive of the religious and immigrant components of occupational stratification. The widening of wage differentials at Waltham Watch, particularly as between blue- and white-collar occupations, carries with it the same implication. It is possible that the rising capital requirements for going into business also fostered more pronounced socio-economic differences. This possibility, however, hinges on the rates of asset accumulation from rising incomes, a trend obscured by the likely onset of tax evasion.

The explanation of the increase in assets needed to set up a business may, like a number of other trends, be associated in the first instance with the growth of population. As the population grew, the volume of business activity also grew. For shopkeepers this probably meant that they had to carry larger inventories than had been customary at an earlier date. In the service trades, the rise in demand probably necessitated larger investments in tools and equipment so that each customer could be served more quickly. Whether in the form of larger inventories or increased stocks of tools and equipment, the growth of population required increased levels of investment.

Population growth was by no means alone in prompting this development. Rising incomes also played a part, as did population density. Had the growing population been spread over a wider physical area, it would have been possible to satisfy the rising demand for goods and services by establishing a larger number of firms at previous capitalization levels. As it was, the limited funds, or perhaps the limited ambitions, of even successful small businessmen fostered competition within an area of dense settlement. But the investment stakes required to compete effectively did rise. If over time it also became harder to accumulate savings, then it would have become progressively harder to escape wage-earning status. The data available allow for no resolution of this issue.

As against the tendency for religious and/or socio-economic differences to become more structured in the realms of residence, voluntary associations, and occupations, such differences became strikingly less marked in the realms of politics and local government. Although there continued to be an anti-Catholic bloc within the local Republican Party and among the factions which contended for municipal offices, the nativist majority of the 1850's was steadily eroded. For their part, Catholic voters lined up at an early date behind the Democratic Party; but it would be erroneous to see in this a species of religious segregation. The local party caucus became neither wholly or even predominantly Catholic. And even Republican standard-bearers in the 1870's and 1880's actively solicited the votes of Catholics.

Religion aside, both local party caucuses were at all times composed of men of widely diverse occupation-income and asset standings. In the absence of any alternative explanation of this, it seems clear that the men of Waltham did feel bound by the American tenet which held them to be equals politically. This principle, however, did not extend to the selection of party candidates, for in this there was a clear preference shown men of long residence who possessed assets and were either independent businessmen or professionals. Political equality thus always applied to voting and to nominating, but not to standing for elective office.

The change from a town meeting to a mayoral-aldermanic city government in 1885 was the proximate cause of the very considerable increase in the representativeness of elected public officials. To the extent that this change was occasioned by population growth and its attendant problems, the deepening of popular participation in public affairs also owed something to industrial and urban development. But although the structural change in governmental forms may have been a by-product of growing numbers, the change in the kinds of men standing for and elected to public office must have been brought about by other factors. The election of aldermen from wards, given the degree of residential segregation, was in itself bound to produce some change. The question nonetheless remains as to why, within the framework of wards, voters did not continue to nominate and elect assetted shopkeepers and professionals. Why did they, in the realm of politics, cease to honor the very attributes by which they increasingly sought to differentiate men in other realms?

Since there is no warrant for holding that blue-collar workers were more highly esteemed in 1890 than they had been in 1850, their election to public office at the latter date must have flowed either from socioeconomic bloc voting or from a lowered esteem for public affairs. Without a doubt, there was religious bloc voting, since wards composed predominantly of Protestant residents returned Protestant aldermen and wards with a preponderance of Catholic residents elected Catholic aldermen. And if there was religious bloc voting, is it not likely that there was also socio-economic bloc voting?

But did the Waltham Watch wards, for example, elect watch workers in preference to shopkeepers or professionals because they believed such men would better represent their interests or because it little mattered who represented their interests so long as they were represented? If the former was the case, it could be contended that more diverse candidates were elected because status differences were of greater, not lesser, importance to the electorate. Alternatively, if blue-collar workers could be elected because the public service had become tarnished or less estimable, then socio-economic differences did lose their significance in political life at the very same time that they came to bear added weight elsewhere.

It might at first glance appear inconsistent to maintain that the conduct of public affairs sustained a loss of prestige during a period when the variety and levels of public activity were so considerably expanded. But of all the species of bigness which Americans are known to have prized, big government was never among them. This generalized aversion to government may be viewed as one of long standing. It is in the concrete experience of the men of Waltham, however, that evidence of their growing disenchantment with *their* government must be found.

Waltham voters did not elect blue-collar aldermen to the extent that they did because they preferred them to men of higher socio-economic status. They did so because the men of higher status became increasingly reluctant to stand for election. The rising scale and complexity of municipal affairs and the factioning of the polity had transformed elective public office into a specialized activity which attracted more men with political career ambitions and fewer men whose interest in public affairs was thought to be selfless. It was the rise of politics and of politicians that demeaned the public service in the eyes of the Waltham citizenry.

The origins of this development may be traced back to the first attempts by Irish Catholics to gain representation in town government. The very need of the Catholic population to lay a claim to representation meant that there was no longer one public but two, and that elected representatives might have been expected now to serve the interests of different publics. Added to the factioning precipitated by this development, the growth of the public sector embodied some of its own sources of disaffection. An inbred fear of government and an unwillingness to pay taxes with alacrity or to see tax rates rise were among the most obvious pressure points touched by growth. But much if not most of the unease created by the expansion of government probably stemmed from the sustained rise in expenditures in those activities where the existence of problems was itself strongly resented. For example, it was comparatively hard to begrudge the monies spent for road building and maintenance, for sidewalks, for pure water supplies, and for garbage removal. The city was growing and these were among the necessary costs of expansion. In contrast, the expenditures aimed at such problems as truancy, crime, disorderly conduct, and indigency were probably much more intensely resented because problems of these sorts were created by "bad" people. This is not to say that taxpayers did not want more police protection, street lights, truant officers, and a poor farm, but that they disparaged those who occasioned their need and resented the expense which such needs entailed.

That the people who were so frequently involved in anti-social behavior (and being poor unto indigency in a society which appeared to offer so many income opportunities was as much a species of anti-social behavior as being drunk and disorderly), that these miscreants were so often Irishmen and/or new to the town and/or assetless added fuel to the fires of religious prejudice and "free rider" worries. Governmental services provided to such people could be interpreted as a form of pandering, as if, illogically, crime would disappear if there were no more policemen and poverty cease with the ending of welfare expenditures. Hence, those elected to provide public services, as well as the tax obligations which the provision of services necessitated, were less fully honored, at least in part, because such services were less noble. As in the days of kings, it was the messenger who brought unhappy tidings who suffered the vengeance of his hearers.

If the foregoing interpretation is correct, it may be said that the public ideal—the sense that individual men owe something of themselves to the collectivity of men—was diminished as the public grew increasingly less ideal. As population scale and religious, socio-economic, and residence longevity differences brought about a politicized and more problematic collective existence, it became easier to leave public affairs to the "politicians" and to turn one's energies more exclusively to the pursuit of self-interests. Even the most formal discharge of public responsibilities, the payment of taxes, suffered. For now, in addition to the perhaps normal reticence of men to part with income without direct personal benefit, taxes carried the added burden of misgivings toward portions of the public served.

But, it may be asked, is not widespread physical mobility alone always likely to weaken or destroy the reigning public ideal? Since most moves are predicated upon the expectation of self-aggrandizement in one form or another, since in this sense physical mobility is a self-seeking and self-serving act, is it not likely that movers will attach greater weight to their own interests, to the neglect of a concern for society as a whole? This is undoubtedly true to some degree. However, movers are not wholly or even largely free to do as they please at their points of arrival. Because of their newness and strangeness, the primary burden of adjustment rests upon them. And while a group of movers may coalesce to introduce institutions which ease this burden, their efforts even in this regard will be fundamentally influenced by the character of their new setting. Just as many of the demographic trends in the Waltham population were shaped by the longer-term residents because in-migrants tended to duplicate the characteristics of out-migrants, so in Waltham society those men, firms, and institutions with long-standing commitments to the city had a disproportionately larger influence upon affairs than did the more transient elements in the population. It was this "home guard" of comparative stability, which shaped the character of the community to which in-migrants had to adjust. The major impact of the physically mobile took the form of the reactions of the more permanent residents and of established institutions to their presence.

The evidence bearing upon the persisting population indicates that it was a population of successful men. This is probably why many of them were so keenly disturbed by the presence of the problems of truancy, crime, drunkenness, and indigency. For such problems were known to stand as barriers to success. Yet, on the basis of their own positive experiences, there was no justification for problems of these sorts. There was ample opportunity for all, and only a perversity of character could lead men from the path of achievement. By thus ignoring the very real constraints that might limit the ability of some men to exploit opportunities, it remained possible to believe that any man who failed to achieve material success did so because of his own personal shortcomings.

The logic of this view worked not only to define a lack of success (and certain forms of behavior held to be inimical to success) as abnormal, but to define material accumulation, along with certain other forms of behavior, as normal. In keeping with the declining authority of Protestant religious ideas and institutions, it may be presumed that, in Waltham as elsewhere, the pieties of work, thrift, self-reliance, and diligence were gradually stripped of their spiritual imperative and refashioned as guidelines for secular ambition. But among the most important consequences of defining the achievement orientation and material accumulation as normal, three stand out. These were, first and most obviously, to make the men of Waltham less unashamedly materialistic. The second was to produce so high a regard for concrete results that high productivity became a norm. And the third was to preclude the crystallization of stratification patterns into a hard and fast social class system.

That material accumulation was a prevailing lifetime goal is borne out most clearly by the evidence that most physical migrants lacked assets while most persisters had or came to have assets. On the assumption that most men engage in physical mobility only for good and sufficient reasons, this pattern implies that materialistic ambitions were often strong enough to prompt movement while successful accumulation was an important deterrent to movement.

In addition, Waltham's materially successful men were disproportionately recognized and honored in positions of trust and leadership. They were the emulated, the yardstick of achievement by which men could define their social standing. It was partly for this reason that homeownership was so highly prized. Nothing so visibly evidenced accumulation as owning real property. Nothing so tangibly suggested the aura of permanence, or the absence of any need to move again. In a society where large numbers of men felt compelled to move about in search of opportunities, those who had already met with success testified to their accomplishment by assuming commitments which indicated their physical immobility.

Since material possessions are almost universally employed in defining social standings, the mere adoption of a material standard cannot be said to have differentiated the men of Waltham from contemporary English or French or German townsmen. It could be maintained that what led them to be more openly materialistic was the comparative abundance of the natural resources at their disposal. But the essential difference arose from the fact that the other criteria employed in the definition of social standings in most European countries were either absent entirely or of much weaker significance in Waltham. The combined forces of settlement by immigrants, of high levels of internal migration, and the ideal of political equality had stripped lineage and tradition of the weight they had carried elsewhere. Because it mattered less who a man's family had been or what it had accomplished in the past, it mattered more what a man did and was accomplishing now and what his prospects for the future were. As we have seen, most of the men ever resident in Waltham were strangers to it. Their origins, blood lines, and family histories were unknown and unknowable unless they chose to tell. Even among the very longest term residents, family pasts garnered little prestige unless shored up by contemporary accomplishments, for many a man had equally early American antecedents. Hence the best gauge of a man's social standing turned on his current occupation, income, and asset position, and on his likelihood of achievement in the future. It was the irrelevance of the past which made the materialistic dimensions of the present so distinctly important in the social evaluations of older men and estimates of the potential for material success in the future so critical in the ranking of younger men.

One direct consequence of tying individual social identifications so strongly to present and future material achievement was to establish a premium upon results at the expense of a lesser concern for the authority of procedural and technical precedents, often to the practical neglect of very real human interests. Perhaps this is nowhere more graphically illustrated than in the development of the Boston Manufacturing Company. It will be recalled that when it was initially established, this company could not employ many children because its production processes demanded so high a level of worker input. As a result, the company had to break with prevailing industry employment practices and to staff its mills with transient young women. Over time, however, the labor requirements of machine-tending were reduced by technological advance. Because it was now both feasible and profitable to do so, the company increased its employment of children. It fostered child labor even though at the very same time the social value placed upon education was rising and the first questions about the consequences of child labor for the children involved were being raised.

The temptation to attribute this train of events to the character of a particular form of economic organization should be tempered by the awareness that men in most walks of life strove quite as much as corporate managers to exploit the opportunities they confronted with the rewards rather than the costs or the methods uppermost in their minds. Industrial workers, for example, worked harder and faster than their European counterparts, not simply because employers drove them to it, but because they too were in a hurry to arrive in the material terms that garnered an acceptable social standing. It was as if everything had to be accomplished in one lifetime, for men who themselves lived without substantial and binding ties of custom and tradition with the past had good reason to doubt their own consequence for posterity. As the actual experience of mobility weakened the bonds with what had been, and as mobility expectations implicitly involved a readiness to dissolve such bonds, so the changes bred by industrial and urban development, by innovation, and by the expansion of knowledge insured that the future would be a world apart from the present. Existence, for many men, was the brief span between a forsaken past and a volatile future, whose meaning and importance resided in the tangible accomplishments of a lifetime. In contrast, those men whose lives were significantly linked with the past and whose futures were prefigured in non-materialistic terms—the Catholic Church was the outstanding embodiment of such linkages in Waltham—were less driven by the demons of contemporary achievement.

The major social consequence of vesting material accomplishment with so much importance was that classes could find no footing. For social classes are necessarily self-conscious constructs. They can only exist if, and to the extent that, there exists an awareness on the part of some men that they share a social standing that sets them apart from other men. And when men cannot perpetuate the exclusivity of their standing, they have no grounds for such an awareness. There cannot be a "we" and a "they" if the "they's" are free to become, wish to become, can become, and do become "we's."

Traditions which limit freedom, which sap ambition by constraining access to opportunities, and which heavily discount contemporary achievement would thus appear to be prerequisites of a system of social classes.

A present and a future circumscribed by the sanctification of the precedents of the past are required to sustain a class order. Most of the men in Waltham and in much of the rest of the country owed nothing to the past.

Or did they? Was not the freedom to pursue their own destiny their most valuable inheritance? The difference lay in that such a legacy was liberating rather than constraining. It encouraged men to discount the past in the very act of encouraging them to remake their future. In this sense, the freedom which came to be viewed as an elemental given in the social system militated against the formation of classes. At any one moment of time, men might display widely divergent levels of achievement, so that there could be no question but that the society was stratified. Momentary differences, however, were just that. Intra-generational and inter-generational mobility were expected to alter—and did alter—the relative standings of many men, and economic growth had the demonstrable consequence of improving the absolute standings of most men. No socio-economic standings were fixed or immutable. Religious differences alone survived intact through time, but these transcended the materialistic bases of class formation.

Playwright Eugene O'Neill once commented: "I am going on the theory that the United States, instead of being the most successful country in the world is its greatest failure. . . . Because it has always been in a state of rapid movement it has never acquired real roots. Its main idea is that everlasting game of trying to possess your own soul by the possession of something outside it, too. America is the foremost example of this because it happened so fast here and with such enormous resources. The Bible has already said it much better: 'For what shall it profit a man if he shall gain the whole world, and lose his own soul?'"

If this "soul" is that link with eternity forged by lives imbedded in a rooted and hallowed past and aspiring to an idealized future, one would have to agree with O'Neill's description. There are, however, substantial grounds for disagreeing with his judgment. Among them is that while it may be dangerous to live without a past, this remains to be seen. The price in misery which roots have exacted, the very abuses of a rigid class order which O'Neill himself detested are, on the other hand, known in full measure. But how very American of O'Neill to have contrasted the country's experience with idealized possibilities rather than with other realities!

The massive grinding poverty, the personal debasement, and the peril to life which have so often characterized industrialization were notably absent in Waltham. We know of no comparable village in Georgian England or Bismarckian Germany or Stalin's Russia whose transformation was accompanied by so little pain and suffering. This is not to say that life was without its torments here. But on any international scale, immense change was wrought at a human price so low as to beggar comparison. Sizeable elements of a population were able to realize their ambitions for success and security. Two antagonistic religious groups hammered out a way to live together in peace. An opportunity-laden future was bequeathed to the next generation. Even the problems which were also part of that legacy were accompanied by a positive and self-confident outlook. Clearly, when compared with other realities, Waltham was the scene of a human victory.

Appendix I
Research Methods

This appendix provides a detailed statement of the procedures followed in the collection and analysis of the data presented. It elaborates upon some of the problems of data reliability and methodology which were given only the briefest mention in the text. With the advantage of hindsight, it also includes suggestions of how future studies of a similar nature might improve upon some of the methods employed.

The study population was generated by preparing a data card for each male appearing in the 1850, 1860, 1870, and 1880 manuscript federal census returns, in the manuscript Massachusetts census returns for 1865, and in the Waltham tax rolls for 1890. Cards of different colors were used for each cohort to insure against confusion.

Of necessity, it was assumed that the enumerations in the censuses and the 1890 tax rolls were complete. Even if this assumption was incorrect, little or nothing could be done in a practical way to compensate for deficiencies in the census listings. It should be recognized, however, that any under-enumeration would serve to bias estimates of physical mobility upward and estimates of persistence downward. How great under-enumerations may have been and whether the rate of under-enumeration declined as census-taking techniques improved are questions for which no conclusive answers can be provided. On the basis of the evidence that most of the men who appeared, in a census year, on the tax rolls but not in the census were men without assets, it may be inferred that census shortcomings affected the poorer and therefore the most physically mobile portions of the population.

A facsimile of the 4 × 6-inch data card prepared for each male is provided below.

CATEGORIES ON DATA CARDS

HH#——In each census, households were numbered serially in order of their enumeration. This number was recorded on each card as an aid to identifying members of the same family after the cards had been organized alphabetically. Reference to this number also made it possible to find an individual in the census if the need arose to re-examine his census entry. In the 1870 and 1880 censuses, Waltham was divided into census tracts, each with its own serial numbering. For these censuses, tract numbers as well as household numbers were recorded.

The 1890 tax rolls were published on a ward-by-ward basis, and these ward numbers were recorded. An individual who owned property in more than

182

HH#	NAME ALT			AGE
HH STAT	__HEAD __SGLE __DEP	OCCUPA		RATE
NATIV		PA NAME NATIV RES	MA NAME NATIV RES	
RELIG	__PROT __CATH	TAX HOME O	DEATH	
FROM		TO		
ROLES				

one ward was reported in each. In such cases, the cards were amalgamated to avoid duplication, and the ward number of residence (signified by the one in which the poll tax was paid) was entered.

NAME, ALT——Names were recorded directly from the censuses and the 1890 tax rolls. Where doubts arose, either because the handwriting in the census was difficult to read or because it was believed that a name might have been misspelled, alternate possibilities were also recorded. Since the censuses reported sex, it was possible to use this designation as well as first names to insure that only males were included. Names about which there was some uncertainty were checked against the tax rolls and against earlier and later censuses in an effort to clarify spellings insofar as was possible.

AGE——Ages were recorded directly from census reports. Given the unreliability of the age reports of older men in particular, age data was not of much use in matching such men between censuses and between the death rolls and the censuses.

HH STAT——Household statuses were recorded in the following manner: It was assumed that all members of a household who had the same last name were members of the same family. A male was classed as the head of a household if he was married and if the entries immediately following his entry indicated the presence of a wife and/or children. Widowers were also classed as household heads when so identified. All males 16 and older with occupational listings were recorded as single whether they lived in a family unit or not. All males under age 16 were classed as dependents as were males under 20 who lived in family units but had no occupational listing.

OCCUPA——Occupations were recorded as listed in the censuses. For 1890, the occupation listed in the city directory of that year was recorded. As indicated in the study, census occupational listing were often quite ambiguous. In some instances, the census takers recorded place of employment rather than the nature of employment in the occupation column. The payrolls of Waltham Watch and Boston Manufacturing were used to correct for this deficiency insofar as their employees were concerned. In other instances, census takers designated an occupation but failed to indicate whether a man was an employee, an employer, or self-employed within that occupation. Examinations of the census schedules for agriculture and manufacturing made it possible to draw such distinctions in some but by no means in all cases. Overall, the occupational data probably resulted in an understatement of skill and occupational status levels.

RATE——Payroll data for Waltham Watch and Boston Manufacturing were employed to draw distinctions between unskilled and skilled workers and between workers and supervisors within these two companies. These broad classes rather than the pay rates themselves were recorded.

NATIV——All censuses reported place of birth by country for the foreign born and by state for the native born. The nativity of children under three years of age provided the only concrete evidence of the points of departure of in-migrants into Waltham. The identical sort of evidence was also available from the place of birth information included in the recorded deaths of children under three.

Because nativity figured importantly in the designation of religion, it was important in some cases to know the nativity of a male's parents. This was particularly true of males born in Canada and in Britain. Later in the period, it was also true for native-born Americans.

PA NAME, NATIV, RES——These data, for both fathers and mothers, were collected from a variety of sources. Once collected from any one source, parentage information was transferred onto the cards of persisting males for those years when it was not otherwise available. The 1880 census alone reported the names and nativities of the parents of all enumerated persons. For previous census cohorts, parentage information was available from the census only for those males whose parents were also enumerated. The published birth records for the period prior to 1850 made it possible to collect this information for almost all Waltham-born males who were in residence in 1850. Post-1850 death records reported the names and nativities of parents and provided yet another source of information. In practice, parents' residence data were collected only for those males whose families were long-standing residents of the city. This made it possible to view old Waltham families as a distinct grouping.

RELIG——Religion was initially inferred from an individual's nativity and/or that of his parents. Most native-born males were classed as Protestants, as were most foreign-born males from all countries except Ireland. Irish-born males and males born in the United States and abroad of Irish-born parents were classed as Catholics. German-born males were not classified for want of evidence as to whether they came from the Catholic or

Protestant portions of Germany. The small numbers of Jewish and Muslim males were also not classified.

The largest shortcoming of associating nativity with religion was that it undoubtedly led to the classification of some Irish Protestants as Catholics. To reduce this error, and most particularly among persisting males, lists of Protestant church leaders and of leaders in voluntary associations believed to be exclusively Protestant (e.g., the Masons, church clubs, the Y.M.C.A., the British-American Association, etc.) were checked against reported nativity. Inferred religious affiliations were then adjusted accordingly for all family members. Thus, in the population as a whole, the numbers and proportions of Catholics are probably overstated, while among the persisting population the numbers and proportions are more nearly accurate.

TAX——Tax payments, net of poll taxes, were recorded from manuscript tax rolls. As indicated in the study, the reliance upon tax payments as an estimate of wealth created a number of problems. First, there was the problem of data reliability in view of what appears to have been a growing tendency to evade personal property taxes. Second, there was the problem that the distribution of assets overstated disparities in assets to the extent that such a distribution was not adjusted for age, marital status, and kinship. Third, there was the problem that assets came increasingly over time to be held in the names of females. This increased the difficulty of reconciling asset-holding with kinship.

In practice, nothing could be done to adjust the data for trends in tax evasion. Nor was the data in any way altered to correct for the bias in distribution or for female asset holding. These problems were simply noted and their consequences indicated.

HOME O——When the tax rolls indicated that assets included homeownership, this was recorded by entering a check mark.

DEATH——The municipal death rolls reported deaths in Waltham (and outside of it in the cases of war-related deaths during the Civil War) along with sufficient demographic detail to permit fairly accurate matching between the deceased and census enumerations. Once matched, the year of death was recorded on the data card.

FROM, TO——Where information from any source was found which indicated either the last previous place of residence of in-migrants or the next place of residence of out-migrants, such information was entered. In practice, most of the information collected bore upon the originating points of in-migrants. Most of this data was taken from census reports of the birth places of children under three and from birth place information reported for children under three listed in the death records.

ROLES——Men who served in elected offices in the local government and voluntary associations had their service recorded here. Government records, newspaper reports, city directories, and the minutes of a number of voluntary associations provided this information.

Where the censuses reported a physical disability or illiteracy, this was noted on the bottom line. The only practical use of such information was the evidence it provided to the effect that illiteracy was uncommon and most likely to be a characteristic of older Irish immigrants.

No effort was made to check state records for legal name changes. The small numbers of men and boys sent out of town to prisons, asylums, and reform schools was also ignored. Both of these omissions would serve to increase the physical mobility tallies and to decrease the persistence tallies, but they cannot have done so to any significant degree.

Persistence was recorded by entering the letter P on the left side of the card under ROLES when signifying appearance in the preceding census and on the right side when signifying appearance in the succeeding census. The completed card files were searched through by hand one at a time in the effort to detect persistence. In the cases of men and boys who persisted as members of a family unit, it was fairly easy to detect persistence, because an individual could be identified as a member of the unit. Single, unrelated males were the most difficult to trace for two reasons, namely, the frequency of name duplications (e.g., there were as many as seven Patrick Kelly's and John Smith's in the 1880 census) and the unreliability of age reports. If any error was made here, it was on the side of underestimating persistence.

Once the data cards had been completed, the information they contained (excepting RATES, PA and MA RES, FROM and TO, and ROLES) was transferred onto computer punch cards. To minimize the errors that might arise, the simplest codes that could be devised were employed where coding was necessary. The only raw data that were substantially altered in this process were the occupational data. Here it was necessary to conserve computer storage space by amalgamating occupations. For example, all carpenters, masons, plumbers, electricians, etc., were amalgamated as building tradesmen. All watch workers and textile workers were amalgamated under those headings, and so on. The distinctions of skill levels made in the text rest upon pro-rations of the proportions of skilled and unskilled known to have existed on the basis of payroll records, or were estimated.

A computer program was then designed to provide tallies of the characteristics of each enumerated male population. Once this was completed, the punch cards were reorganized to include only persisters. A new program then provided a print-out of all persisters starting with the men of the 1850's who remained 10 years, then those who remained 20, 30, or 40 years. Next came the men of the 1860's, then of the 1870's, and the 1880's. When it became obvious that there were too few pairs of fathers and sons for meaningful inter-generational comparisons, the card file was re-examined and altered to include persisters who were absent from only one intervening census. Inter-generational mobility tallies were then made manually using the persistence print-outs. It was at this point that information bearing upon leadership roles and power wielding was entered. Most of those whose original data cards indicated such roles were found among the persisters.

Retrospectively, the largest shortcoming in these procedures was an error of omission. The initial computer program neglected to tally the characteristics of out-migrants. This problem was circumvented by netting out the characteristics of persisters from each census cohort, but it would have been simpler to have collected the tallies directly.

In making tallies of asset mobility among persisters, any increase in assets was taken as an improvement. Since the asset data always took the form of tax payments, they could not easily be adjusted for price changes, and they were not adjusted. This means that asset mobility was probably overstated in any comparisons which ended with 1870, but that it was probably understated for comparisons which ended with either 1880 or 1890. In addition, the procedures employed made no allowance for relative shifts in asset holding. Men who improved their asset positions in dollar terms were classed as upwardly mobile even though their assets grew at rates below the average.

In conclusion I would like to recommend that future efforts of the sort undertaken here devise some means to treat families as well as unrelated individuals as the units of study. This will present a number of methodological problems, but I believe that it will reduce a number of other problems and add greatly to our understanding of mobility processes and their consequences.

Appendix II
Occupational Classifications

BLUE-COLLAR UNSKILLED:

Apprentice
Baker's Helper
Basket Mkr.
Bedstead Mkr.
Blind Mkr.
Book Binder
Boot & Shoe Wkr.
Bottler
Brewery Wkr.
Broom Mkr.
Brush Mkr.
Carpet Layer
Chalk Mkr.
Chemical Wkr.
Cigar Mkr.
Coal Yard Wkr.
Collars/Cuff Mkr.
Cook
Crayon Mkr.

Dredger
Farm Laborer
Fisherman
Gas/Light Co.
Glass Wkr.
Hat Wkr.
Hotel Wkr.
Iceman
Janitor
Laborer
Lash Mkr.
Laundry Wkr.
Leather Wkr.
Mariner
Meat Packer
Metal Trades (part)
Milkman's Helper
Miller's Helper
Miner

Needle Wkr.
Paper Mkr.
Paver
Porter
Pruner
Railroad Wkr.
Servant
Slipper Mkr.
Soldier/Sailor
Stocking Mkr.
Street Car Driver
Street/Roads Wkr.
Teamster
Textile Wkr. (part)
Umbrella Mkr.
Waiter
Warehouseman
Watchman
Watch Wkr. (part)

BLUE-COLLAR SKILLED:

Building Trades
Foreman
Garment Cutter
Harness Mkr.

Metal Trades (part)
Printing Trades
Railroad Fireman
Telegrapher

Textiles Wkr. (part)
Upholsterer
Watch Wkr. (part)

WHITE-COLLAR UNSKILLED:

Baggage Master
Butler
Canvasser
Clerk
Collector

Customs Insp.
Messenger
Nurse
Piano Tuner
Press Clipper

Recruiter
Salesman
Sexton
Travel Agent

188

White-Collar Skilled:

Actor	Drawing Master	Secretary
Bookkeeper	Newspaper Reporter	Stenographer
Draftsman	Paymaster	Surveyor

Self-Employed:

Apothecary	Fish Mkt.	Photographer
Artist	Florist	Piano Mkr.
Auctioneer	Grocer	Plumbing Shop
Baker	Gunsmith	Poultry Mkt.
Banker	Hardware Dealer	Phrenologist
Barber	Harness Shop	Printing Ofc.
Barkeeper	Hostler/Stabler	Real Estate/Insurance
Billiard Saloon Prop.	Huckster	Restorator
Boardinghouse Keeper	Ice Cream Business	Shoe Store
Boat Builder	Incubator Business	Showman
Bowling Saloon Prop.	Marble Business	Stationer
Builder	Merchant	Stock Broker
Butcher Shop	Milkman	Tea Store
Clairvoyant	Miller	Tobacconist
Clothier	Milliner	Undertaker
Confectioner	Mill Supplier	Upholsterer
Contractor	Mover	Variety Store
Dentist	Musician	Veterinarian
Excursionist	Nurseryman	Violin Mkr.
Farmer/Gardener	Optician	Yeoman

Managers-Officials:

Bank Pres.	Manager	Treasurer
Depot Master	Naval Officer	YMCA Secty.
Government Official	Sea Captain	

Technical-Professional:

Architect	Coastal Surveyor	Publisher
Attorney	Editor	Teacher
Chemist	Engineer	
Clergyman	Physician	

Industrial Employers:

Manufacturer

Index

Age: distributions, pre-1850, 8-9, 11-12; 1850-90, 19, 34-36; and migration, 38; and assets, 89
Ancient Order of United Workmen, 150
Appleton, Nathan, 5
Arrests, 158-59
Assets: distributions, pre-1850, 9, 12-13; 1850-90, 15-18, 44-46, 80-92; mobility, 96-102

Banks, Nathaniel, 119
Bathhouse, 140
Birth Rate. See Fertility differentials
Black population, 11, 149
Board of Health: role of, 130; 1885 survey by, 137-38
Boston: influence of, 1, 132; commuters to, 16, 136
Boston Manufacturing Company: early development, 2-3, 6, 9-11; work force, 40-41, 62, 71, 164; agents, 118; child labor, 178-79
Buttrick, Francis, 91

California gold rush, 19
Capital requirements, 57, 63, 173-74
Catholic church: earliest, 11; as neighborhood center, 137; place of in community, 155-57
Censuses, 30-31
Charles River, 1-2, 5
Child labor, 59-60, 150, 178-79
Children, dependent, 34
Churches: number and sects, 10-11, 141; roles in community, 141-46, 147; stratification, 152
Civil War, 41, 52, 149-50
Commuters, 16, 42-43
Cooperation, 150
Crime, 158-59

Davis & Farnum Foundry, 60, 134
Death rate, 11, 20
Deaths, 25-27, 87, 160
Dennison, Aaron, 6, 52, 133

Discrimination, ethnic-religious, 57-62, 121-24, 136-37, 158-63
Division of labor, 50-54. See also Fission of tasks; Specialization
Drunkenness, 158-59

Eaton, Thomas B., 63-64, 162
Education: early, 10; attitudes toward, 58-60; and labor force, 170-73. See also School board
Elgin, Illinois, 41
Everett Literary Association, 148-49, 157

Family formations, 85-89
Farmer's Club, 150-51
Farming, 1-2, 64, 150-51
Fenian Brotherhood, 150
Fenian Sisterhood, 150
Fertility differentials, 33-35
Fission of tasks, 51-52, 72-74
Fitchburg Railroad, 9-10, 13-14
Flood, Rev. Bernard, 156
"Free riders," 125-27, 176-77
French, Daniel, 160

Gissing, George, 132
Grand Army of the Republic, 129, 149

Hastings, Josiah, 158, 160
Hill, Rev. Thomas, 10, 127, 147n
Homeownership, 90, 98-102, 133-34, 137, 168, 178
Housing, Company, 3, 74, 133-34
Housing stock, 11, 14-15, 136

Incorporation, 110, 115
Infant mortality, 25
Inheritance, 92
In-migration: pre-1850, 6, 8, 13-15, 18-19; 1850-90, 27-30; net, 8, 10, 15, 25-31, 165-66; gross, 26, 30-31; origins of, 32-33; and religion, 35-38; and assets, 37-38, 87; contribution of to wealth, 84; summary of, 165-66

Irish Catholics: numbers, 9, 11, 15, 33; persistence, 46, 101–2; employments, 60–64; mobility, 96–102; politics, 105, 121–25; living conditions, 137–40; changes in, 162–63; summary, 166–67

Jackson, Patrick Tracy, 4
Job assignments, 51, 59–60, 62, 71–72, 179
Job training, 58, 62

Kindergartens, 109
Knights of Labor, 74, 149

Labor force: at Boston Manufacturing and Waltham Watch, 40–42, 73, 115, 153–55; entry into, 58–60, 167, 172
Land annexation, 13–14
Leary, Timothy, 122–23
Local government, 104–18, 174–76
Longevity. See Persistence
Lowell, Francis Cabot, 5

Marriages, 11, 45, 85, 89
Moody, Paul, 5

Names: street, 5; given, 162
Natural increase: pre-1850, 10–11, 14; 1850-90, 25–26, 29–30
Neighborhoods, 136–37
Newspapers, 157–58
Newton Chemical Company, 14, 60, 134

Occupational mobility, 50–76, 96–102, 166
Occupations, 50–57; and income differentials, 90
Old families, 48, 98–99
O'Neill, Eugene, 180
Out-migration: destinations, 19n, 38, 42; rates, 19, 26–27, 29–30, 35–38, 85

Paine, Robert Treat, 134
Party regularity, 119–20
Persistence, 8, 18, 35, 43–49, 85–87, 167, 177–78
Phillips, Wendell, 149
Police, 21, 158–59
Political factioning, 120–23
Poor relief, 21, 128–29
Population, 23–25, 29, 32–35
Power: and social mobility, 92–93, 96–102; in public affairs, 117–18
Professionalization, 110, 128
Proliferation, 50
Protestant sectarianism, 11, 141–47
Public officials, 10, 20–21, 110–15, 121, 128, 174–76

Real wages, 65, 89
Republican majority, 119
Residence patterns: earliest, 6; and transportation, 42–43, 136; changes in, 132–38; and discrimination, 137–38; summary of, 170
Ripley, Rev. Samuel, 10
Robbins, Royal E., 52, 91–92, 118, 133–34, 153
Robert's Paper Mill, 134
Rumford Institute, 4, 21

St. Mary's. See Catholic church
St. Patrick's Day, 162
St. Patrick's Mutual Relief Society, 147–48, 156
Sanitation, 138–40
Savings, 64–65
School board, 108–9, 127–28. See also Education
Self-employment, 42, 63–64
Sex distributions, 8, 20
Skill requirements, 57–59
Slippage, 30–31
Social leadership, 93–94
Social mobility, 77–103, 177–81
Social Space, 77
Sovereigns of industry, 150
Specialization, 51, 72–74, 152–55. See also Division of labor
Status, 77–79
Steward, Ira, 149
Stratification, 140, 152, 169
Street lighting, 109–10

Taxes: evasion of, 81–84, 89–92; administration of, 82, 106
Temperance, 147–48
Town Improvement Society, 129
Trolley line, 43, 118
Truancy, 108, 150

Union Club, 149
Unionism, 74, 149–50

Vacations, 42
Vocational school, 108, 171
Voluntary associations, 93–102, 141–56
Voting, 119–20

Waltham Cotton and Woolen Factory Company, 2–6
Waltham Naturalization Association, 122–23
Waltham System, 3–5
Waltham Watch: work force, 40–41; development, 52–54; money and real wages, 65, 89; employee activities, 152–55. See also Robbins, Royal E.

Wards, 140
Watch Factory Relief Association, 147–48, 154

Watchmakers' school, 59
Water Commission, 138–40

THE JOHNS HOPKINS UNIVERSITY PRESS

This book was composed in Baskerville text and Sans Serif display type by the Jones Composition Company from a design by Victoria Dudley. It was printed on S. D. Warren's 60-lb. 1854 paper, regular finish, and bound in Joanna Arrestox cloth and Curtis Tweed-weave by The Maple Press.

Library of Congress Cataloging in Publication Data

Gitelman, Howard M.
  Workingmen of Waltham.

  Includes bibliographical references.
  1. Labor mobility—Waltham, Mass.—History.
2. Waltham, Mass.—Social conditions. I. Title.
HD5726.W26G57   331.1′27′097444   74-6822
ISBN 0-8018-1570-3